Social Theory Since Freud

'Anthony Elliott is quickly emerging as a one-person industry, intent in all of his writings to demonstrate both the relevance and the importance of psychoanalytic theory for social analysis.'

Thesis Eleven

'Anthony Elliott has once again provided a lucid and critical examination of the relationship between psychoanalysis and social theory. While many writers are still catching up with Lacan's work, Elliott explains the major advances to be found in post-Lacanian theory, and shows how it offers a new view of subjectivity and the "imagination" attuned to the complexities of contemporary social life.'

Professor Stephen Frosh, *Birkbeck College, London*

'Comprehensive and challenging, *Social Theory Since Freud* explores major developments in western thought since Freud mapped out the unconscious. It is an authoritative synopsis of the Frankfurt School, Castoriadis, Lacan, Laplanche and Kristeva. In pursuing the legacy of Freud, Anthony Elliott shows convincingly that the imagination is central to rethinking the relationship between social theory and psychoanalysis.'

Bryan Turner, *Cambridge University*

In this compelling book, Anthony Elliott traces the rise of psychoanalysis from the Frankfurt School to postmodernism. Examining how path-breaking theorists such as Adorno, Marcuse, Lacan and Lyotard have deployed psychoanalysis to politicize issues like desire, sexuality, repression and identity, Elliott assesses the gains and losses arising from this appropriation of psychoanalysis in social theory and cultural studies.

Moving from the impact of the Culture Wars and recent Freud-bashing to contemporary debates in social theory, feminism and postmodernism, Elliott argues for a new alliance between sociological and psychoanalytic perspectives. Drawing in particular from the thought of key contemporary psychoanalytic thinkers such as Julia Kristeva, Jean Laplanche and Cornelius Castoriadis, *Social Theory Since Freud* opens the way for a new approach to the creativity of action.

Anthony Elliott is Professor of Sociology at the University of Kent at Canterbury. His recent books include *Concepts of the Self* (2001), *Psychoanalytic Theory: an introduction* (2002, 2nd Edition), *Critical Visions* (2003) and *Subject to Ourselves* (2004, 2nd Edition).

Social Theory Since Freud

Traversing social imaginaries

Anthony Elliott

Routledge
Taylor & Francis Group

LONDON AND NEW YORK

First published 2004
by Routledge
2 Park Square, Milton Park, Abingdon,
Oxon OX14 4RN

Simultaneously published in the USA and Canada
by Routledge
29 West 35th Street, New York, NY 10001

Routledge is an imprint of the Taylor & Francis Group

© 2004 Anthony Elliott

Typeset in Garamond by
Keystroke, Jacaranda Lodge, Wolverhampton
Printed and bound in Great Britain by
Cromwell Press, Trowbridge, Wiltshire

British Library Cataloguing in Publication Data
A catalogue record for this book is available from the British Library

Library of Congress Cataloging in Publication Data
A catalog record for this book has been requested

ISBN 0–415–27164–9 (hbk)
ISBN 0–415–27163–0 (pbk)

For Oscar

Contents

Preface and acknowledgements

The discerning reader may notice that, in tracing the intellectual stock-market fortunes of psychoanalysis in social theory and critical cultural studies, the title of this work makes a play on Lacan's paper 'The agency of the letter in the unconscious or reason since Freud'. In doing so, I signal a shift of intellectual mood – away from the current orthodoxy of French Freudianism in the academy. Moving beyond Lacan's Freud necessarily entails, I argue, an encounter with the wider social and political ramifications of psychoanalysis – in social theory in particular and the social sciences in general.

I would like to thank Charles Lemert – for his support and friendship, and for enriching contemporary social theory. This volume is in no small way influenced by the example set by his writing, particularly *Dark Thoughts* (Routledge, 2002), even though the bulk of this material was drafted before I came to see the degree to which style can considerably influence substance – hence some extensive redrafting!

During my work on this book, I have benefited from the conversation, input and advice of many people at the following institutes where I have lectured on Freud and social theory: the Northern Californian Society for Psychoanalytic Psychology; the Psychoanalytic Institute of Northern California; the San Francisco Institute of Psychoanalysis; the Boston Institute of Psychoanalysis; the Melbourne Institute of Psychoanalysis; the Tavistock Institute, London; the Centre for Psycho-Social Studies, UWE; and, the Centre for Psycho-Social Studies, Birkbeck College, University of London.

I should like to thank the British Academy for the award of a grant that facilitated the completion of this project. The book was finished during a period I spent as Distinguished Visiting Professorial Fellow in the Faculty of Social Sciences at La Trobe University, Melbourne. I would particularly like to thank Dennis Altman, Judith Brett and Peter Beilharz for making my stay at La Trobe such a friendly and productive one. Others who have contributed to the book, either directly or indirectly, whom I should like to thank include Jean and Keith Elliott, Nick Stevenson, Anthony Moran, Paul du Gay, Alison Assiter, Fiore Inglese, Simon Skacej, Kriss McKie, Carmel Meiklejohn and Deborah Maxwell.

I would specially like to thank Charles Spezzano, Sean Homer and Jeff Prager for their assistance and input into this book. I have also benefited through conversations with the following: Jane Flax, Janet Sayers, Stephen Frosh, Paul Hoggett, Jessica Benjamin, Nancy Chodorow, Stanley Gold, the late Judith Linnane, Lynne Segal and Patricia Clough.

Marie Shullaw, who commissioned the book, proved a patient and insightful editor. Her successor at Routledge, Gerhard Boomgaarden, has been marvellously supportive. Preparation of the manuscript was carried out by Liz Wood, who has contributed much to the project, with considerable dedication, grace and patience.

Some parts – sections and pieces – are previously published and reprinted here by permission of the publishers or by prior agreement. These parts have appeared in the following: *The Psychoanalytic Quarterly, Meridian, American Imago, Revista De Psicoanaslisis, Journal of the Universities Association for Psychoanalytic Studies, Thesis Eleven* and *Psychoanalytic Studies*. Other traces are from contributions to previous edited collections, including Bryan S. Turner (ed.), *The Blackwell Companion to Social Theory* (Blackwell, 2000); Anthony Elliott (ed.), *Freud 2000* (Cambridge: Polity Press, 1996); and, M.-C. Durieux and A. Fine (eds), *Sur Les Controverses Ameraines Dans La Psychanalyse* (Paris: Presses Universitaires De France, 2000).

Beyond all else, the book owes to Nicola, Caoimhe and Oscar – the last of whom did little to assist the writing, but who nevertheless gets the dedication.

Anthony Elliott

Introduction
Imagination in the service of the new

Those who speak of 'imaginary', understanding by this the 'specular', the reflection of the 'fictive', do no more than repeat, usually without realizing it, the affirmation which has for all time chained them to the underground of the famous cave: it is necessary that this world be an image *of* something.

(Cornelius Castoriadis, *The Imaginary Institution of Society*)

The unconscious is not structured as a language.

(Jean Laplanche, *Seduction, Translation and The Drives*)

The one who seemed to hypostatize language as a control lever of therapy ultimately gave language the least possibility to express itself there, as if the extralinguistic rebounded and sent transference and countertransference, patients and analysts, back to prelinguistic psychical representations or acting without representation.

(Julia Kristeva, *The Sense and Non-Sense of Revolt*)

The 1980s and 1990s witnessed a remarkable resurgence of psychoanalytically-inspired social and cultural theory on both sides of the Atlantic, largely under the impact of the linguistic or discursive turn in the social sciences and humanities. Central to this revival of interest in psychoanalytic theory was the reinterpretation of Freud developed by France's leading psychoanalyst, Jacques Lacan. For many, the theoretical advantages of Lacan's Freud concerned, perhaps above all, his inflation of the role of language in the constitution of the psyche, an inflation which appeared to fit hand in glove with the 'linguistic turn' of the social sciences (and which allegedly permitted French psychoanalysis to cut around a range of tricky issues arising from biology and the body). At any rate, and notwithstanding that the heyday of Lacanianism had pretty much come and gone in French psychoanalytic circles by the time of Lacan's death in 1981, this linguistification of Freud proved especially conducive to some progressive political circles concerned with critiquing – among other topics – the crisis of paternal authority, controversies over gender categories as well as the rise of identity-politics. Indeed, for some considerable period of time, it seemed that theory just wasn't Theory unless the name of Lacan was referenced.

The 'turn to Lacan' proved particularly compelling to various thinkers in the academy, from feminists to film theorists, who brought French psychoanalytic concepts to bear on topics like cross-dressing and spectatorship, queer politics and cyborgs.

This politicization of psychoanalysis through the spectacles of Lacanianism was, for some critics at least, deeply ironic. For one of the foremost achievements of Freud's uncovering of the unconscious imagination was his innovative application of clinical concepts to the spheres of culture, literature, politics and art, that which he termed 'applied psychoanalysis', a kind of model of pure psychoanalytic criticism which right to this day (and notwithstanding the efforts of psychoanalysts the world over to flatten and depoliticize the operational categories of Freudianism) serves to underscore the social and political ramifications of repressed desire and the radical imagination. In addition to Freud's speculations on culture and politics, there have been many and various social scientists, philosophers and cultural critics who have developed the founder's ideas, extending and applying them. Wilhelm Reich, Herbert Marcuse, Theodor Adorno, Erich Fromm, Erik Erikson, Phillip Rieff, Talcott Parsons and Jurgen Habermas: all of these thinkers, in differing ways, drew from Freud to underscore the intertwining of the erotic and symbolic, the unconscious and sociality, repression and daily life. And so it was that, in terms of the academy at least, astonishing, and painfully insufficient, the radical political edge of psychoanalysis came to be celebrated only after Freud had been respectably translated into French, and perhaps more to the point translated (largely by Lacan) into the dense, and at times difficult, conceptual terrain of structuralism and post-structural linguistics.

And yet the political irony runs deeper than this. For at an earlier historical juncture, specifically during the late 1960s and early 1970s, the very same Lacan had figured as a source of inspiration for theoretical and political debate on the left. Many of the new cultural ideas of that time had their roots in Lacan's proto-structuralist disclosure of the place of subjectivity in the structure of language, particularly as set out in his papers and seminars dating from the 1950s and 1960s. The political attraction of Lacan's structuralist rewriting of Freud, according to Fredric Jameson (1988: 82), was that it was 'not locked into the classical opposition between the individual and the collective, but rather able to think these discontinuities in a radically different way'. Translation of the Lacanian psychoanalytic model into social theory was perhaps nowhere more methodologically detailed, and politically fine-tuned, than in the work of Louis Althusser, who set out a vigorously anti-humanist account of ideology. Such work had various beneficial effects, and inspired a range of theoretico-political projects (see Frosh, 1999; Elliott, 2002). And yet the negativism accorded to culture under this Lacanian aesthetic, while perhaps offering a degree of solace to those political radicals attempting to grasp the failures of various political struggles of the period, was profoundly jaded. At its bleakest, the Lacanian Symbolic was deployed to underscore the inevitability of social order and political domination as a fundamental structure of human desire – such that the more capitalism unleashed a tediously uniform culture across the world, the more women and men aggressively turned their longings, aspirations and desires back upon themselves in a repressive act of heightened self-subjection. Fortunately, and at the same time, culture itself entered into a direct confrontation with such theoretical proclamations, primarily through unleashing a global challenge to the notion that we had entered a world comprising a singular, soulless cultural mentality. Difference and diversity were central to this newer cultural dynamic, one inaugurated by and conducive to a multi-billion-dollar communications sector and popular culture industry. From a theoretical standpoint, it seemed fairly clear that the anti-humanist, hyper-structuralist reading of Lacan's Freud was palpably unable to come to grips with such a world of accelerated communications and technology, of intensive globalization, and of new cultural departures (most notably post-feminism and postmodernism). An anti-humanist, structuralist theorization of the inevitability of self-subjection, not to mention the sidelining of possibilities for resistance, subversion and transgression, was, in short, radically out of kilter with the monumental social changes unleashed by the forces of globalization.

Which brings us back to the 1980s and early 1990s – the very highpoint of the politicization of psychoanalysis – and the issue of what guaranteed the ongoing ascendancy of Lacan's reading of Freud over other theoretical models during this time. Social theorists and cultural analysts of various political orientations found that the untroubled days of hyper-structuralism had run their course by about the late 1970s, at which time many went in search of new theoretical maps for engaging with the dawning postmodern era. Some turned to Derrida, some to Lyotard, and many became devotees of Foucault. For those steeped in the language of psychoanalysis, however, it became necessary to trade Lacan's early analyses of the symbolic determination of the subject for his late mediations on sexual fantasy, as a kind of papering over of the traumatic kernel of desire itself. This marked, in effect, the arrival of Lacan Mark II, of a postmodern Lacan. In one sense, this shift from a hyper-structuralist to a post-modern reading of Lacan brought social theory and cultural studies closer to the action of that dramatic speed-up of communications, culture and capitalism which was unfolding throughout the West. Against the backdrop of the ruth-less colonizing commercial activities of transnational corporations and the dominance of image, information and ideas within a media-driven culture, a postmodern Lacanianism insisting on the emptiness of desire seemed just what was demanded for the purposes of radical political critique. Such personal detachment and political disenchantment was given powerful expression by a group of authors who, for want of a better label, might be termed the 'Lacanian mafia': Slavoj Žižek, Renata Salec, Joan Copjec, Richard Boothby and others. All of these authors, in quite different ways, offered slick, stylized theories of the fate of subjectivity that postmodern culture seemed unable to refuse, namely a linking of various Lacanian motifs (the impossibility of desire, the lack haunting subjectivity, the traumatism of the signifier) with the very idea of a global age that had inaugurated a supposedly post-political condition. The appeal of this postmodern or post-structuralist version of Lacan, roughly speaking, was that it seemed not only more in tune with contemporary cultural developments, but also offered a range of key theoretical concepts (from *objet petit a* to the notorious mathemes) that engaged multi-dimensional social realities in a fashion that other theoretical currents seemed unable to comprehend.

Where there was theoretical exchange and cross-disciplinary dialogue, one of the most controversial was that staged between Lacanianism and historicism, particularly as represented in the writings of Foucault. We can find just such a postmodern cross of Lacan and Foucault in Joan Copjec's *Read My Desire: Lacan Against the Historicists*, which is worth briefly considering here for what it indicates about the status of imagination in contemporary critical studies. In a world racked with contingency and ambivalence, Copjec argues, it is a mistake to think that what is on the surface is merely the level of the superficial. On the contrary, postmodern culture glitters at the edge of its surfaces – in media images, computational signs, globalized codes. According to Copjec, this is why Foucault was right to reject the 'repressive hypothesis' put forward by Freud (and other sexual radicals) that culture is inherently oppressive. Rejecting the conventional understanding of power as an external force that exerts itself upon society, Foucault came to appreciate that power is also an instrument in the production of sexuality and of pleasure. From this angle, sexuality is understood as an effect of cultural discourses and technologies aimed at regulating bodily management and of constructing 'sex' as the secret core of the self. Contemporary examples might include discourses of political correctness, or developments in human reproductive technologies, as indicating the extent to which sexual life has become thoroughly permeated by knowledge–power systems. Sexuality and sexual difference are thus an outcrop of historically variable discourses in which individuals find themselves located. Yet transformations at the level of human sexuality involve much more than alterations in discourse – however important that is. It is here that Copjec breaks with Foucault, rejecting the view that political resistance arises at the very limit of power/knowledge networks. Drawing from Lacan and his late seminars on the tactile stuff of desire – bodily fluids, human organs, fetishized objects – Copjec argues 'while sex is, for psychoanalysis, never simply a natural fact, it is also never reducible to any discursive construction, to sense, finally'. Sex, therefore, is not the limit of sexuality. There is always a kind of leftover from, or failure of, desire. Invoking Lacan, this leftover is conceptualized by Copjec as lack, a traumatic absence arising from the loss of maternal love.

Unlike some of her wilfully apolitical, sloganizing associates in the Lacanian mafia, Copjec's writing is sociologically engaged, attempting to raise questions of the imaginary horizons of life in a world where imagination itself often seems formulaic and degraded. In applying her psychoanalytic insights to film, media studies, the commodity form as well as feminism and sexual difference, Copjec's purpose is to highlight the degree to which the imaginary relation of the subject to social relations and cultural processes has been poorly theorized. She argues, in particular, that cultural theorists have consistently misread Lacan: there is in Lacan's teachings a depth as regards the imaginary constitution of the subject that shows up the meagreness of accounts that continue to speak of 'decentred subjects' and 'subject effects'. Or so she claims.

Of what, exactly, does this renewed, more fruitful, encounter between Lacanianism and culture consist? Here Copjec's answers are particularly defective, contrasting as she does the standard Lacanian emphasis on the subject as a discursive effect with a revised Lacanian/postmodern/feminist account of identity formation that, in the end, still situates subjectification as subjection. She is especially deft, it must be said, when it comes to dismantling the standard Lacanian account of the subject's narcissistic relation to otherness and sociality. For example, she points out that while Lacan's classic essay on the mirror stage theorizes the child's narcissistic apprehension of experience, it is in fact in Lacan's late writings and seminars that the French master details the lures of the imaginary – particularly in relation to the concept of the gaze. And yet if only such textural sophistication made a tangible contribution to rethinking imagination! For pretty much the same fate afflicts the conceptualization of the imaginary in Copjec's revised Lacanianism as it did in the more orthodox appropriations of French psychoanalysis that she criticizes. Lack, misrecognition, gap, absence, superegoic law: a single word to sum up all of these might be negativism. The informing idea that it is from the mirror-like gaze of the other that the traumatic, impenetrable constitution of the subject arises can only retain a semblance of sense if we continue to evade the problem of human creation, of the subject's imaginary construction of a world for itself, not to mention the issue of the content of Lacanian theory and its epistemological claims (see Castoriadis, 1984). Certainly saying, as Copjec (1994: 32) does, that 'the speaking subject cannot ever be totally trapped in the imaginary' doesn't get us very far, and only pushes the issue of the productivities of radical imagination further back.

What, then, have been the intellectual consequences of Lacanianism? The theoretical hegemony of Lacanianism within the academy is now over. There are several reasons for this, one of which concerns the rise of object-relational and Kleinian theory in the social sciences and humanities – of which more shortly. Yet even for those, and there are indeed many, who have traded their beloved Parisian Freud for, say, a postmodern reading of Klein or a post-theory celebration of Winnicott, there remains still missing – for the most part – a conceptual appreciation of the philosophical (and for that matter political) gains and losses of Lacan's version of psychoanalysis. Many of the ideas of Lacan – especially his rewriting of Oedipus in structuralist mode – remain of incomparable value. Those to whom Lacanianism suggests either the failure of Theory or the abuse of Freudianism are, it seems, often likely to trivialize the whole project of a radical political psychoanalysis; they are also likely to downgrade the political importance of Lacan's achievement of establishing repressed desire and sexuality as legitimate objects of debate in both the academy and public political life. That said, there are numerous respects in which the losses of social theory's engagement with Lacanianism outweigh the gains, and these are worth briefly mentioning.

A number of social theorists have taken issue with the philosophical premises of Lacanian psychoanalysis, including amongst others Paul Riceour, Jean-François Lyotard, Luce Irigaray and Gananath Obeyesekere. Such theorists have tended to put the Freudian objection against Lacanianism that the unconscious is resistant to ordered syntax. At it crudest, or at least this is so in some versions of this argument, Lacan actually suppressed the deeply subversive implications of Freud's uncovering of unconscious imagination by structuralizing desire, and thus reduced the repressed unconscious to a free play of signifiers. In a previous book, *Social Theory and Psychoanalysis in Transition*, I argued that Lacan's linguistic or post-structuralist reintepretation of the Freudian unconscious has, in fact, been formulated in diverse ways, with some versions stressing the primacy of the Symbolic order and inflating the role of language in psychical life, while other versions have emphasized the illusions and snares of the Imaginary order and thus have granted a kind of primacy to fantasy over and above the emotional contours governing reflective subjecthood. Not all Lacanian theory is of this either/or kind, though it is accurate to say that the most influential advocates of French psychoanalysis tend to emphasize either a more fluid or deterministic reading of Lacan's concepts. As I see it, and notwithstanding the more interesting and innovative interpretations of this intellectual tradition, there are good reasons to reject the philosophical premises of Lacanian psychoanalysis. As I have argued at length previously (Elliott 1999, 2002, 2003), there are two core premises of Lacan's Freud which should be rejected: first, that 'lack' transcendentally pierces and frames in advance the production of desire; second, that the conscious/unconscious dualism is best approached as a linguistic relation. I shall not be concerned with an overall appraisal of the philosophical premises of Lacanianism here; however much of what I do argue in this book concerning the future direction of dialogue between social theory and psychoanalysis is informed by my previous writings. Certainly, the present argument that social theory requires a new approach to the creativity of action, one in which radical imagination and the unconscious moves to the fore, arises directly out of my previous critiques of Lacanian social thought, as set out in both *Social Theory and Psychoanalysis in Transition* and *Subject to Ourselves*. This book focuses accordingly in detail on thinkers such as Cornelius Castoriadis, Julia Kristeva and Jean Laplanche whose work on imagination is, in my view, central to rethinking the crucial debate between social theory and psychoanalysis.

Moving beyond such received ideas in psychoanalytic studies, the guiding impetus that informs the present study is that one can reasonably claim that Lacanianism is in error in making language and the unconscious imagination indissociable, as though drive and desire lacked any representational contours prior to Lacan's 'law' of symbolization. In fact, some of the most interesting developments in contemporary psychoanalysis persuasively show that the status of the psychic representative prior to representation, and certainly prior to the psyche's Oedipal enmeshment within language and symbolization, may be regarded as having a kind of unconscious (or what Castoriadis has termed the *human Nonconscious*) all of its own. This argument is complex and will be developed in detail in Chapter 3. But, for our present purposes, it is worth noting that such clinical and theoretical insights derive largely from one of the main alternatives to Lacanian-inspired cultural studies, namely the various relational and intersubjective accounts of subject-formation offered in object-relations theory and Kleinian psychoanalysis. Rejecting the Lacanian emphasis on the determination of linguistics or discursive codes in the construction of subjectivity, a range of psychoanalytically-inspired social theorists and cultural critics have argued that the intrasubjective and intersubjective constitution of desire is far more complex, differentiated and nuanced than is dramatized in French psychoanalytic theories. In some approaches, it is the intersubjective constitution and reproduction of psychic life which is especially significant, with theorists referring to 'the shadow of the Other' (Jessica Benjamin), 'the analytic Third' (Thomas Ogden), the relational force of 'thinking in fragments' (Jane Flax), or the transformational 'power of feelings' (Nancy Chodorow).

Theories of imagination

Not all imaginative acts are pleasurable, and not all forms of activity are necessarily creative. One may derive pleasure from painting or playing the piano, but it is likely that there are some not so pleasant associations connected with such activities too: for example, getting stuck in one's attempt to visualize or represent something anew in the act of painting is likely to generate unpleasure, and the repetitive aspect of practice has caused many budding musicians to give the game away. Yet from a psychoanalytic angle – which is inevitably concerned with the question of unconscious pleasure, or its derivatives – the crux of the matter lies elsewhere. From a psychoanalytic point of view, activities can not be exhaustively assessed on the basis of one's conscious state of pleasure, since there are necessarily unconscious preoccupations and representations to take into account also. More significantly, such unconscious desires and affinities – if you like, the representational dream-work of the self – can regularly be at odds with one's conscious ideals. In one sense, therefore, it may be the case that the self derives unconscious pleasure from the momentary discontent of getting stuck, or losing one's way, in the artistic process known as creation. Indeed, such 'jamming' of conscious preconceptions and preoccupations can be crucial to the emergence of genuine creativity.

These may not be especially radical insights, but for those who have come to psychoanalysis from the disciplines of, say, literary criticism, philosophy or cultural studies, my comments may give pause for thought, since implicit in what I have said about pleasure and the unconscious is a different take on the relationship between imagination and creativity. In what follows I want to elaborate a conception of imagination which is always in the service of the new, of the past recreated, of repetitious social practices always revised, of traditions and canons of culture reelaborated, and of social things renewed. I do so in the knowledge that there could be nothing more fanciful than to have the last word on imagination, if only because (as I argue throughout this book) the imaginary gives the slip to all attempts at conceptual closure or fixed interpretations. Moreover, it would be cute to pretend that a defence of the imagination is, in our current time, especially politically pressing or historically urgent: like 'democracy' or 'freedom', the word 'imagination' is something everyone seems to favour automatically as a personal and social good. And yet, as we know, the imaginary has long been something of a dirty word in psychoanalysis, at once derivative and distorted, as that which entraps the subject in chronic mis-recognitions of self, others and world. In the Lacanian gospel, which as noted has been one of the most authoritative readings of Freud in the social sciences and humanities, we are stuck with a repetitive imagination, an imaginary anchored in the haunted specular. From such a viewpoint, to speak of the imaginary as creative, as where creation comes from, can only be seen as a Utopian or infantile longing to put a stop to the unconscious. In terms of the imaginary fabrications of psyche and society, however, the situation, I maintain, is quite the contrary.

In formulating an alternative account of the creative power of imagination I have throughout this book drawn upon ideas from quite divergent sources. To take up other theoretical speculations on the experience of subjectivity, imagination and cultural production, as a first approximation, I want to begin with the way in which the imaginary is at one with the sense of innovation and of impending change, whether in the psyche itself or in the affective struc-turation of social things. I shall begin with three recent psychoanalytical formulations: three theoretical constructs concerning the imaginary, which I shall in turn seek to unloosen for what these narratives have to offer for a theory of creation. These three theoretical formulations are associated with studies by Cornelius Castoriadis, Julia Kristeva and Jean Laplanche, who have all written the most interesting and influential contemporary works on psychoanalysis and the imagination. In what follows, the work of these psychoanalysts will be introduced in order to provide a basis for further critical discussion of the nature of imagination, and especially of the unconscious in social relations, throughout the book.

Cornelius Castoriadis: radical and social imaginaries

The first formulation is taken from Castoriadis,[1] who in an interview in 1991 reflected on the 'incessant flux' of the imagination thus:

> The 'presubjective' world is a compact, blind, and dull mass; the blossoming forth of the imagination is a local explosion that digs into this mass a hole, that opens an interior space within it, a chamber that can swell enormously. And this chamber is not a room; it is a kind of cylinder, since it is, at the same time, *a time*. It therefore also has a fourth dimension; and

that means that it constitutes, for itself, the inner linings of the cylinder, an organised world . . . there are olfactory objects, tactile objects that are, at the outset, much more important than visual objects. I am not fixated on the 'scopic'; one of the gross inadequacies of Lacan's conception of the imagination is his fixation of the scopic. For me, if one is speaking of stages that are worked out, the *imagination* par excellence is the imagination of the musical composer (which is what I wanted to be). Suddenly, figures surge forth which are not in the least visual. They are essentially auditory and kinetic – for there is also rhythm. There is a marvellous excerpt from a letter by Mozart cited by Brigitte Massin, in which Mozart describes how he composes. Like every self-respecting composer, he composes, obviously, in his head. When deaf, Beethoven heard – imagined – in his head. A true composer writes and hears chords, chordal progressions, as I, in closing my eyes, can review some scene or imagine some scene, bringing into mutual presence characters who have never really been present to each other. Mozart explains that the piece composes itself in his head, and he says the following hallucinatory thing: when the piece is finished, it is all laid out simul-taneously before him in its progression. He hears in one moment the beginning, the middle, the end of the first movement of the sonata. As Galileo says of God, the proofs we arduously traverse step by step are laid out before Him *instantaneously*. That is an imagination. When Mozart says, I have the entire piece laid out in my head, it is not that he sees the score, it is that he hears the totality of the piece. That appears incomprehensible to us because our musical imagination is rather poor: to be able to hear simultaneously the beginning of the *symphony in G minor* and the minuet. Nor is there anything 'visual' in the social imaginary. The social imaginary is not the creation of images in society; it is not the fact that one paints the walls of towns. A fundamental creation of the social imaginary, the gods or rules of behaviour are neither visible nor even audible but *signifiable*.

(Castoriadis, 1997: 182–3)

Castoriadis's reflections on the imaginary principally concern, one might say, the ways in which a world (at once emotional and social) somehow or other comes to be ordered and organized from groundlessness or chaos; about the creation of imagination from 'dull mass'; about creation and invention as a consequence of an 'explosion that digs into this mass a hole'. This involves for Castoriadis the creation of 'something' out of 'nothing', an eruption of imaginary significations that shapes the psyche of individuals and the culture of society itself. The constitution of these imaginary determinations manifests the creativity that appertains to the psyche as such, and that 'opens an interior space within it'.

Clearly a great deal could be said about the links between imagination and the auditory and kinetic in Castoriadis's reflections, with all this implies of an overvaluation of visual objects in psychoanalysis. And, more pertinently to the focus of this book, how the fetishization of the scopic in Lacanian psychoanalysis has led to a harmful neglect of the creativity of the psyche. Freud emphasized, of course, that *visual memory* is fundamental to the unconscious and its expressive processes of condensation, displacement and representation – especially in that aspect of his corpus where he conceived of fantasy in terms of his model of the dream. In some versions of Freud, dreams are the linchpin for an easy fit between representation and imagination. 'As an analogue of the mind', writes Harvie Ferguson (1996: 7) in *The Lure of Dreams*, 'the dream came to represent *both* reflection *and* imagination. Indeed, the plasticity of the dream not only brought to life a picture of the world; its succession of images also revealed the normally hidden process of representation itself'. In Freud's approach, however, the visual domain was not all. For sensory elements also figured in Freud's construction of the dream-work and, by extension, the imagination. The Freudian subject may dream visually, and only be able to report the dream in words, yet the sharpness of the visual perception is an upshot of heterogeneous domains of representation (sensations, affects, verbal and non-verbal representations).

Indeed the creativity of social imaginary significations is Castoriadis' central theme from beginning to end. The imaginary, he insists, is not a question of harmonious representation, of 'the creation of images in society', but of the productive energies of self-creation, which generate social imaginary significations and the institutions of each particular society. What is radically imaginary about the psychic process of every individual is precisely the representational pleasure of the unconscious monad, initially closed upon itself, and subsequently forced to shift from self-generating solipsistic fantasy to the shared meanings of society. To the radical imaginary of the psychic monad corresponds what Castoriadis terms the 'social imaginary', an aesthetics of imagination that holds together the primary institutions of society (language, norms, customs and law) and the forms of relation through which individuals and collectivities come to relate to such objects of investment.

Julia Kristeva: the melancholic imagination

In her sharp biography *Melanie Klein*, the European psychoanalyst Julia Kristeva[2] also writes about what makes for creative imagination:

> The unconscious or preconscious fantasy is present in all psychic activities and behaviours, so much so that the fantasy is an 'active presence of fantasy scenes'. Such a fantasy is, strictly speaking, bound up with motivity, taste and food aversions, the sharpness of the perception (particularly the visual perception) of the primal scene, the image of the body, voice-song-and-speech, sporting activities, concert-show-and-film attendance, educational and intellectual activities, neurotic symptoms, and, in the end, the entire organisation of the personality. Not only is the totality of psychic life *impregnated* with fantasies, but in the child whom Klein listened to and analysed, the fantasy – that is, the fantasy that preceded repression – is

united with psychic life, because this fantasy and this life, 'the representative of the earliest impulses of desire and aggressiveness, are expressed in and dealt with by *mental processes far removed from words* and conscious relational thinking'.

(Kristeva, 2001a: 140)

Kristeva's reflections are in one sense primarily concerned with the presence of fantasy and unconscious work, all to do with the imagination of sensational life. The psychic work of representation is a universal feature 'present in all psychic activities and behaviours', by no means restricted to the therapeutic relationship, nor to particular aspects of mental functioning, such as the standard psychoanalytic menu of day-dreaming or erotic imaginings. Rather, it is our ordinary experiences – from sporting activities to the practicalities of learning and education – that are saturated with this originary imagination. All psychic activity, says Kristeva, is 'impregnated with fantasies'.

What is clear in Kristeva's account of fantasy is that this imaginary domain is inextricably interwoven with the motions of pleasure and unpleasure, the most primitive impulses of desire and aggressiveness which bring a world of subjectivity into being in the first place. Freud astutely captured the theatrical dynamics of sensational life in terms of the logics of dreaming; and it is these affective processes (the dream-work) which for Kristeva dominate the mental apparatus from start to finish. Yet what might Kristeva be gaining by drawing attention to the imaginary resilience – the creative representational refashioning of the senses – of everyday life? And what, we might ask, is gained by thinking of what happens to our wishes (inseparable from figure and fantasy) in categories that emphasize the pro-linguistic: fantasy life is 'expressed in and dealt with by *mental processes far removed from words* and conscious relational thinking'. Would this not be the other side of language, which is the representational flux of the unconscious ego?

Kristeva conceptualizes what she refers to as the 'proto-fantasy' as a kind of oscillation of the imagination, with the human subject internally divided, split between infantile narcissism and the other's lack. Strictly speaking, if representation is an 'active presence of fantasy scenes', this is because desire, for Kristeva as for Lacan, is the desire of the Other. To desire the Other is a kind of fashioning, an imagining of what the other dreams, an imitating, an identification with the other's desire. Notwithstanding that it is the inescapability of imaginary misrecognition that leaves the human subject to impute an imaginary fullness to the other's desire which, in fact, pertains only to the representation (that is, the imaginary plenitude that the subject itself desires), the point is that there would be no meaning, not to say anything of the possibility for self-knowledge, without these imaginative fashionings.

Kristeva has written in great depth about the length people will go to in creating obstacles to pleasure; in doing so, she has reformulated Freud's account of Oedipal desire as a general theory of the constitution of the subject and its baroque imaginings. I examine Kristeva's theories in the opening chapter, and critically engage with her path-breaking account of primary identification in Chapter 3. Here I want to emphasize that her reflections on the unconscious or preconscious fantasy – in the above quotation – captures something important about the imaginary making and taking of pleasure in daily life. In Kristeva's reckoning, the psychoanalytic theory of fantasy is about the human subject's imaginings that inform, say, perceptions of the body, imaginings about how one sounds and speaks, imaginings about one's sporting prowess, imaginings about pop stars and celebrities, imaginings about educational advancement and intellectual recognition, imaginings about where one is headed or what may be wrong with one's life.

More than any other psychoanalyst, perhaps more than Freud's foundational insights, Kristeva captures the complex ways people use their imagination to make life meaningful. For Kristeva, individuals are captured by, or in thrall to, their unconscious fantasies – these radically strange, foreign social dreams. Such fantasies, in addition to constituting intercourse between unconscious dreams and practical life, are the very imaginings of imagination. I examine Kristeva's theoretical approach in considerable detail at various points of this book partly because, in my view, she offers us an exemplary social theory of the creativity of imagination. Yet there are now a number of highly original conceptual departures that underscore the creativity of the psyche, and in one sense it is possible that not even Kristeva adequately accounts for what the French psychoanalyst Jean Laplanche – to whom I now turn for a final formulation on the imagination – underscores concerning the importance of creation to social thought.

Jean Laplanche: imaginary seductions

Laplanche was one of the first post-Lacanians to write of the strange trans-formations – the condensations, displacements and reversals – of unconscious repression, which results in the formation of an internal foreign other, of what Freud called a thing-presentation, or, if you will, the depths of imagination itself.[3] He has been one of the few major psychoanalytic thinkers, period, to focus on the irreducible creativity of unconscious work, by which he means specifically the field of symbolizing activity. His psychoanalytic work, to a considerable degree, represents a series of reflections on the ontology of determinism within Freudianism, and I shall examine how some of his central ideas may be relevant to social theory in Chapters 2 and 3.

For the moment, it is appropriate to detail Laplanche's account of the internal otherness – an unconscious of strange, foreign bodies – at the centre of psychic life. As he writes:

> What guarantees the alien-ness of the other? Can one affirm here, with Lacan, the priority of language? If for my part, I speak rather of a 'message', this is for at least two well-defined reasons: *firstly*, the message can just as easily be non-verbal as verbal; and for the baby it is principally non-verbal.

Secondly, emphasising 'language' effaces the alterity and individuality of the other in favour of transhistorical structures.

(Laplanche, 1997: 660)

There are a couple of things to note here. Laplanche, like Kristeva, rejects the linguistic imperialism of Lacanian doctrine: 'the message can just as easily be non-verbal as verbal'. So too, like Kristeva, Laplanche distances himself from a concern with 'transhistorical structures' (phylogenesis, language) in favour of the essential uniqueness and individuality of human imagination. In shifting away from Lacan and back to Freud – returning to prelinguistic psychical representatives or fantasmatic constructions made of images and split from words – Laplanche will emphasize that in the act of *psychic translation* the singular individual *creates* in the strongest sense of the term.

It could be said that Laplanche is out to provide a social theory of our *struggle for representation* in the field of symbolizing activity – which, in a sense, has been the subject of all psychoanalytic theories since Freud unearthed the unconscious logics of the dream. For in his preoccupation with the problem of translation – by which is meant the psychic forcefield of representations, resemblances, contiguities, condensations and reversals – Laplanche's work plays ingeniously on a subtle, but definite, relation between human subjects in the context of symbolic and social formations. For Laplanche, it is essential to grasp that the infant is, from the beginning of life, presented with what he calls 'messages' (both verbal and non-verbal) by parents, messages which the infant is ill-equipped to adequately deal with or understand on an emotional plane. It makes perhaps less difference what the soft caresses of a mother actually signify as regards the self-understandings of the adult, though part of Laplanche's interest turns on the way parents always convey far more than they consciously intend. What matters in Laplanche's scheme is that the infant has been addressed or called with a message, a message which is at once exciting and mystifying.

The striking feature of Laplanche's theorization of the message as enigmatic is its sheer open-endedness. His account of the psychosexual development of the individual subject in terms of the ongoing emotional work of translation and retranslation would make no sense were it not for the recognition that, because of the small infant's initially limited ways of trying to emotionally process proffered messages, psychic life is always, necessarily, imaginative, creative, inventive. Unlike the iron determinism of the early Lacan's emphasis on the Symbolic subjection of the subject, it is the mystifying element of the message that for Laplanche sparks imaginative associations in the child. What is inescapable for the infant – and then subsequently for the adult – is that such mystifying messages demand continual psychic work, are in need of continual translation. Indeed, Laplanche himself has acknowledged that he came up with the concept of 'message', with all this implies of the need for translation, in order to overcome the rigid determinism of psychoanalysis in France since Lacan. I try to keep this aspect of Laplanche's work to the forefront when examining his contributions in Chapters 2 and 3.

The argument of this book

Castoriadis, Kristeva and Laplanche are not alone among those theorists of the contemporary age who have wrestled with the question of imagination as well as individual and social transformations affecting imaginary life. Fortunately, for academic social science but also for the demands of practical social life, there have been a growing number of voices raising pressing political issues about the conditions and consequences of our imaginative interpersonal relations in a postmodern world of fragmentation and fracture. Such authoritative voices today include, to mention only a few: Judith Butler, Drucilla Cornell, Slavoj Žižek, Homi Bhabha, Christopher Bollas, Lynne Segal, Fredric Jameson, Stephen Frosh, Luce Irigaray, Elizabeth Grosz, Nancy Chodorow, Jane Flax, Charles Spezzano, Thomas Ogden and Jessica Benjamin. Each has drawn from psychoanalysis to develop a particular angle on the changing relations between self and society in the contemporary epoch. Each has focused on specific problematics of current social conditions – from feminism to postmodernism, from psychotherapy to literature – in rethinking the terms of both individual and collective imaginaries.

Yet the contributions of Castoriadis, Kristeva and Laplanche do stand out, in a most definite way, in terms of both the comprehensive and courageous fashion in which each details forms of the radical imaginary. Castoriadis conceives of individual imaginaries as ineluctably interwoven with social-historical imaginaries. Kristeva thinks of human imagination in terms of a permanent state of psychic questioning, of unconscious transformations, an endless dialectic of semiotic and symbolic restructurings. And Laplanche places the imagination squarely in relation to the demands of interpersonal bonds, the ceaseless work of imaginative, symbolizing activities. Critical social theory now faces the challenging work of sifting through the core insights of these three psychoanalytic-cultural pioneers, both for resituating subjectivity in the wake of post-structuralism and postmodernism and for reassessing the culture it is critiquing. Through extended engagement with the works of Castoriadis, Kristeva and Laplanche, this book is intended as a contribution to that task.

My own *Social Theory and Psychoanalysis in Transition*, along with its more popularizing companion volume *Psychoanalytic Theory: An Introduction*, as well as my subsequent foray into the terrain of postmodernism in *Subject to Ourselves*, had their inspirational roots in these alternative theoretical orientations. Endebted in particular to Castoriadis's notion of the imaginary domain of human creation, as well as Kristeva's recasting of the subversive aspects of unconscious transformations, I sought in these works to address questions about both the representational production of the subject and the affective structure of social things – questions that I felt had been largely ignored, sidestepped, displaced or more generally repressed by more orthodox traditions.

This book is intended as a critical response to the paradoxes raised by the current orthodoxy in psychoanalytically-inspired social and cultural theory. I try to spell out why I think this orthodoxy is insufficient in grasping the most crucial questions of our current global political predicament. A critical poetics of social imaginaries transcending the current orthodoxy is, I argue, an urgent concern of social theory, and to that end I draw extensively from the writings of Castoriadis, Kristeva and Laplanche to sketch the contours of how this situation might be remedied. The opening chapter sets the stage by developing a critical overview of the encounter between psychoanalysis and contemporary theory in general, as I traverse various accounts of the social imaginary. The central standpoints examined include (1) critical theory, with emphasis on the importance of psychoanalysis, social theory and philosophy for emancipatory thought; (2) post-structuralist interrogations of the production of subjectivity and identity; and, (3) various feminist readings of psychoanalysis and masculinist assumptions in western social theory. In Chapter 2, I consider some of the ways in which Freud has been situated in the social field in contemporary intellectual discourse, paying special attention to the 'culture wars' and debates over trauma and memory which shaped the 1990s. By framing this contemporary turn away from Freud in a wider psychoanalytic context, I consider some implications of the rise of 'anti-psychological psychology'.

The subsequent chapters seek to reconstruct some of the core concepts of contemporary psychoanalysis in the light of recent social theory. Chapter 3, in introducing several novel conceptual revisions, begins by examining the tensions between concepts of fantasy and representation on the one hand, and the ideas of creativity, creation and imagination on the other. Among the issues raised are questions about the constitution of representation; the debate in post-Kleinian and post-Lacanian circles over the hypothesis of a proto-fantasy, or instituting representation; and the structuration of representation with reference to primary repression and identification. The current preoccupation with the pre-Oedipal register, and especially the notion of primary repression, is critically appraised, and it is here that I introduce the theorems of *rolling identification* and *representational wrappings of self and other*. I introduce such terminological innovation, or neologisms, to refer in a general way to the study of the imaginary constitution of the subject, linking the psychic origins of the human subject to the foundational force of intersubjectivity and culture. The scope and nature of this critique of the Freudian conceptual field is then directly explored with reference to recent debates in sexuality studies, feminism and postmodernism. In the final part of the book, in a dialogue that reflects further on these terminological innovations, I attempt to articulate the theme of the social imaginary in relation to processes of language, symbolization, cultural reproduction and political domination.

Pretext
You'll never dream the same dream twice

A classical political dichotomy, that of the relation between the individual and society, lies at the heart of social theory and the philosophy of social science. This opposition between self and society, between private and public, is particularly evident in the writings of a range of major classical and contemporary social theorists seeking to explain the individual's relation to social institutions, cultural processes and historical forces. In confronting the problem of the relation between self and society, what emerges from much of the existing literature is either a conceptual dynamic that emphasizes the power of the individual in her or his relations to both interpersonal relationships and social forces, or a dynamic in which the external world is taken as constitutive of individual identities, actions, practices, beliefs and values. An either/or logic rules. Personalizing things gives way to subjectivizing them, while institutionalizing them gives way to objectivism. Either way, one term of this political dichotomy is raised over and above the other term – such that this enforced binary division comes to appear inevitable. And yet each approach does retain certain strengths and limitations. The first approach, that which posits the individual as the prime object of analysis, rightly emphasizes the creativity, knowledgeability and reflectiveness of human agents, yet typically downgrades issues of social relations and institutional reproduction. The second approach, that which puts society centre stage, rightly emphasizes the variety of structuring socio-historical forces in the constitution of the subject, yet typically neglects the complexities of human subjectivity, of action and agency.

This political dichotomy, not without relevance for the discourse of psychoanalysis itself, contains a number of striking ironies. For one thing, the similarities between these supposedly contending viewpoints become plain when looked at from the vantage point of psychoanalytic theory. The fixed, absolute conception of subjectivity as purely self-legislating and omnipotent, for example, in individuals-first approaches merely inverts the overinflated image of institutional power and cultural determination in society-first approaches. Where then to locate identity? On the side of individuals, or of society? And what if this dichotomous way of posing the issue concerning the relation between self and society is itself part of the problem – that is, a kind of symbolic violence? 'Socialisation', argues Cornelius Castoriadis, 'is constitutive of the human being. What is stupidly called in political, philosophical and economic theory the 'individual' – and which is opposed there to society – is nothing other than the society itself' (Castoriadis, 1997: 187). In other words, what individuals-first and society-first approaches call the 'individual', as a kind of shorthand for the singular human being, is for Castoriadis nothing other than the trace of the social itself – an introjection of successive strata of socialization, cultural codes and ideological perspectives, as well as social co-ordinates and pragmatic presuppositions.

Once you start thinking of the structuring of social differences and cultural prohibitions like this, psychoanalysis appears less as an alternative theory of self/society divisions, and more as a dismantling of the very conceptual divisions created by the classical political dichotomy I've been sketching. Could it be that what passes between subjectivity and the outside is kept fixed or rigid in much social theory because the social scientist fears a blurring of categories, classifications, knowledge itself? What does the dynamic unconscious actually do, in any case, to the classic political dichotomy? In Castoriadis's formulation, as noted, self and society are on the same analytic divide as regards the thinking of social differences. This essentially Freudian reading of culture stresses that if there is a fundamental deadlock or antagonism operating here it is not that between self and society, but rather between the psychic and social. It is precisely this issue of the fluidity, conflict and division of the unconscious mind, and with it that of the distribution of psychical energy in self/society interlockings, that remains unaddressed in mainstream social science perspectives. Particularly in objectivistic or deterministic versions of social thought, such as Marxism or functionalism, the actions, ideas and psychic processes of individuals are cast as susceptible to the forces of social structures, yet curiously those same structures are seen as free of the impacts of psychic process.

Perhaps nowhere more so does psychoanalysis demonstrate the blatant inconsistencies of the traditionalist self/society division than in its interrogation of the dreamy unconsciousness of sleep. It is not by accident that

Freud founded the theory of psychoanalysis upon the study of dreams, as it is in conditions of sleep that the hallucinogenic form of our unconscious thoughts shatters the hold of prohibitions issuing from the conscious mind. In *The Interpretation of Dreams*, Freud (1900, S.E. 5: 507) explains the central differences of the dreaming mind from the consciousness of waking life thus: 'It is not that [the unconscious] is more negligent, more unreasonable, more forgetful, more incomplete, say, than waking thought; it is qualitatively different from it, and so at first not comparable to it. It does not think, calculate, judge in any way at all.'

One might suppose that Freud, in insisting on the uncontrollable representational swirl of our dreaming minds, pits the repressed energies of unconscious desire against our more conscious forms of self-knowledge. If he had chosen to do so in his study of dreams, he would certainly have been drawing from a rich philosophical tradition – from Kant's proclamation that 'the madman is a waking dreamer' to Schopenhauer's summation 'the dream a brief madness and madness a long dream'. Yet Freud thought otherwise. The interweaving of parts of the mind – conscious reflection, the not-quite-consciousness of daily life and dreamy unconsciousness – is never so simple a matter as the psychic world obliterating its own trace within a social relation or instituted structure, nor is it simply a matter of the individual's mechanical socialization into society's practices, norms and prohibitions. This, then, is where Freud's challenge to social theory enters – in the unconscious no man's land of conflict, division and uncanniness; in discerning the outermost boundaries of society and history in the inner linings of the psyche, as well as the limits of childhood infantile wishes and the unconscious in the social process of institutionalization.

Differentiating self and psyche is central to Freud's *The Interpretation of Dreams*. Dreaming, says Freud, protects the individual's sleep: 'The dream is *the guardian of sleep, not its disturber.*' Yet if it is the dream which facilitates sleep of the self, the same cannot be said for the dreamer – or, more precisely, the psychic agency that dreams. 'What is repressed', writes Freud, 'does not obey the wish to sleep'. Though he didn't say it quite like this, Freud's idea is that part of the mind is always at work – dreaming is simultaneously a result of sleeping and of not-sleeping. One example of the psyche's productivity during sleep is that which Freud terms 'secondary revision', which simply put involves unconscious revision of frightening or disturbing dream images, one function of which is the facilitation of sleep. Another thing to which the unconscious of the sleeper is most fully awake is a kind of sensory vividness, which ultimately springs from the subject's earliest childhood recollections – what Freud termed the 'lasting traces' of the prehistoric period of emotional life. It is as if in the dreamy world of sleep part of the mind is most awake, scanning, collecting and retranscribing our remembered impressions (which for Freud stretch all the way back to the first or second year of life) to facilitate a kind of unconscious dream network of elaborations, representations, paths.

But if it is so that part of the mind travels back to our earliest childhood recollections when we dream, there is also a sense in which we move forward. Castoriadis describes this as a 'surging forth' of radical imaginings, the unconscious unrestrained. Granting the unconscious infinite extension, Castoriadis says the dreamer-to-be not only carries around a complex history of memories, but that she or he is continually selecting and scrutinizing psychical objects throughout the day in order to extend paths of dream life. Such unconscious scanning of the 'day's residues' is the terrain on which past and present conduct their hallucinogenic intercourse in the self's dream life, but always with the creative energies of the subject for reforming, retranscribing and transforming to the fore. This 'surging forth' of the dreamer's energized, representational overdeterminations thus always outstrips what is already there – that is, the raw stuff of recollections and residues. This unconscious surging toward some form of presentation or elaboration is creative in the strongest sense of the term; it is the creation *ex nihilo* of hallucinogenic figures and forms. 'Sleep', as Proust wrote, 'is the only source of invention.' Or, as Castoriadis (following Heraclitus) says: 'You will never dream the same dream twice.'

One of the most important reasons, then, that it is no longer as plausible as it once was to think of individuals and collectivities as antithetical is that both are constituted to their roots through the domain of the social imaginary. In the broadest possible sense, the social imaginary – expressed through the constitution and reproduction of a world of representations, signfications and affects – is what renders our understanding of the terms 'individual' and 'society' possible. This indeterminate creativity of imagination, the uncanny exhilarations and difficulties of living, both with ourselves and with others, has of course been a principal theme of various key intellectuals that link psychoanalysis with sociology, politics and history. What psychoanalysis has done to and with social critique has been the subject of numerous studies (see, for example, Frosh 1999; Elliott 1999, 2002). What I am more concerned to re-examine in the opening chapter that follows is what psychoanalysis has disrupted in the dominant sociological picture of social doing and the making of society.

Psychoanalysis has sometimes been mindful of the social contexts and cultural scripts that influence, and powerfully shape, the lacing together of the social-historical and psychic worlds. But as much as Freud tried to refine what he called 'applied psychoanalysis', it remains the case that the core discovery of psychoanalytic practice and theory – the repressed unconscious – is what philosophers, social theorists and cultural analysts have time and again wrestled with. How then to make and break the links between psychoanalysis and critical social theory? In what follows I focus primarily on European social theorists and philosophers who have initiated a critical poetics of the social imaginary. The work of these authors comprise a movement of enquiry which stretches from Freud's foundational twinning of sexuality and death in the life of the unconscious mind, through the radical structuralist and post-structuralist reworkings of Lacan, Althusser, Irigaray and Kristeva, and on to more recent conceptualizations of the postmodern imaginary in the writings of Deleuze, Guattari and Lyotard.

1 Social theory since Freud
Traversing social imaginaries

Freud's theory is in its very substance 'sociological'. Freud's 'biologism' is social theory in a depth dimension that has been consistently flattened out by the Neo-Freudian schools.

(Herbert Marcuse, *Eros and Civilisation*)

In psychoanalysis nothing is true except the exaggerations.

(Theodor Adorno, *Minima Moralia*)

Freudian analysis is the steadfast penetration of the injured psyche. It takes so seriously the damage that it offers nothing for the immediate.

(Russell Jacoby, *Social Amnesia*)

Social theory has the task of providing conceptions of the nature of human agency, social life and the cultural products of human action which can be placed in the services of the social sciences and humanities in general. Among other problems, social theory is concerned with language and the interpretation of meaning, the character of social institutions, the explication of social practices and processes, questions of social transformation and the like. The reproduction of social life, however, is never only a matter of impersonal 'processes' and 'structures': it is also created and lived within, in the depths of an inner world, of our most personal needs, passions and desires. Love, empathy, anxiety, shame, guilt, depression: no study of social life can be successfully carried out, or meaningfully interpreted, without reference to the *human element* of agency. Modernity is the age in which this human element is constituted as a systematic field of knowledge. That field of knowledge is known as psychoanalysis.

Psychoanalysis, a product of the culture of late nineteenth-century Europe, has had a profound influence on contemporary social thought. Psychoanalysis, as elaborated by Freud and his followers, has been enthusiastically taken up by social and political theorists, literary and cultural critics, and by feminists and postmodernists, such is its rich theoretical suggestiveness and powerful diagnosis of our contemporary cultural malaise. The importance of psycho-analysis to social theory, although a focus of much intellectual debate and controversy, can be seen in quite specific areas, especially as concerns contemporary debates on human subjectivity, sexuality, gender hierarchy and political debates over culture. Indeed, Freudian concepts and theories have played a vital role in the construction of contemporary social theory itself. The writings of social theorists as diverse as Erich Fromm, Herbert Marcuse, Louis Althusser, Jürgen Habermas, Julia Kristeva, Luce Irigaray, and Jean-François Lyotard all share a Freudian debt. Yet there can be little doubt that the motivating reason for this turn to Freud among social theorists is as much political as intellectual. In a century which has witnessed the rise of totalitarianism, Hiroshima, Auschwitz, and the possibility of a 'nuclear winter', social theory has demanded a language which is able to grapple with modernity's unleashing of its unprecedented powers of destruction. Psychoanalysis has provided that conceptual vocabulary.

Freud and the interpretation of the social

Freudian psychoanalysis is of signal importance to three major areas of concern in the social sciences and the humanities, and each of these covers a diversity of issues and problems. The first is the *theory of human subjectivity*; the second is that of *social analysis*; and the third concerns *epistemology*.

Freud compels us to question, to endeavour to reflect upon, the construction of meaning – representation, affects, desires – as pertaining to human subjectivity, intersubjectivity and cultural processes more generally. Against the ontology of determinacy which has pervaded the history of Western social thought, Freud argues that this world is not predetermined but is actively created, in and through the production of psychical representations and significations. The psyche is the launching pad from which people *make meaning*; and, as Freud says, the registration of meaning is split between the production of conscious and unconscious representation. Another way of putting this point is to say that meaning is always *overdetermined*: people make more meaning than they can psychically process at any one time. This is what Freud meant by the unconscious: he sought to underscore radical ruptures in the life of the mind of the subject which arises as a consequence of the registration and storing of psychical representatives, or affective signification.

Freud's underwriting of the complexity of our unconscious erotic lives has been tremendously influential in contemporary social and political theory. A preoccupation with unconscious sources of human motivation is evident in social-theoretical approaches as diverse as the critical theory of the Frankfurt School, the sociological departures of Talcott Parsons and the philosophical postmodernism of Jean-François Lyotard. Indeed, the theme of the decentring of the subject in structuralist and post-structuralist traditions derives much of its impetus from Lacan's 'return to Freud' – specifically, his reconceptualization of the conscious/unconscious dualism as a linguistic relation. But while the general theme of the decentred subject has gained ascendancy throughout the academy, much current social-theoretical debate has focused on the detour needed to recover a sense of human agency as well as to account for multi-dimensional forms of human imagination. In Kristeva's discussion of the semiotic dimension of human experience, the imagination is primarily assessed in terms of the semiotic structuration of psychic space. In Ricoeur, it is a series of claims about the hermeneutics of imagination, giving of course special attention to the narratives of ideology and utopia, experience and norm. In Deleuze, it is part of an attempt to reconnect the productivities of desire to the affective force-field of postmodern culture.

This leads, second, into a consideration of the complex ways in which Freud's work has served as a theoretical framework for the analysis of contemporary culture and modern societies. The Frankfurt School, to which I shall turn in detail shortly, was for many years the key reference point here. Well before the rise of Lacanian social theory, Theodor Adorno, Herbert Marcuse and Erich Fromm articulated a conception of psychoanalysis as an account of self-divided, alienated individuals, which was understood as the subjective correlate of the capitalist economic order. While Marcuse's work became celebrated in the 1960s as offering a route to revolution, it has been Adorno's interpretation of Freud which has exercised perhaps most influence upon contemporary scholars seeking to rethink the psychic ambivalences of modernity itself (see, for example, Dews, 1995; Žižek, 1994). In this connection, Adorno's thesis that psychoanalysis uncovers a 'de-psychologization' of the subject is now the subject of widespread discussion (Whitebook, 1995). Those who share this vision of modernity place emphasis on the rise of consumer society, the seductive imagery of mass media and the pervasiveness of narcissism.

Some versions of Freudian-inspired social theory, however, have stressed more creative and imaginative political possibilities. Against the tide of Lacanian and postmodern currents of thought, several general frameworks for understanding modernity and postmodern culture as an open-ended process have emerged (for example, Cornell, 1991, 1993; Frosh, 2002; Elliott, 2003, 2004). What is distinctive about this kind of Freudian social thought is its understanding of everyday life as a form of dreaming or fantasizing; there is an emphasis on the pluralism of imagined worlds, the complexity of the intertwining of psychical and social life, as well as alternative political possibilities. This insistence on the utopic dimension of Freudian thought is characteristic of much recent social and cultural theory; but it is also the case that various standpoints assign a high priority to issues of repression, repetition and negativity. Freud was, of course, much concerned with emotional problems generated by repetition, the actions people cannot stop repeating or the narratives people cannot stop recounting. He understood such repetitions as symptomatic of a failure to remember, the closing down of creative imagination. For Freud, the aims of analysis centred on the uncovering of the deep psycho-logical forces of such repressed motivations; free association, the pleasures of imagination and the freedom to explore fantasy are at once method and outcome in psychoanalysis. Such concerns are also central to contemporary social and political thought, as Freud has been drawn upon with profit to map the paths through which individuals and collectivities remember and repress the past, at once psychical and social-historical.

For many social critics, the power of imagination is inescapably situated within the project of modernity, played out at the level of identity-politics, feminism, postmodern aesthetics and the like. Notwithstanding current techniques of domination and technologies of the self, there are many who claim that the postmodern phase of modernity unleashes a radical experimentation with alternative states of mind and possible selves. At the core of this perspective there is an interpretation about the restructuring of tradition as well as transformations of personal identity and world-views which necessarily alter the conditions of social life today. (The thesis of modernity as a reflexive process of detraditionalization is proposed by Giddens, 1991 and Beck, 1992.) Broadly speaking, traditional ways of doing things are said to give way to actively debated courses of action, such that individuals confront their own personal and social choices as individuals. On this account, there is a reflexive aware-ness of an internal relation of subjectivity to desire, for personal identity is increasingly defined on its own experimental terms. Such an excavation of the psychological conditions of subjectivity and intersubjective relations clearly has profound implications for the nature of contemporary politics as well as the democratic organization of society (see Elliott 2004).

Finally, social thought has been revitalized through its engagement with Freud as a form of emancipatory critique. This concern is motivated by a conviction that critical social theory should offer paths for transforming self and world in the interests of autonomy. Habermas (1972) is perhaps the most important social theorist who has drawn from Freud in developing a model of emancipatory critique in social analysis. Freudian theory, in Habermas's interpretation, is directed towards freeing the patient from the repetition compulsions that dominate her or his unconscious psychical life, and thereby altering the possibilities for reflective, autonomous subjectivity. However, a reading of the emancipatory dimensions of Freudian psychoanalysis which is more in keeping with a postmodern position is one in which desire is viewed as integral to the construction of alternative selves and possible collective futures. In this reading, it is not a matter of doing away with the distorting dross of fantasy, but rather of responding to, and engaging with, the passions of the self as a means of enlarging the radical imagination and creative life.

In this opening chapter, I shall briefly summarize some of the core trajectories of psychoanalytic theory, and then examine the relevance and power of psychoanalysis in terms of social-theoretical debates in the human sciences. Throughout, I will attempt to defend the view that psychoanalytic theory has much to offer social theorists, including feminists and postmodernists, in the analysis of subjectivity, ideology, sexual politics, and in coming to terms with crises in contemporary culture.

The legacy of Freud

It is now more than a century since psychoanalysis emerged under the direction of a single man, Sigmund Freud. Freud, working from his private neurological practice, founded psychoanalysis in late nineteenth-century Vienna as both therapy and a theory of the human mind. Therapeutically, psychoanalysis is perhaps best known as the 'talking cure' – a slogan used to describe the magical power of language to relieve mental suffering. The nub of the talking cure is known as 'free association'. The patient says to the analyst everything that comes to mind, no matter how trivial or unpleasant. This gives the analyst access to the patient's imagined desires and narrative histories, which may then be interpreted and reconstructed within a clinical session. The aim of psychoanalysis as a clinical practice is to uncover the hidden passions and disruptive emotional conflicts that fuel neurosis and other forms of mental suffering, in order to relieve the patient of his or her distressing symptoms.

Theoretically, psychoanalysis is rooted in a set of dynamic models relating to the human subject's articulations of desire. The unconscious, repression, drives, representation, trauma, narcissism, denial, displacement: these are the core dimensions of the Freudian account of selfhood. For Freud, the subject does not exist independently of sexuality, libidinal enjoyment, fantasy, or the social and patriarchal codes of cultural life. In fact, the human subject of Enlightenment reason – an identity seemingly self-identical to itself – is deconstructed by psychoanalysis as a fantasy which is itself secretly libidinal. Knowledge, for Freud as for Schopenhauer and Nietzsche, is internal to the world of desire. In the light of Freudian psychoanalysis, a whole series of contemporary ideological oppositions – the intellect and emotion, commerce and pleasure, masculinity and femininity, rationality and irrationality – are potentially open to displacement.

In order to detail an accurate map of the intersections between psychoanalysis and social theory, it is necessary to outline some of the basic concepts of Freudian theory. These concepts have become so familiar that they require only a schematic commentary. (For more detailed treatments see Rieff, 1959; Ricoeur, 1970; Gay, 1988; Frosh, 1999; Elliott, 2002.) Moreover, the theoretical ambiguities and political ambivalences pervading Freud's work will be noted only in passing, although many issues arising from these will be discussed in depth later in the book.

'All our conscious motives are superficial phenomena: behind them stands the conflict of our drives. . . . The great basic activity is unconscious. Our consciousness limps along afterward.' It was Friedrich Nietzsche, not Freud, who wrote this. Similarly, Romantic poets, such as Goethe and Schiller, and nineteenth-century philosophers, such as Schopenhauer and Feuerbach, also placed the determinate effects of unconscious passion at the centre of human subjectivity. Freud was aware of these insights, and often referred to them in his own writings, although he was also sceptical about the Romantic idealization of the unconscious.

If these poets and philosophers looked at the nature of unconscious passion in terms of the aesthetic, Freud traced repressed desire in terms of human sexuality and the psyche. Freud's originality is to be found in his critical analysis of the unconscious as *repressed*. One of Freud's most substantial findings is that there are psychical phenomena which are not available to consciousness, but which nevertheless exert a determining influence on everyday life. In his celebrated metapsychological essay 'The unconscious' (1914a), Freud argued that the individual's self-understanding is not immediately available to itself, that consciousness is not the expression of some core of continuous self-hood. On the contrary, the human subject is for Freud a *split* subject, torn between consciousness of self and repressed desire. For Freud, examination of the language of his patients revealed a profound turbulence of passion behind all draftings of self-identity, a radical *otherness* at the heart of subjective life. In discussing human subjectivity, Freud divides the psyche into the unconscious, preconscious and conscious. The preconscious can be thought of as a vast storehouse of memories, most of which may be recalled at will. By contrast, unconscious memories and desires are cut off, or buried, from consciousness. According to Freud, the unconscious is not 'another' consciousness but a separate psychic system with its own distinct processes and mechanisms. The unconscious, Freud comments, is indifferent to reality; it knows no causality or contradiction or logic or negation; it is entirely given over to the search for pleasure and libidinal enjoyment. Moreover, the unconscious cannot be known directly, and is rather detected only through its effects, through the distortions it inflicts on consciousness.

Freud's unmasking of the human subject as an endless flow of unconscious love and loathing is pressed into a psychoanalytic deconstruction of inherited Western conceptions of ontology. Rejecting the idea that consciousness can provide a foundation for subjectivity and knowledge, Freud traces the psychic effects of our early dependence on others – usually our parents – in terms of our biologically fixed needs. The infant, Freud says, is incapable of surviving without the provision of care, warmth and nourishment from others. However – and this is fundamental in Freud – human needs always outstrip the biological, linked as needs are to the attaining of pleasure. Freud's exemplary case is the small child sucking milk from her or his mother's breast. After the infant's biological need for nourishment is satisfied, there is the emergence of a certain pleasure in sucking itself, which for Freud is a kind of prototype for the complexity of our erotic lives. As Freud (1940: 154) writes:

> The baby's obstinate persistence in sucking gives evidence at an early stage of a need for satisfaction which, though it originates from and is instigated by the taking of nourishment, nevertheless strives to obtain pleasure independently of nourishment and for that reason may and should be termed *sexual*.

From this angle, sexuality is not some preordained, unitary biological force that springs into existence fully formed at birth. Sexuality is *created*, not prepackaged. For Freud, sexuality is 'polymorphously perverse': subjectivity emerges as a precarious and contingent organization of libidinal pleasures, an interestingly mobile set of identity-constructions, all carried on within the tangled frame of infantile sexuality.

Any emotional investment put into an object or other becomes for Freud a form of self-definition, and so shot through with unconscious ambivalence. In a series of path-breaking essays written on the eve of the First World War, Freud tied the constitution of the ego to mourning, melancholia, and grief. In 'On Narcissism: an introduction' (1914), Freud argued that the ego is not simply a defensive product of the self-preservative reality principle, but is rather a structured sedimentation of lost objects; such lost loves are, in turn, incorporated into the tissue of subjectivity itself. The loss of a loved person, says Freud, necessarily involves an introjection of this absent other into the ego. As Freud (1923: 28) explains the link between loss and ego-formation:

> We succeeded in explaining the painful disorder of melancholia by supposing that [in overcoming this hurt] an object which was lost has been set up again inside the ego – that is, that an object-cathexis has been replaced by an identification. At that time, however, we did not appreciate the full significance of this process and did not know how common and how typical it is. Since then we have come to understand that this kind of substitution has a great share in determining the form taken by the ego and that it makes an essential contribution towards building up what is called its 'character'.

Ego-identity is constituted as a fantasy substitution, through multiple, narcissistic identifications with significant other persons.

We become the identities we are in Freud's view because we have inside us buried identifications with people we have previously loved (and also hated), most usually our parents. And yet the foundational loss to which we must respond, and which in effect sets in motion the unfolding of our unconscious sexual fantasies, remains that of the maternal body. The break-up or restructuring of our primary emotional tie to the maternal body is, in fact, so significant that it becomes the founding moment not only of individuation and differentiation, but also sexual and gender difference. Loss and gender affinity are directly linked in Freud's theory to the Oedipus complex, the psyche's entry into received social meanings. For Freud, the Oedipus complex is the nodal point of sexual development, the symbolic internalization of a lost, tabooed object of desire. In the act of internalizing the loss of the pre-Oedipal mother, the infant's relationship with the father (or, more accurately, symbolic representations of paternal power) becomes crucial for the consolidation of both selfhood and gender identity. Trust in the intersubjective nature of social life begin here: the father, holding a structural position which is outside and other to this imaginary sphere, functions to *break* the child/mother dyad, thus refering the child to the wider culture and social network. The paternal prohibition on desire for the mother, which is experienced as castration, at once instantiates repressed desire and refers the infant beyond itself, to an external world of social meanings. And yet the work of culture, according to Freud, is always outstripped by unconscious desire, the return of the repressed. Identity, sexuality, gender, signification: these are all radically divided between an ongoing development of conscious self-awareness and the unconscious, or repressed desire. (For further discussion on this point see Ricoeur, 1970: 211–29.)

Freud's writings show the ego not to be master in its own home. The unconscious, repression, libido, narcissism: these are the core dimensions of Freud's psychoanalytic dislocation of the subject. Moreover, it is because of this fragmentation of identity that the concept of identification is so crucial in psychoanalytic theory: the subject creates identity by means of identification with other persons, located in the symbolic context of society, culture and politics. The psychoanalytic dislocation of the subject emerges in various guises in contemporary social theory. In the critical theory of the Frankfurt School, it is part of an attempt to rethink the powerlessness of identity in the face of the objectifying aspects of contemporary science, technology and bureaucracy. In Habermas, it is a series of claims about the nature of distorted intersubjective and public communication as a means of theorizing repressive ideologies. In Lacan, it is a means for tracing imaginary constructions of self-concealment, as linked to the idea that language is what founds the repressed unconscious. In Lacanian and post-structuralist feminism, it is harnessed to a thoroughgoing political critique of sexual difference and gender hierarchy. In the postmodern works of Deleuze and Guattari, and of Lyotard, it is primarily a set of sociopolitical observations about psychic fragmentation and dislocation in the face of global capitalism.

Psychopathologies of rationality: the Frankfurt School

Most conversations these days in social theory and philosophy are about 'endings'. The end of history, the death of the subject, the disintegration of metaphysics, the disappearance of community, the fragmentation of political power: all such 'endings' play the role of a symptomatic element which allows us to perceive a widespread sense of political pessimism, of an overwhelming irrationality, of generalized anomie and groundlessness, that permeates postmodernity. Against this backdrop, psychoanalytic social theory has been credited by some observers with going against the grain of the contemporary critical climate, rejecting the manic celebration of fragmentation and dispersion in postmodernism, and instead addressing the profound political difficulties of finding new paths for the radical imagination in order to further the project of autonomy. Indeed, psychoanalysis in recent years has been drawn upon in order to rethink the new and the different in contemporary social life. This turn to psychoanalysis has been undertaken in the name of both conceptual adequacy and political proficiency. At a conceptual level, the turn to Freud reflects a growing sense that social theory must address the libidinal, traumatic dimensions which traverse relations between self and other, identity and non-identity, subjectivity and history. At a political level, the turn to Freud is more strategic: given the flattening of the political imagination and the rising fortunes of technocratic rationality, psychoanalysis is for many a potentially fruitful arena for radical political engagement at the current historical juncture.

Freud's relevance to social critique remains perhaps nowhere better dramatized than in the various writings of the first generation of critical theorists associated with the Frankfurt Institute of Social Research. The Frankfurt School, as it came to be called, was formed in the decade prior to the Nazi reign of terror in Germany, and not surprisingly many of its leading theorists conducted numerous studies seeking to grasp the wave of political irrationalism and totalitarianism sweeping Western Europe. In a daring theoretical move, the School brought Freudian categories to bear upon the sociological analysis of everyday life, in order to fathom the myriad ways that political power imprints itself upon the internal world of human subjects and, more specifically, to critically examine the obscene, meaningless kind of evil that Hitler had actually unleashed. Of the School's attempts to fathom the psychopathologies of fascism, the writings of Adorno, Marcuse and Fromm particularly stand out; each of these authors, in quite different ways, drew upon Freudian categories to figure out the core dynamics and pathologies of post-liberal rationality, culture and politics, and also to trace the sociological deadlocks of modernity itself. The result was a dramatic underscoring of both the political dimensions of psychoanalysis and also the psychodynamic elements of public political life.

The philosophical backdrop to the Frankfurt School's engagement with Freud and psychoanalysis was spelt out in particular detail by Adorno, who sketched along with co-author Max Horkheimer – in *Dialectic of Enlightenment* – a bleak portrait of the personal and political pathologies of instrumental rationality. Humanization of drives and passions, resulting in the transformation from blind instinct to consciousness of self, was for Adorno necessary to release the subject from its enslavement to Nature. But, in a tragic irony, the unconscious forces facilitating the achievement of autonomy undergo a mind-shattering repression that leaves the subject marked by inner division, isolation and compulsion. The Janus-face of this forging of the self is clearly discerned in Adorno's historicization of Freud's Oedipus complex. According to Adorno, the bourgeois liberal subject repressed unconscious desire in and through oedipal prohibitions and, as a consequence, achieved a level of self-control in order to reproduce capitalist social relations. But not so in the administered world of late modernity. In post-liberal societies, changes in family life means that the father no longer functions as an agency of social repression. Instead, individuals are increasingly brought under the sway of the logic of techno-rationality itself, as registered in and through the rise of the culture industries. The concept of 'repressive desublimation' is crucial here. The shift from simple to advanced modernity comes about through the destruction of the psychological dimensions of human experience: the socialization of the unconscious in the administered world directly loops the id and the superego at the expense of the mediating agency of the ego itself. As Adorno summarized these historical developments in identity-constitution: 'The prebourgeois world does not yet know psychology, the oversocialised knows it no longer.' Repressive desublimation functions in Frankfurt School sociology as that psychic process which links what Adorno called the 'post-psychological individual' to the historical emergence of fascism and totalitarian societies.

It was against this psychoanalytic backdrop that Adorno and Horkheimer theorized the self-cancelling dynamic of the civilizing process in *Dialectic of Enlightenment*, proposing a structural fixity in which all forms of rationality and identity are constituted through a violent coercion of inner and outer nature; or, to put the matter in a more psychoanalytic idiom, subjectivity and inter-subjectivity are always-already the direct outcrop of the heteronomous, hypnotic power of superego law. Accordingly, the search was now on within the first generation of critical theory to locate the good Other of instrumental reason. In this connection, Adorno reserved a privileged place for high art as dislocating repressive types of logic and bringing low all forms of 'identifying' thought. Marcuse, for a time, thought that it might be possible to recast sexual perversion, and specifically the domain of fantasy, as somehow prefigurative of a utopian social order – on the grounds that the primary processes slipped past the net of the reality/performance principle.

These and other images of Utopia arose from the School's intriguing blend of Marxism and Freudianism. And yet the issue of *critique* – specifically the vantage-point from which the School launched its devastating condemnation of capitalist culture – has dogged followers of Frankfurt sociology. In *Perversion and Utopia*, the American philosopher Joel Whitebook writes of the perfor-mative contradiction in Frankfurt School sociology between asserting that identity is necessarily as rigid, spiritless and abstract as the reified object it dominates in the administered world on the one hand, and of confidently maintaining that an in-depth psycho-social critique of these processes can be undertaken on the other hand. Something is amiss here (from which world, exactly, were the Frankfurt School analysts able to critique such systematic pathologies?), and for Whitebook the answer lies in the Frankfurt School's global portrayal of all subjective synthesis as violence or domination. Developing upon perspectives advanced by the work of those associated with the second generation of critical theory, specifically the writings of Albrecht Wellmer, Whitebook argues that Adorno mistook distortions of language in contem-porary rationalism for language as such, and was therefore led to deny the social-historical gains of discursive rationality *tout court*. (Like Wellmer's *The Persistence of Modernity* (1991), Whitebook's *Perversion and Utopia* is an attempt to release the frozen potential of the first generation of Critical Theory from its aporetic confinement to the philosophy of consciousness, but in a manner that fully incorporates psychoanalysis into a theory of intersubjectivity.) Injecting Freudian psychoanalysis into Webarian social theory, Adorno is said by Whitebook to have effectively pitted unconscious rage against the non-identical – registered in the administered world's blind 'compulsion for unity', the manic articulations of which arise precisely at that historical moment in which the psychological possibilities for reflexivity are rendered superfluous. But there are considerable difficulties with the interpretation that the 'psychological' dimensions of liberal individualism have been replaced by the 'post-psychological' individual of the administered world of late capitalism. These difficulties include, among others, Adorno's reductionistic reading of psychoanalysis as a 'psychological theory' (but see Žižek, 1994).

What has been of incomparable value, however, is the School's analysis of why human subjects, apparently without resistance, submit to the dominant ideologies of late capitalism. The general explanatory model developed by the Frankfurt School to study the socio-psychological dimension of the relation between the individual and culture has received considerable attention in social theory (Jay, 1973; Benjamin, 1977; Held, 1980; Elliott, 1999). In what follows, I shall concentrate principally on the social-theoretical reconstructions of psychoanalysis offered by Fromm and Marcuse.

Erich Fromm

Fromm, who had been practising as an analyst since 1926 and was a member of the Frankfurt Psychoanalytic Institute, sought in his early studies to integrate Freud's theory of the unconscious with Marxist sociology. Influenced by Wilhelm Reich's book *Character Analysis*, which connects society to the repressed unconscious, Fromm became preoccupied with the cultural consequences of sexual repression, as well as the mediating influence of the family between the economy and the individual. According to Fromm, Freudian psychoanalysis must supplement Marxism in order to grasp how social structures influence, indeed shape, the inner dimensions of human subjectivity. Fromm's concern with the effects of repression, however, differed substantially from the analysis worked out by Reich. In Fromm's view, Reich had been unable to develop an adequate theory of social reproduction because he had reduced Freud's theory of sexuality to a monadic focus on genital sexuality. Yet Freudian psychoanalysis, Fromm maintained, was fundamentally a 'social psychology'. For Fromm, the individual must be understood in his or her relation to others.

The bourgeois nuclear family, Fromm says, is pivotal to understanding the links between individual repression, cultural reproduction and ideological domination. An agency of social reproduction, the family is described as 'the essential medium through which the economic situation exerts its . . . influence on the individual's psyche' (Fromm, 1932: 483). Fromm contends that the family implants regression at the heart of subjectivity, sustains economic conditions as ideology, and infuses perceptions of the self as submissive, self-effacing and powerless. The central message of Fromm's early work is that the destructive effects of late capitalism are not only centred in economic mechanisms and institutions, but involve the anchoring of domination within the inner life and psychodynamic struggles of each individual.

As the 1930s progressed, Fromm became increasingly sceptical of orthodox Freudianism. He strongly criticized Freud's notion of the death drive for its biological reductionism, and argued that it only served to legitimate at a theoretical level the destructive and aggressive tendencies of capitalism. Significantly, Fromm also became influenced by neo-Freudian analysts – such as Harry Stack Sullivan and Karen Homey – who stressed larger social and cultural factors in the constitution of selfhood. This emphasis on cultural contributions to identity-formation was underscored by Fromm in his major books, *Escape from Freedom* (1941) and *The Sane Society* (1956), both of which argued the idea of an essential 'nature of man', a nature repressed and distorted by capitalist patterns of domination.

Although Fromm's early studies on the integration of individuals into capitalism were broadly accepted by other members of the Frankfurt School, his subsequent, more sociological diagnosis of an essential human nature twisted out of shape by capitalism was strongly rejected. Marcuse, for example, charged Fromm (and other neo-Freudian revisionists) with undoing the critical force of Freud's most important ideas, such as the unconscious, repression and infantile sexuality. According to Marcuse, Fromm's revisionism underwrites the smooth functioning of the ego only by displacing the dislocating nature of the unconscious. Marcuse (1956: 240–1) sums up the central point in the following way:

> Whereas Freud, focusing on the vicissitudes of the primary drives, dis-
> covered society in the most concealed layer of the genus and individual
> man, the revisionists, aiming at the reified, ready-made form rather than
> at the origin of the societal institutions and relations, fail to comprehend
> what these institutions and relations have done to the personality that they
> are supposed to fulfil.

Fromm's attempt to add sociological factors to psychoanalysis, says Marcuse, results in a false political optimism as well as a liquidation of what is truly revolutionary in Freud: the discovery of the repressed unconscious.

Herbert Marcuse

Marcuse, like Fromm, views psychological and political repression as deeply interwoven. For Marcuse, Freudian psychoanalysis is relevant for tracing the exercise of domination upon the inner world of the subject, for understanding how capitalism and mass culture shape personal desires, and for analysing the possibilities of human emancipation. Unlike Fromm, however, Marcuse rejects the view that sociological and historical factors must be added to Freudian theory. Instead, Marcuse seeks to unfold the liberative potential in Freud's work from the inside out, in order to reveal its radical political edge.

Marcuse's reconceptualization of psychoanalysis seeks to develop the 'political and sociological substance' of Freud's work (Marcuse, 1956: xii). His analysis proceeds from an acceptance of some of the core claims of psychoanalysis. These include the theory of the unconscious, the conflict between the pleasure and reality principles, the life and death drives, and the view that civilization entails sexual repression. Marcuse contends, however, that Freud was wrong about the permanent cultural necessity of psychological repression. Marcuse agrees that all social reproduction demands a certain level of repression. Yet what Freud did not see, Marcuse argues, is that capitalism creates a crippling (though impermanent) burden of repression. From this angle, individuals are in fact adapting to the destructive forces of capitalist domination, forces that masquerade as the 'reality principle'.

These provocative ideas are developed by Marcuse in his classic *Eros and Civilization* (1956) and *Five Lectures* (1970). The key to Marcuse's interpretation of Freud is the division of repression into 'basic' and 'surplus'. Basic repression refers to that minimum level of libidinal renunciation deemed necessary for facing social life. What this means, in short, is that a certain amount of repression underlies the constitution of the 'socialized subject', a subject capable of sustaining the business of social and sexual reproduction. By contrast, surplus repression refers to the intensification of restraint created in and through asymmetrical relations of power. Marcuse points to patriarchy (especially in terms of family relationships) and to the workplace as socio-symbolic fields containing a surplus of repression. This repressive surplus, says Marcuse, operates through the 'performance principle', a culturally specific form of reality structured by the economic order of capitalism. For Marcuse, the destructive psychological effects of this principle are highly consequential. 'Performance' recasts individuals as mere 'things' or 'objects', replaces eroticism with genital sexuality, and fashions a disciplining of the human body (what Marcuse terms 'repressive desublimation') in order to prevent repressed desire from interfering with capitalist exchange values.

Marcuse presses this reinterpretation of Freud into a critical theory of the psychic costs of modernity. In Marcuse's view, the massive social and industrial transformations which have occurred in the twentieth century – changes in systems of economy and technology as well as cultural production – have produced a radical escalation in psychological repression. The more technocapitalism has advanced, he argues, the more repression has become surplus. The immense productive capacities released from technology, modernism and monopoly capitalism have been turned back upon the individual subject with a vengeance. As a consequence, the personal sphere is subject to decomposition and fragmentation. According to Marcuse, the psychoanalytic division of the individual into id, ego, and superego is no longer relevant. A weakening in patriarchal authority within the bourgeois nuclear family, accompanied by the impact of the mass media and commodified culture, has led to an authority-bound, easily manipulable subject. Subjecthood, in conditions of late capitalism, is rendered a mere functional component of the system of domination.

Notwithstanding this bleak picture of the contemporary epoch, Marcuse was optimistic about social change. In one sense, he used Freudian psychoanalysis against itself, to trace the emancipatory potentials of modernity. He argued that the performance principle, ironically, generates the economic and social conditions necessary for a radical transformation of society. That is, the material affluence generated by capitalism opens the way for undoing surplus repression. Emancipation for Marcuse is linked to a reconciliation between culture, nature, and unconscious pleasure, what he termed 'libidinal rationality'. The preconditions for the realization of libidinal rationality include the overcoming of the split between pleasure and reality, life and death, and a recovery of repressed needs and aspirations. Through changes in fantasy structures and the social context, Marcuse says, society can become re-eroticized.

Marcuse's analysis of contemporary ideological pressures toward 'surplus repression' contains many insights, but it is also clear that there are important limitations to his approach. For one thing, he fails to point in anything but the most general way to how ideology transforms repression from 'basic' into 'surplus', and so it is far from easy to grasp the complex ways in which culture implants political domination upon the emotional economy of subjects. (For a detailed discussion of this and related psycho-political difficulties in Marcuse's work, see Elliott, 1993). Similarly, the argument that reason or rationality can be located in repressed drives (the notion of 'libidinal rationality') is underdeveloped. Marcuse's work fails to analyse in any substantive way intersubjective social relationships. Instead, his vision of political autonomy is one in which repressed drives become liberated, and thus transfigurative of social relations. From this angle, some critics have suggested that Marcuse's conception of the relation between repressed desire and social transformation is individualistic and asocial in character (see Held, 1980; Chodorow, 1989).

Contemporary critical theory: Habermas's reading of Freud and the theorem of distorted communication

An attempt to overcome some of the core theoretical and political limitations of the Frankfurt School, while also retaining Freudian psychoanalysis as an exemplar for critical social theory, is to be found in the writings of the contemporary German philosopher, Jürgen Habermas. Influenced by Marcuse in particular, Habermas uses psychoanalytic theory to supplement and enrich critical theory as concerns the analysis of social power and ideological domination. Habermas, like Marcuse, agrees with Freud that the development of social organization and productive economic forces has required a certain amount of psychological repression. But in conditions of late modernity, says Habermas, as the constraints of economic scarcity are overcome, we begin to witness the radicalizing possibilities of the transformation (and perhaps eradication) of social repression.

Perhaps somewhat strangely, most of Habermas's major contributions to a radical appropriation of psychoanalysis for social critique – stemming from the late 1960s especially, but also through the 1970s and into the 1980s – fail to profit from the pivotal research conducted by the first generation of critical theorists on the psychopathologies of European rationalism and the Enlightenment. Rather than seeing the substantive claims of psychoanalysis as a political resource for critical social theory, Habermas instead develops a methodological interpretation of Freudian psychoanalysis as linked to the objectives of critical theory. In one important sense, as will be highlighted in subsequent discussion, Habermas's reconceptualization of Freud has many elements in common with Lacanian psychoanalysis, though the final result is radically different. Like Lacan, Habermas conceives of psychoanalysis as a theoretical and methodological structure which traces public, intersubjective communication. Also like Lacan, Habermas argues that the unconscious is essentially linguistic in character. In contrast to Lacan, however, Habermas argues for the possibility of emancipation through the recovery of the repressed unconscious. By developing a literalist understanding of psychoanalysis as the 'talking cure' – that is, that the unconscious can be made conscious via speech – Habermas seeks to link the overcoming of social repression to transformations in structures of communication and public political discourse.

Ideology, says Habermas, is a structure of communication that has become systematically bent out of shape by power. Distortion marks the point at which social rationalization intrudes into everyday life, or of what Habermas terms the 'lifeworld' – the domains of cultural reproduction, socialization and personal identity. Like the early Frankfurt School, Habermas argues that the increasing penetration of a rationalizing, bureaucratizing logic into cultural life has degraded social relations and the autonomy of personhood. The uncontrolled growth of anonymous systems of administration and economy increasingly reach into every sphere of social life. But this besieging of the lifeworld by economic and administrative subsystems is not just a matter of social domination: on the contrary, such pathology becomes incorporated into the rigid, monotonous character of contemporary identity-patterns. Indeed, Habermas speaks of an 'inner colonization of the lifeworld', which suggests that desire and passion are increasingly colonized and controlled by the ideological dictates of the social system itself.

Habermas regards psychoanalysis as a discourse that traces the communicative distortions of social power and ideology upon subjectivity. In *Knowledge and Human Interests* (1972), he argues that unconscious repression is an effect of linguistic distortion. 'The ego's flight from itself,' says Habermas, 'is an operation that is carried out in and with language. Otherwise it would not be possible to reverse the defensive process hermeneutically, via the analysis of language' (1972: 241). In this communications reading of Freud, repression is understood as a process of *excommunication*. Drawing on Alfred Lorenzer's psychoanalytic research on linguistic pathologies, Habermas claims that the unconscious is constituted through an excommunication of language from public, intersubjective relations through a process of privatization. The unconscious, on this reckoning, is conceived as that which is excluded from public, intersubjective communication. As Habermas (1972: 223) argues: 'The psychically most effective way to render undesired need dispositions harmless is to exclude from public communication the interpretations to which they are attached.' From this angle, Habermas contends that emancipation entails the *elimination of unconscious distortions of communication* in order to secure a self-reflective movement toward political autonomy.

As with the first generation of critical theorists, and especially Marcuse, Habermas's recasting of repression as a process of excommunication has significantly stimulated and influenced contemporary social theory. In contrast to the individualistic interpretation of Freud developed by Marcuse, Habermas's communications reading of psychoanalysis directly confronts the intersubjective nature of repressed desire, thus making the psychoanalytic tradition more immediately relevant to the concerns of social theory. However, a number of important objections have been made of Habermas's use of psychoanalysis. First, it appears that Habermas conflates repression with the unconscious, and thus fails to consider the importance of other unconscious processes and mechanisms such as fantasy, wish-fulfilment, projection, introjection and the like (see Giddens, 1979; Whitebook, 1989). Second, and related to this criticism, Habermas's linguistic reconceptualization of the psyche, like Lacan, erases the prelinguistic realm of unconscious passion, thereby screening from view the role of affect in the constitution and reproduction of social practices (see Elliott, 1999). Finally, by discarding these vital elements of the Freudian conceptual field, Habermas is left with an account of the unconscious which is essentially negative and constraining – which is why he argues that, at a collective level, the unconscious must be made conscious! What this overlooks, of course, are the creative dimensions of unconscious fantasy and affect; these are dimensions of psychical experience, I contend, which are fundamental to social life and critical self-reflection (see Elliott, 1999: chapter 3).

Returning to Freud: Jacques Lacan

Many psychoanalytic theorists have identified loss as central to self-constitution. From the fall from pre-Oedipal Eden, in which the small infant becomes separated from the maternal body, through alarming and painful terrors of the Oedipal constellation, and onto subsequent adult disappointments, rejections and negations: loss infiltrates all emotional transactions between self and others, and so in a sense is at the root from which desire flows uncontrollably. Yet while the intricate connections between loss and selfhood have been underwritten throughout the history of psychoanalysis, perhaps the most remarkable contribution remains that elaborated by the French psychoanalyst Jacques Lacan. The world of illusion which we fashion to avoid the traumatic and impenetrable mysteries of loss are for Lacan the very stuff out of which we are made. For Lacan, the individual subject is constituted in and through loss, as an excess of lack. In a radical revision of Freud, largely through a widening of the horizons of psychoanalysis to embrace structuralist linguistics and poststructuralist theories of discourse, Lacan makes lack the cause which ensures that as human subjects we are continually falling short, failing, fading and lapsing.

The writings of Lacan have been widely regarded (especially in the English-speaking world) as inexhaustibly complex, and one reason for this may be that Lacan himself believed it necessary to fashion a theoretical discourse at odds with itself in order for psychoanalysis to do justice to the rich vagaries of emotional life. Another reason concerns the immense conceptual shifts inaugurated by Lacan, shifts in the language of psychoanalysis away from the world of biology and toward the study of language and human speech, away from the deterministic forces of instincts and appetites and toward the analysis of structures and culture. In taking psychoanalysis in this largely anti-biological direction, Lacan was dazzlingly eclectic, in his writings borrowing one moment from the structuralist anthropologist Claude Lévi-Strauss and the next from the philosopher Maurice Merleau-Ponty, while in his seminars putting to work the insights of the linguist Roman Jakobson and recontextualizing Hegel's master/slave dialectic for the analysis of human desire. The work of Lacan and his followers will be returned to in the context of feminist and postmodern theories discussed later in the chapter. At this point, it is necessary to consider the main features of Lacan's revision of Freud.

The world of sense-perception, for Lacan as for Freud, is born from immersion in a sublimely opaque realm of images, of very early experience of imaginings and imagos, of primitive fantasies of the body of another. It was noted earlier that Freud viewed the small infant, from the very start of life, in a symbiotic relation with the maternal body. At this preindividualistic, premimetic stage of life, the infant makes no distinction between itself and the maternal body, or between a space that is inside and outside. Instead, the infant's world consists of a merging of itself and the maternal body. Lacan calls this realm, caught between wonderful delight and terrifying anguish, the Imaginary. The Imaginary for Lacan is a prelinguistic, pre-Oedipal register, solely visual in operation and in which desire slides around and recircles an endless array of part-objects – breasts, lips, gaze, skin. According to Lacan, this imaginary drafting of the world of illusion, of wholeness, is broken apart once the infant comes to identify with, and introject, things or objects beyond itself, thus shifting beyond the lures of the Imaginary. This primordial moment of separation is devastating, a loss so painful that it results in a *primary repression* of the pre-Oedipal connection to the maternal sphere, a repression which in one stroke founds the repressed unconscious. Once severed from primary identification with the pre-Oedipal mother, the infant is projected into the realm of language, the differences internal to signification that Lacan calls the Other, or the Symbolic order. The Symbolic in Lacan's theory is a plane of received social meanings, logic, differentiation. Symbolization and language permit the subject to represent desire, both to itself and to others. Yet the representation of desire, says Lacan, is always stained by a scar of imaginary, maternal identification. As speaking subjects, our discourse is always marked by lack, the repressed unconscious. 'The unconscious' says Lacan, 'is the discourse of the Other.'

Lacan theorizes the imaginary tribulations of self-constitution largely through a novel consideration of Freud's theory of narcissism. In 'The mirror stage as formative of the function of the I' (1949), Lacan contends that the infant apprehends a sense of bodily unity through the recognition of its image in a mirror. The 'mirror' provides the infant with consoling image of itself as unified and self-sufficient. As Lacan (1977:1) puts this:

> unable as yet to walk, or even to stand up, and held tightly as he is by some support, human or artificial . . . he nevertheless overcomes in a flutter of jubilant activity, the obstruction of his support and, fixing his attitude in a slightly leaning-forward position, in order to hold it in his gaze, brings back an instantaneous aspect of the image.

This reflecting mirror image is not at all, however, what it seems. Lacan says that what the mirror produces is a 'mirage of coherence', an alienating *mis-recognition*. In short, the mirror *lies*. Mirroring leads the infant to imagine itself as stable and unified, when in fact psychical space is fragmented, and the infant's physical movements uncoordinated. The reflecting mirror leads the infant into an unfettered realm of narcissism, underpinned by hate and aggression, given the unbridgeable gap between ideal and actuality. This imaginary drafting of the self, says Lacan, 'situates the agency of the ego, before its social determination, in a fictional direction' (1977: 2).

The imaginary can thus be described as a kind of archaic realm of distorted mirror images, a spatial world of indistinction between self and other, from which primary narcissism and aggressivity are drawn as key building blocks in the formation of identity. But if the Imaginary order is already an alienation of desire, then the same is certainly true of the Symbolic order of language. The Symbolic, says Lacan, smashes the mirror unity of the Imaginary. For Lacan, as for Freud, this happens with the entry of the father into the psychic world of the child. In disturbing the mother–child link, the Oedipal father breaks up the self–other unity of the Imaginary order. For Lacan, language is the fundamental medium which structures the Oedipal process. The child enters the symbolic via language, which ushers in temporal, spatial and logical differences, which are foundational to self and other, subject and object. Language for Lacan is an intersubjective order of symbolization which carries the force of cultural sanctions, of what he terms 'the Law of the Father' – for it is in and through language that the subject attempts a reconstruction of lost, imagined unities.

Rewriting the unconscious and Oedipus in terms of the symbolic dimensions of language, Lacan's theoretical point of reference is the structural linguistics of Ferdinand de Saussure. It is not possible here to provide an adequate exegesis of Lacan's appropriation and reconstruction of Saussure's ideas (see Elliott, 1999); in what follows I shall only emphasize certain aspects of Lacan's use of Saussure's structural linguistics, particularly those aspects most relevant to the concerns of social theory. In Saussurian linguistics, language is explicated as a system of internal differences. In this view, signs are made up of a signifier (a sound or image) and a signified (the concept or meaning evoked). The meaning of a word arises through its differences from other words: a pencil, for example, is not a pen. A book is not a pamphlet, not a magazine, not a newspaper. Words as such do not 'mean' their objects. Language creates meaning only through an internal play of differences. Now Lacan accepts the key elements of Saussure's structural linguistics, but he radicalizes the relation between the signifier and the signified. Lacan will have nothing of the Saussurian search for the signified, or concept, however 'arbitrary' the relation between signifiers that generates meaning may be. Instead, Lacan inverts Saussure's interpretation of the sign, asserting that the signifier has primacy over the signified in the production of meaning. As he explicates this:

> The first network, that of the signifier, is the synchronic structure of the language material in so far as in that structure each element assumes its precise function by being different from the others. The second network, that of the signified, is the diachronic set of the concretely pronounced discourses, which reacts historically on the first, just as the structure of the first governs the pathways of the second. The dominant fact here is the unity of signification, which proves never to be resolved into a pure indication of the real, but always refers back to another signification.
>
> (Lacan, 1977: 126)

In Lacan's psychoanalytic reading, the two orders of discourse are always separated by censorship, marked by a bar of repression. The signified, says Lacan, cannot be elucidated once and for all since it is always 'sinking' or 'fading' into the unconscious; the signified is, in effect, always just another signifier. And for Lacan the signifier is itself coterminous with the unconscious. The unconscious, says Lacan, is 'the sum of the effects of the *parole* on a subject, at the level where the subject constitutes itself from the effects of the signifier' (Lacan quoted in Ragland-Sullivan, 1986: 116).

Language, as a system of differences, constitutes the subject's repressed desire through and through. The subject, once severed from the narcissistic fullness of the Imaginary, is inserted into linguistic and symbolic structures that both generate the unconscious and allow for its contents to traverse the intersubjective field of culture. Access to ourselves and others, however, is complicated by the fact that desire is itself an 'effect of the signifier', an outcrop of the spacings or differences of linguistic structures. From this angle, the unconscious is less a realm on the 'inside' of the individual, or 'underneath' language, than an intersubjective space *between* subjects – located in those gaps which separate word from word, meaning from meaning. 'The exteriority of the symbolic in relation to man,' says Lacan, 'is the very notion of the unconscious' (1966: 469). Or, in Lacan's infamous slogan: 'the unconscious is structured like a language'.

Advantages and limitations of Lacan's theory

Lacan's re-reading of Freud has powerfully influenced contemporary social theory. His emphasis on the centrality of symbolic structures in the constitution of the subject, as well as the disruption caused to these structures through the fracturing effects of the unconscious, has been of core importance to recent debates concerning identity and cultural forms (see, for example, Ragland-Sullivan and Bracher, 1991; Leupin, 1991). His stress on the complicated interweaving of language and desire has been original and provocative. Significantly, it has served as a useful corrective to social-theoretical accounts that portray the self as the site of rational psychological functioning. Moreover, his linguistic reconceptualization of the unconscious powerfully deconstructs theories of representation which presume that mind and world automatically fit together.

There are many limitations, however, with the Lacanian account of subjectivity and social relations. The most important of these, as concerns subjecthood, is Lacan's claim that imaginary identification with the self and others, as forged in the mirror stage, involves an inescapable sentence of alienation. While it is undeniable that Freud viewed miscognition as internally tied to ego-formation, Lacan's version of this process involves a number of substantive problems. Consider the following: what is it that allows the individual to (mis)recognize itself from its mirror image? How, exactly, does it cash in on this conferring of selfhood? The problem with the argument that the mirror distorts is that it fails to specify the psychic capacities which make any such misrecognition possible. That is, it fails to detail how the mirror is constituted as *real* (see Elliott, 1992: 138–6). Related to this is the criticism that Lacan's linguistic reconceptualization of psychoanalysis actually suppresses the radical implications of Freud s discovery of the unconscious by structuralizing it, reducing it to a chance play of signifiers. In this respect, Lacan's claim that the unconscious is naturally tied to language has come under fire (see Ricoeur, 1970; Castoriadis, 1984; Laplanche, 1987). Here it is asserted that the unconscious is the precondition for language and not the reverse. As concerns social theory, the problems in this respect are significant. For it is certainly arguable that, in presenting an account of desire as disembodied and prestructured linguistically, Lacan effectively strips the subject of any capacity for autonomy, reflection and transformation.

Equally serious are the criticisms that have been made of Lacan's account of culture. Lacan's linkage of the 'subject of the unconscious' with the idea of the 'arbitrary nature of the sign' raises the thorny problem of the replication of ideological power. In this connection, Lacan fails to explain how some ideological and political meanings predominate over others in the shaping of the personal sphere. Instead, cultural domination is equated with language as such. It is the subjection of the individual to the symbolic, to the force of the Law, which accounts for the fall of the subject. However, as Dews (1987) argues, Lacan's equation of language with domination seriously downplays the importance of power, ideology and social institutions in the reproduction of cultural life.

Lacanian and post-Lacanian contexts

Lacan's return to Freud has powerfully influenced debates concerning the links between self and society in the late modern age. The emphasis on problems of language and communication in Lacanianism has made this current of thought highly relevant to a variety of social-theoretical issues in the social sciences.

In his essay 'Ideology and ideological state apparatuses' (1971), the French Marxist philosopher Louis Althusser seeks to integrate structural Marxism and Lacanian psychoanalysis in order to understand the working of ideology in modern societies. Althusser traces ideology as a discourse which leads the individual subject to understand itself and others in such a way as to support the reproduction of ruling-class power. Like Lacan, Althusser argues that social forms are experienced, not so much in the public world of institutions, as in the fantasy realm of the imaginary. 'All ideology' represents in its necessarily imaginary distortion is not the existing relations of production . . . but above all the (imaginary) relationship of individuals to the relations of production and the relations that derive from them' (1971: 38–9). From this angle, ideology provides an imaginary centring to everyday life, it confers identity on the self and Others, and makes the individual feel valued within the social, cultural network.

What are the psychic mechanisms which underpin ideology? Echoing Lacan, Althusser argues that ideology functions in and through *mirroring*. Like the Lacanian child in front of its mirror-image, the ideological mirror implants received social meanings at the heart of the subject's world. Yet, as in the mirror stage, the constitution of social forms necessarily involves a misrecognition, since ideology idealizes and distorts the intersubjective world of society, culture and politics. Through a 'subjection' to ideological discourses of class, race, gender, nationalism and the like, the individual comes to *misrecognize* itself as an autonomous, self-legislating subject. Imaginary misrecognition occurs through a process that Althusser terms 'interpellation'. It is in and through ideology that society 'interpellates' the individual as a 'subject', at once conferring identity and subjecting the individual to that social position. This interweaving of signification and imaginary misrecognition, Althusser contends, is rooted in 'ideological state apparatuses', which include schools, trade unions and the mass media, and whose function is to ensure the subjection of individuals to different social positions in modern class-based societies. That human subjects should come to overlook the nature of their real decentred subjectivity, says Althusser, is precisely the function of ideology – thus serving to reinforce the dominant power interests of late capitalism.

The theory of ideology developed by Althusser, with its implicit use of Lacanian psychoanalysis, marks one of the major sources of stimulus in twentieth-century social thought. It sets out an array of ideas about the relations between the personal and social domains, the imaginary and institutional life. Althusser's argument that ideology is an indispensable imaginary medium for social reproduction is provocative and important, and it did much to discredit traditional Marxist theories of ideology as mere false consciousness. Like the unconscious for Freud, ideology for Althusser is eternal. However, it is now widely agreed that there are many problems with Althusser's account of ideology. Most importantly, Althusser's argument about the mirroring distortion of ideology runs into the same kind of theoretical dead-end as does Lacan's account of the imaginary. That is, in order for an individual subject to (mis)recognize itself in and through ideological discourse, then surely she or he must already possess certain affective capacities for subjective response. From a psychoanalytic angle, the psychical capacity for identification, representation and reflection suggests that the relations between the personal and the ideological spheres are extremely complex, and are certainly anything but a simple 'implantation' of culturally controlled and closed social forms – as Althusser's work suggests. The central problem in this respect is that Althusser's theory implies an unsatisfactory notion of cultural domination, one in which subjects are rigidly inserted into the ideological process. (For detailed treatments of Althusser's misreading of Lacanian psychoanalysis see Barrett, 1991: chapter 5; Elliott, 1992: chapter 5.)

Whatever these shortcomings, however, the Althusserian/Lacanian model remains a powerful source of influence in contemporary social theory. Indeed, Althusser's Lacan has recently been examined with new interest that concerns the study of subjectivity, society and culture. Jameson (1990: 51–4) argues for a return to the Lacanian underpinnings of Althusser's social theory in order to fashion what he calls a 'cognitive mapping' of postmodern symbolic forms. So too, Žižek (1989; 1991) recasts the Althusserian model of 'interpellation' in order to trace the fantasy identifications created in and through cultural forms such as media and film.

Feminist psychoanalytic criticism

In recent years, some of the most important conceptual advances in psychoanalytic social theory have come from feminist debates on sexual subjectivity and gender hierarchy. Broadly speaking, the major division in psychoanalytic feminism is between Anglo-American object relations theory on the one hand, and French Lacanian and post-Lacanian theory on the other. Through the object–relations perspective, feminist theorists analyse sexuality and gender against the backdrop of interpersonal relationships – with particular emphasis on the pre-Oedipal child–mother bond. Post-structuralist feminists indebted to Lacanian psychoanalysis, by contrast, deconstruct gender terms with reference to the structuring power of the order of the Symbolic, of language as such. In previous writings, I have explored in detail both the theoretical and political differences between these competing psychoanalytic standpoints in feminism and contemporary sexuality studies (Elliott, 2002, 2003). In what follows,

I shall concentrate for the most part upon developments in feminist theories of sexual difference that draw from, rework or transfigure Lacanian theory. The central concerns that I touch on include an exploration of the political ramifications of psychoanalysis; the psychic forces which affect women's desexualization and lack of agency in modern culture; the relationship between maternal and paternal power in infant development; and the connections between sexuality, the body and its pleasures. For in addressing these issues, feminist psychoanalytic theorists have sought to enlarge their understandings of polarized sexual identities in modern societies and to rethink the possibilities for restructuring existing forms of gender power.

Lacanian psychoanalysis is probably the most influential current in feminist social theory today (cf. Benjamin, 1988; Flax, 1990; and Elliott, 2002, for detailed treatments of the contributions of the object-relations school of psychoanalysis to feminist criticism). In Lacan's deployment of Saussurian linguistics, as noted above, meaning arises from difference. In the order of language, a signifier attains reference to a signified through the exclusion of other signifiers. In patriarchal culture, that which is excluded is the *feminine*: woman is denied a voice of her own. Lacan thus claims, in what is regarded by many as a clear indication of his anti-feminism, that 'The Woman does not exist.' Linking the unconscious with the essentially patriarchal organization of language and culture, Lacan defines the feminine in the negative. Woman as the Other, as something which is outside the symbolic order: this is what gives the masculine unconscious its self-presence as power and authority.

At this point, it is necessary to briefly consider some central features of the Lacanian theory of gender-differentiated subjectivity. For Lacan, as for Freud, the phallus is the marker of sexual difference *par excellence*. The father and his phallus smash the incestuous unity of the mother–infant bond, and thereby refer the infant to the wider cultural, social network. In contrast to Freud, however, Lacan claims to conceptually disconnect the phallus from any linkage with the penis. The phallus, says Lacan, is illusory, fictitious, imaginary. It exists less in the sense of biology than in a kind of fantasy realm which merges desire with power, omnipotence, wholeness. In Lacanian theory, the power that the phallus promises is directly tied to maternal, imaginary space. According to Lacan, the infant wishes to be loved exclusively by the mother. The infant painfully learns, however, that the mother's desire is invested elsewhere: in the phallus. Significantly, this discovery occurs at the same time that the infant is discovering itself in language, as a *separate subject*. In this connection, it is important to note that Lacan says that *both* sexes enter the symbolic order of language as castrated. The infant's separation from maternal space is experienced as a devastating loss. The pain of this loss *is* castration, from which sexual subjectivity becomes deeply interwoven with absence and lack.

Lack, therefore, cuts across gender: both boys and girls undergo castration. Yet to enter the symbolic, says Lacan, is to enter the masculine world. For Lacan, sexual identity is established through a privileging of the visible, of having or not having the phallus. As Lacan puts this: 'It can be said that the [phallic] signifier is chosen because it is the most tangible element in the role of sexual copulation . . . it is the image of the vital flow as it is transmitted in generation' (1977: 287). Lacan thus underwrites the constitution of masculinity as phallic and femininity as non-phallic. In this scenario, the feminine is on the outside of language, culture, reason and power. Yet, since meaning arises only out of difference, Lacan infuses this argument with a subtle twist as concerns gender. Man's self-presence as phallic authority, says Lacan, is secured only through the exclusion of the feminine. The displaced feminine makes the masculine as phallic power exist, yet it also threatens its disruption. At the limit of the symbolic order, the feminine at once maintains and subverts existing forms of gender power.

Lacan was not much interested in the social application of his theories. But this has not prevented feminists from making critical appropriations of Lacanian psychoanalysis for rethinking the social theory of gender. Interest in Lacan's ideas for feminism was initiated in the English-speaking world by Juliet Mitchell, who in *Psychoanalysis and Feminism* (1974) uses Freud and Lacan to explore the contemporary gender system. In Mitchell's Lacanian-based feminism, an analysis of sexual politics is developed which stresses that the symbolic order of language creates sexual division. Gendered subjectivity, for Mitchell, is necessarily tied to a fundamental loss: that of maternal, imaginary space. In this connection, the phallus, as 'transcendental signifier', functions as an imaginary lining or construction which masks the lack of the human subject at the level of sexual division. Yet the crucial point, according to Mitchell, is that these imaginary scenarios position males and females within unequal gender relations. Man is constituted as a self-determining, autonomous agent, and woman as the lacking Other, as sexual object. Using Lacanian theory against itself, however, Mitchell also explores potentialities for gender transformation. Though the phallus may stand for entry to the symbolic order, Mitchell claims, it is an imaginary object that either sex can secure once and for all. Seen as a transactional negotiation of identity, the phallus need not be tied to male domination. Mitchell thus concludes: 'Some other expression of the entry into culture than the implication for the unconscious of the exchange of women will have to be found in non-patriarchal society' (1974: 415).

Though generating much interest at the time, most commentators would now agree that Mitchell's analysis of gender contains serious theoretical and political difficulties. It seems to assume, for example, that the social reproduction of sexuality and gender is a relatively stable affair, without allowing room for the contradictions and ambiguities of split subjectivity and the unconscious. This involves important political implications. For if women are symbolically fixed in relation to masculinity as the lacking Other, via a repression of desire, then it remains far from clear as to why women would ever feel compelled to question or challenge the contemporary gender system. This point can be made in another way. The Lacanian specification of the feminine as that which is always defined negatively – lack, the Other, the dark continent – carries a number of theoretical and political ambiguities. On the one hand,

Lacan's doctrines have been a valuable theoretical resource for feminists analysing how women are rendered the excluded Other in patriarchal discourse and culture. On the other hand, the recurring problem for feminism when set within Lacanian parameters is that all dimensions of human sexuality become inscribed within the signifier and therefore trapped by the Law. Lacan's reduction of the feminine to mere oppositeness implies that woman can be defined only as *mirror* to the masculine subject, and thus can never escape the domination of a rigidly genderized discourse.

In opposition to Lacan, however, a number of French feminists have recently sought to articulate an alternative vision of female sexual subjectivity in French psychoanalysis. This approach to revaluing the feminine is generally referred to as post-Lacanian feminism, though it is worth briefly expanding on this label. This branch of feminist psychoanalysis is generally considered 'Lacanian' because theorists associated with it adopt a broadly structuralist interpretation of gender categories, situating woman as the excluded Other of masculinist discourse and culture. Yet this approach is also 'anti-Lacanian' since such theorists tend to oppose the view that woman can only be defined as the mirror opposite of the masculine subject, and thus never escape the domination of a rigidly genderized discourse. Broadly speaking, post-Lacanian feminists evoke a positive image of femininity, an image that underscores the multiple and plural dimensions of women's sexuality. Hélène Cixous, for example, speaks of the rhythms, flows, and sensations of the feminine libidinal economy, contrasting this with the exaggerated masculinist stress on genital sexuality. Woman, says Cixous, has the 'capacity to depropriate unselfishly, body without end, without appendage, without principal "parts" . . . Her libido is cosmic, just as her unconscious is worldwide' (1976: 95). Similarly, Luce Irigaray locates the feminine in the multiplicity of bodily sensations arising from the lips, vagina, clitoris, breasts. In contrast to the imperial phallic compulsiveness of male sexuality, women's capacity and need for sexual expression resides in the multiplicity and flux of feminine desire itself. As Irigaray says of woman: 'Her sexuality, always at least double, is in fact *plural*' (1977: 102). Women, argues Irigaray, need to establish a different relationship to feminine sexuality, establishing a range of displacements to patriarchy through writing as a cultural practice. Speaking the feminine, for Irigaray, can potentially transform the oppressive sexed identities of patriarchy. In her more recent work, particularly *An Ethics of Sexual Difference* (1993) and *To Be Two* (1999), Irigaray situates the renegotiation of identities in the frame of ethics, specifically the dilemma of recognizing the Otherness of the other sex. An ethics of sexual difference, she argues, would respect the Other in her or his own right, with regard to considerations of finitude, mortality, creation and the divine.

Finally, we can find another meeting point of feminist and psychoanalytic theories in the work of Kristeva, who elaborates the idea of a specifically feminine mode of being which dislocates patriarchal language and culture. In *Revolution in Poetic Language* (1974), Kristeva contrasts the Lacanian symbolic, the Law which the father embodies, with the multiple libidinal forces of the 'semiotic'. The semiotic is a realm of prelinguistic experience – including feelings, drives and rhythms experienced by the infant in its pre-Oedipal relation to the mother. According to Kristeva, our semiotic longing for the pre-Oedipal mother, though repressed with entry to the symbolic, remains present in the unconscious and cannot be shut off from society and culture. The semiotic, Kristeva says, is present in the rhythms, slips and silences in speech; and it is subversive of the Law of the Father since it is rooted in a pre-patriarchal connection with the feminine. Yet Kristeva denies that the feminine semiotic has any intrinsic link with gender, because it stems from the pre-Oedipal phase and is thus *prior* to sexual difference. Thus, if the semiotic is 'feminine', it is a femininity that is always potentially available to women and men in their efforts to transform gender power. Kristeva looks to the semiotic as a means of subverting the male-dominated symbolic order. She finds a clear expression of the semiotic in the writings of avant-garde authors, such as Mallarme, Lautréamont and Artaud, writing which she feels defies patriarchal language. Kristeva also locates semiotic subversion in pregnancy. The psychic experience of giving birth, Kristeva says, reproduces 'the radical ordeal of the splitting of the subject: redoubling of the body, separation and coexistence of the self and of an other, of nature and consciousness, of physiology and speech' (1986: 206).

In her more recent work, especially *Black Sun* (1989) and *New Maladies of the Soul* (1993), Kristeva situates the emotional turmoil produced by contemporary culture with reference to depression, mourning and melancholia. In depression, argues Kristeva, there is an emotional disinvestment from the Symbolic, from language as such. The depressed person, overwhelmed by sadness, suffers from a paralysis of symbolic activity. In effect, language fails to substitute for what has been lost at the level of the psyche. The loss of loved ones, the loss of ideals, the loss of pasts: as the depressed person loses all interest in the surrounding world, in language itself, psychic energy shifts to a more primitive mode of functioning, to a maternal, drive-orientated form of experience. In short, depression produces a trauma of symbolic identification, a trauma which unleashes the power of semiotic energy. In the force field of the semiotic – rhythms, semantic shifts, changes in intimation – Kristeva finds a means to connect the unspoken experience of the depressed person to established meaning, thereby facilitating an emotional reorganization of the self.

The foregoing feminist theories represent one of the most important areas of contemporary psychoanalytic criticism. They help explain, more clearly than conventional Lacanian accounts, the ways in which dominant sexual ideologies penetrate everyday life, and also explore the radicalizing possibilities of a feminine transformation of gender. But assumptions are made in these theories which need to be questioned. For one thing, the male-dominated Law is opposed in these accounts either by the woman's body or the subversive relationship of women to language. However, some feminists have argued that this merely reinstates a 'female essence' prior to the construction of sexual subjectivity, and is therefore in danger of reinforcing traditional gender divisions through an unintended biologism (see Moi, 1985; Frosh, 1987; Flax, 1990; Elliott, 1992).

Related to this is the concern that these theories erase the mediating factors which link fantasy and social reality, either by displacing the psychoanalytic account of the construction of sexual difference (as in the case of Irigaray and Cixous), or by essentialism (as with Kristeva's merging of the semiotic and motherhood). (For further discussion on these points see Benhabib and Cornell, 1987; Cornell, 1991.)

Psychoanalysis and postmodern theory

The Enlightenment reading of psychoanalysis – represented in, say, Habermas's rendition of Freud's epigram 'Where Id was, there Ego shall become' as cultur-ally prefigurative of the possibility for undistorted communication – has come in for sustained criticism in recent years. One of the sources of the suspicion of modernist psychoanalysis, with its characteristic emphasis on maximizing an individual's freedom, derives from the Lacanian argument that the notion of the autonomous ego is itself an imaginary construct. Some authors and analysts associated with the postmodern turn of recent theorizing rework the Lacanian order of the Imaginary and apply it to culture and knowledge in general, reinterpreting warnings of the death of the subject as a kind of dawning realization that the whole category of subjectivity is itself illusory. The postmodern critique, which combines elements from the philosophical standpoint of post-structuralism with elements of anti-psychoanalysis, tries to dismantle the distinction between consciousness and the unconscious, cultural prohibitions and repressed libido, subjugation and liberation. In postmodern conditions, with its dramatic speed-up in technologies, the subject is not only *decentred* but *desubjectivized* as well. What this means, at least in its more thoroughgoing versions, is a radical deconstruction of the notion of subjectivity itself. How can psychoanalysis, after all, conceivably represent the subject as a bundle of organized dispositions, affects and appetites, when contemporary society is marked in its entirety by fluidity, pluralism, variety and ambivalence? A radical assault on fixed positions and boundaries of all imagination, the postmodern re-writing of psychoanalysis underscores the fluid and multiple trajectories of libidinal enjoyment. The indeterminacy of desire, repetition, the death drive, bodily zones and intensities: these are core elements of the postmodern celebration of the multidimensional and fragmented aspects of our contemporary imaginary.

Broadly speaking, the aim of postmodern psychoanalysis is to rethink the relationship between desire and politics in a way which opens possibilities for social transformation. In this respect, Lacanian psychoanalysis has been sharply criticized by postmodernists as having politically reactionary implications. In their celebrated postmodern treatise *Anti-Oedipus* (1977), Gilles Deleuze and Felix Guattari contend that the Lacanian account of desire, insofar as it binds the subject to the social order, works in the service of repression. Psychoanalysis, in this sense, functions in the service of capitalism, as a kind of vortex around which the unconscious becomes bent out of shape. As Deleuze and Guattari see it, the Lacanian underwriting of lack is almost the opposite of desire, lack being for them just a capitalist ploy by which consumerism can plug the alleged hungers of desire. They argue that psychoanalysis, both Freudian and Lacanian, functions to *personalize desire*, referring all unconscious productions to the incestuous sexual realm of the nuclear family. Oedipal prohibitions, on this reckoning, are just the signifiers which chain desire to normative representations – the point at which we come to desire what capitalism wants us to desire. By contrast, Deleuze and Guattari seek to critique this psychoanalytic privileging of desire rooted in lack as a *product* of Law. They argue that desire in fact precedes representation: there is nothing at all personal to the flows of libido, which continually burst out anew. Perhaps the most striking feature here of Deleuze and Guattari's use of psychoanalytic concepts lies in their attempt to give full throttle to the flows of libidinous energy: a social theory in which the absolute positivity of unconscious productions is underscored, and in which schizophrenia is taken as a potentially emancipatory model.

Deleuze was one of France's most celebrated philosophers of the late twentieth century, and his co-author Guattari was a radical psychoanalyst, opposed to orthodox (both Freudian and Lacanian) theory. *Anti-Oedipus* was a courageous, poetic attempt to explode the normative power of categories like Oedipus and castration in psychoanalysis from the inside out, using psychoanalytic concepts against the colonizing conceptual logic of psychoanalysis itself. Deleuze and Guattari trace the 'free lines' of schizophrenic desire as affirmative force, pure positivity, a series of enabling rhythms and intensities as well as transforming possibilities. From this angle, the schizoid process is what enables libidinal pulsations to be uncoupled from systems, structures or cultural objects, which may in turn transform the production of the political network, making it no longer unfold according to the repressive functioning of Law. Rejecting the rigid and closed worlds of Oedipus and capitalism, Deleuze and Guattari wish to speak up for schizophrenia over neurosis, the flows of desire over lack, fragments over totalities, differences over uniformity. 'Schizophrenia', they write, 'is desiring production at the limit of social production' (1977: 35). Against the Oedipalizing logic of capitalist discourse, where desire is channelled into prescribed pathways, Deleuze and Guattari argue that the impersonalized flows of schizoid desire can herald a radical transformation of society.

Similar theoretical directions are taken in the early writings of the French philosopher Jean-François Lyotard, who argues that political society is itself secretly libidinal. Whereas Deleuze and Guattari argue that desire is codified and repressed in and through capitalism, Lyotard views contemporary society as an immense desiring system. As he sees it, the postmodern is a vast libidinal circuit of technologies, a culture swamped with seductive signs and images. In underscoring the indeterminacy of intensities, Lyotard effects a shift in focus away from theories of representation and structures of the psyche and toward bodily intensities and erotogenic surfaces. In his book *Libidinal Economy* (1993), Lyotard constructs the excitations of libido on the model of the Moebius strip, conceptualized as an endless series of rotations, twistings and contortions. The upshot of this, in political terms, is a series of arguments about how best to extract libidinal pleasure and intensity from postmodern culture. 'What would be interesting', writes Lyotard,' would be to stay where we are, but at the same time to grab all opportunities to function as good conductors of intensities' (1974: 311).

In terms of postmodernism, the work of Deleuze and Guattari, and of Lyotard, underscores the point that contemporary experience is an experience of fragmentation, dislocation, polyvalency. From this angle, the belief that social transformation may be linked to the undoing of hidden meanings or discourses (as suggested in psychoanalytic social theory from Marcuse to Habermas) appears as little more than an ideological fantasy. By contrast, truth in postmodern psychoanalysis is located in the immediacy of libidinal intensity itself. The unconscious cannot be tamed or organized; desire needs no interpretation, it simply *is*. Moreover, it is within the diffuse, perverse, and schizophrenic manifestations of desire that new forms of identity, otherness, fantasy and symbolism can be found.

The issues raised by postmodern psychoanalysis are important, especially when considered in the light of contemporary social transformations such as globalization and new communications technology. It is not apparent, however, that such theories generate any criteria for the critical assessment of social practices, politics, or value positions. As Dews (1987) points out, the dissimulation of libidinal intensities urged in many currents of postmodern psychoanalysis is something that can be ideologically marshalled by both progressive and reactionary political forces. Significantly, the view that desire is *ipso facto* rebellious and subversive is premised upon a naive naturalism, one that fails to examine the social, cultural and political forms in which unconscious passion is embedded (see Frank, 1984). Moreover, there is little consideration of the potential harm, pain and damage that psychical states of fragmentation and fluidity may comprise.

Pretext
Perplexing messages of the social

To be self-reflexive of one's actions and doings in an instituted world of social things and cultural relations is, in some sense, to be committed to an ongoing structured process of events-in-the-world. However minimal the degree of self-awareness of an individual, it could be said that a structured space is created wherever the activities of human agents are worked out; the assumed or taken-for-granted stocks of practical knowledge of an individual, when linked to other non-cognitive, perhaps unconscious, forms of experience, are fundamental to the constitution, reproduction or transformation of structured possibilities of action, as well as the making and remaking of structural constraints upon action or agency. Or, to reverse the running order of this subject/object binary, we might say that the structuring of structures is subjectively creative, is a way of cultivating dispositions, of generating forms of action. 'The structures constitutive of a particular type of environment', as Pierre Bourdieu aptly put it, 'produce *habitus*, transposable *dispositions*, structured structures predisposed to function as structuring structures, that is, as principles of the generation and structuring of practices and representation which can be objectively "regulated" and "regular" without in any way being the product of obedience to rules' (Bourdieu, 1977: 72).

Our inherited sociological language of the reflexive relations between acting subjects and structured objects has in various ways, perhaps somewhat ironically, not been especially helpful for grasping the imaginative psychical and political possibilities inherent in this structuring of structured subjectivities or identities. In fact, various traditions of social thought have tended to cancel out what can be imaginative, novel, exhilarating or disturbing about reflexivity. In some intellectual contexts, what can be dismaying about reflexivity of subjective dispositions and representations – that is, an awareness of the split or divided nature of psychic experience – is, in effect, disowned through an elevation of structures over and above the cognitive, practical and unconscious forms of knowledge of human subjects. In what I shall term the Big Brother sociological diagnosis – an outlook, I should add, that influenced various traditions of social theory for some 20 or 30 years – the activities of agents in the social field were treated as the outcome of a conjunction of psychological and social-historical determinants, in which the latter controlled the former through processes of socialization or ideological interpellation. In some approaches, such an objectivistic sociology of structures led to a wholesale liquidation of human imagination of creative action: for example, in Parsons's functionalism, in which the subject was reduced to a cultural dope, or in Althusser's Lacanian-inspired version of structuralism, in which the individual was recast as an ideological dope.

Repositioning the relation between subject and society through a psychoanalytic way of thinking offers a very different perspective. We might say that who one is in a structured world of social differences is an indeterminate consequence of structures that, in turn, have the symbolic power that they do because of the human subject's psychic openness, unconscious representations and emotional investments. The psychic world of socially and historically constituted human subjects are thus not reducible to the fantasies or representations of the individual alone, nor to the brute materiality or reality of political forces or cultural events. The presence of radical imagination and unconscious fantasy in the life of the subject is crucial, and must be theorized in relation to the inter-personal complexities of communication, the emotional processing of dialogue and the primary, if inaccessible, power of the Other.

This emphasis on the primacy of imaginative creativity, or our unconscious capacity for puzzlement and wonder, differentiates the psy-choanalytic conception of cultural reproduction from other conceptions that ignore the contentious and disturbing role of the repressed uncon-scious in social life. Particularly instructive in this context is Laplanche's notion of enigmatic signification, by which he seeks to draw attention to the human subject's ongoing psychosexual struggle to translate, interpret and retranscribe the words, gestures and actions that other people leave us with in daily practical life. Though he doesn't quite put it like this, one of Laplanche's key ideas is that other people implant themselves upon our psychic lives in the form of enigmatic questions or provocative enigmas; we all, as subjects of social structures, spend enormous amounts of emotional energy trying to figure out, and come to terms with, the presence of the Other inside us. In a sense, the particular ways in which we puzzle over enigmatic messages coming from the Other help define who we are as subjects.

Most of us, at some point in out lives, have experienced the sense of emotional confusion that arises from feeling trapped within conversational misunderstandings. Whether the conversation is one with a friend, colleague, bankteller or governmental official, this sense of feeling trapped is, in various ways, a result of knowing that, while someone is addressing us, the specifics of the communication seem to have swerved away, or veered off, from the intended addressee. Laplanche, drawing on the Lacanian distinction between a signifier *of* (a specific meaning) and a signifier *to* (a designified communication), argues that enigmatic messages involve a *designification of signifiers*. We might conceptualize this as a kind of draining of what a signifier signifies. On this view, for example, what John is saying to Geoff about his discontent at work might seem very confusing or incoherent to the latter, even though Geoff fully realizes that the communication is directed to him and to him alone. Puzzling over communication in general and the message in particular is for Laplanche at the heart of the problematics of human subjectivity and interpersonal relationships.

In short, Laplanche's stress on enigmatic signification and on otherness in the formation of human subjectivity offers a useful corrective to the orthodox vision of the individual as passively reactive to a social world largely outside of her or his control. In contrast to the Big Brother sociological diagnosis, in which external events and impacts happen *to* the individual, Laplanche's metapsychology underscores the psycho-dynamic processes internal to the individual (involving the translation and retranslation of the Other's perplexing sexual messages) as forces of both human autonomy and heteronomy. With Laplanche's necessarily inventive, meaning-making, imaginative unconscious, the human subject's project is at once to connect to the Other outside and the Other inside. With the insights of Laplanche's trenchant reformulation of Freudian psychoanalysis, we can critically pursue the issue of why so much recent social theory and cultural criticism has been so objec-tivistic, so mechanical, and imagined that the production of subjectivity arises as the mere unproblematic determination of external circumstances. With Laplanche we can at least discuss the idea that ambivalence – at once individual and social – is interwoven with closures and reopenings of the psyche to enigmatic signifiers: that is, to perplexing decentring messages.

There are two key themes that I explore and chart in the chapter that follows. The first theme is that of the relationship between psychoanalytic theory and cultural responses to Freud, particularly the ways in which Freudian ideas have been taken up, contextualized and made banal in the social field in which they are used. To do this, I critically examine recent Freud-bashing in terms of contemporary controversies about traumatic experiences and sexual abuse in childhood. The second theme concerns that of enigmatic messages of the social field and associated traumatizing consequences – of which the recent cultural trend to explain 'external trauma' away as the sole cause of private distress or personal crisis is one signal example.

2 Situating psychoanalysis in the social field

Culture wars, Freud-bashing, memory

'Me', 'Myself', and 'I': All this (psychoanalysis, in short) was nothing but a great egoistic dream – that of 'Sigmund Freud': but also 'ours', that of the throng of parricidal listeners and readers. A subject will be born here, identifying itself with all positions, assassinating everyone and playing all the roles.

(Mikkel Borch-Jacobsen, *The Freudian Subject*)

Remembering everything is a form of madness.

(Brian Friel, *Translations*)

If memories are more like dreams than pieces of reliable documentary evidence, and are disguised representations of forbidden desire, it is as though desire can only be remembered by being successfully forgotten.

(Adam Phillips, *On Flirtation*)

'We live', writes Mark Edmundson, 'in the Age of Freud, a cultural moment in which the critical and descriptive terminologies readiest to use sound with unmistakably Freudian resonances' (1990: 3). From Woody Allen's *Annie Hall* to Jacques Derrida's *The Post Card*, from Marie Cardinal's *The Words to Say It* to Paul Ricoeur's *Freud and Philosophy*: Freud's precepts and conjectures pervade our intellectual life and culture, profoundly influencing our thinking about ourselves, others and the world in which we live. Yet despite – might it be because of? – the profound influence of psychoanalysis over contemporary culture, some critics have recently argued that we had entered a post-Freudian era. A campaign launched against psychoanalysis during the 1990s did much to discredit its critical strength and scientific authority, as well as having inaugurated a culture of Freud-bashing in both the academy and public life. *Time* ran the question 'Is Freud dead?' in 1993. The answer was an unqualified 'yes'. The argument put was that Freud botched many of his clinical cases and failed to prove the efficacy of psychoanalytic treatment. If that was not damming enough, Freud's 'talking cure' was declared obsolete owing to advances in pharmacology.

Broadly speaking, there are two key conceptual currents informing the wars over Freud. One is the presumed political irrelevance of Freudian theory. The other is the supposed scientific laxity of psychoanalytic theory and treatment. The political dead-end of Freud's legacy has been put most forcefully, and indeed unambiguously, by Jeffrey Masson in books such as *The Assault on Truth* and *Against Therapy*. Masson argues that issues of sexual abuse have been suppressed in psychoanalysis. The historical origins of this he locates in Freud's alleged denial of the actuality of sexual violence towards children and women. 'By shifting the emphasis from an actual world of sadness, misery, and cruelty to an internal stage on which actors performed invented dramas for an invisible audience of their own creation', writes Masson, 'Freud began a trend away from the real world that, it seems to me, is at the root of the present-day sterility of psychoanalysis and psychiatry throughout the world' (1984: 144).

In respect of the scientific merits of psychoanalysis, Frederick Crews (a literary critic, and one-time Freudian) launched in 1993 a much-discussed attack on Freud's methodology and epistemology in the *New York Review of Books*. Drawing on Adolf Grumbaum's argument that psychoanalysis is a failed experiment, Crews insisted that Freud's claims cannot be substantiated. He argues that the connections posited by Freud between unconscious repression and human motivation do not hold up and that the links Freud sought to demonstrate between the retrieval of memory and personal well-being failed to conform to acknowledged standards of evidence and logic. In Crews's hands, psychoanalysis is less a doctrine about the emotional dynamics of mind and interpersonal relationships than a reflection of the perverse desires and demented imaginings of a bogus medical practitioner known as Sigmund Freud. As Crews writes in his book *Sceptical Engagements*:

> The only mind (Freud) laid bare for us was his own. Once we have fully grasped that point, we can begin enquiring how such a mind – rich in perverse imaginings and in the multiplying of shadowy concepts, grandiose in its dynastic ambition, atavistic in its affinities with outmoded science, and fiercely stubborn in its resistance to rational criticism – could ever have commanded our blind of consent.
>
> (1986: 86)

The era of Freud, it seems, was blinding; the post-Freudian era promises to bring insight.

I shall not seek in this chapter to develop a systematic analysis of the conceptual distortions and epistemological deficiencies in this campaign against Freud. Such a task has, in any event, already been admirably accomplished elsewhere (for example, two important contributions are Malcolm, 1984 and Frosh, 1997). By situating the Freud Wars in relation to broader psychoanalytic dialogues, however, we can illuminate some of the misleading assumptions which have plagued these debates. Consider the following three quotations from different critics of the recent spate of attacks on Freud. The first is from John Forrester:

Both criticisms – the view that psychoanalysis ignores its patients and the view that psychoanalysis smothers its patients – show towards those patients a profound lack of respect for their more or less average trustworthiness, their mose or less average scepticism, their more or less average powers of resistance to being manipulated, their more or less average independence as moral agents. These criticisms thus enact, as much as put forward as an argument, a deep distrust of anyone ever being a reliable source of evidence about the mind, a deep distrust of anyone ever being an independent moral agent.

(1997: 227–8)

The second quotation is from the American relational psychoanalyst Charles Spezzano interpreting the anxiety inherent in Crews's critique that Freudian psychoanalysis failed to unmask the reality behind appearances:

Crews clearly believed that he had found the truth in Freud; and, when he later realised that the truth had alluded him, he felt betrayed. Had he begun by thinking that Freud had a language to offer, he might have been able to try out this language as a way of talking about literature and then left it behind without the bitterness he came to feel. He went looking for dogma, found it, embraced it, and then discovered that, like other dogmas he had satirised in his earlier writings, this one too did not offer permanent objective truth. Having devoted himself to Freud as the beacon of all truths about life and literature, he sounds, in his rejection of Freud, as if he took it personally when he learned about Freud's questionable encounters with Emma Eckstein and Dora and about Freud having taken seriously some of Fliess's 'Crackpot doctrines'.

(1993: 19)

The third quotation is from Jacqueline Rose, in an article 'Where does the misery come from? Psychoanalysis, feminism and the event', who concentrates on the stakes of representation in Masson's rejection of fantasy in favour of the event or the real:

For Masson, figuration, or fantasy, is the act (fantasy is a denial of the reality of the act). . . . For what is at stake in Masson's rejection of fantasy if not representation as such, the idea of a discourse at odds with itself with no easy relation to the real?

(1993: 103)

Each of these quotations suggests an unacknowledged – perhaps unconscious? – element which at once frames and overdetermines the critical assault on Freud.

Distrust operates at the levels of criticism and enactment for Forrester. For if the central objection to Freud's theories is that they were formulated from the evidence of manipulated or untrustworthy patients, it can also be said that the sceptics' critique projects distrust onto the capacity of human beings to act as moral agents in any meaningful sense at all. Forrester's subversive move is to reveal that the critical assault on Freud is itself grounded in distrust, while noting that the affect of cynicism is projected elsewhere (specifically, onto Freud). Something similar goes on in Spezzano's reading of Crews; for Spezzano, Crews's disillusionment with Freud asserts itself as a rejection of psychoanalysis writ large. The demand for certitude, for Spezzano as for Freud, expresses itself as a desire for absolute control, mastery and domination, the violence of which is projected to the outside. Hence, the process of disillusionment can be experienced as overwhelming, or crushing. In Crews's narcissistic discourse, this seems to be translated thus: 'Because I've given up on Freud, so too should the world. Can't you see – the man's a swindler, a charlatan?' In Rose's reading of Masson, the dualism of inside and outside, of fantasy and reality, is said to suffer outright repression. No fantasy because the event is the ultimate point of reality, of meaning, of truth. In three stages, therefore, we find that the critique issuing from the debates over Freud is a discourse at odds with itself.

Ironically, this inside/outside dichotomy – enacted so violently in the writings of Crews, Masson and others – is actually subverted by Freud's theory of the fundamental and radical nature of human imagination. Freud's most subversive move, notwithstanding reworkings of the theory of psychoanalysis throughout his career, can be traced back to the elaboration of, and ensuing disenchantment with, his 'seduction theory' – the notion that every neurosis conceals a history of actual sexual seduction and trauma. In the autumn of 1897, Freud abandoned the 'seduction theory' – or so it is conventionally understood. Certainly it can be said that at this point of his career, prior to the publication of *The Interpretation of Dreams*, Freud reappraised his understanding of the relation of psychic life to the outer world. Central to this shift in Freud's thinking in particular was a radical revaluation of the internal processings of external reality, and especially of how individuals interpret, frame, and fantasize experience (including memories of sexual experiences in childhood). As John Toews comments:

> The collapse of the seduction theory in the fall of 1897 was marked by a collapse of Freud's confidence in his ability to use evidence from his patients' fantasies in reconstructing the real history of event sequences. . . . [B]ut this collapse was transformed into a 'triumph' by his recognition that fantasies might be read a different way, as signs of the unconscious intentions that produce them rather than as the forgotten events to which they referred. From this perspective the 'embellishment' and 'sublimations' of fantasy were not so much outworks to be demolished as obscure revelations of a different kind of truth, the truths of unconscious psychical activity. They were openings into a hidden world of 'psychic reality' that was not passive and objective but active and subjective, a world of unconscious psycho-sexual desire.
>
> (1991: 513)

Once Freud granted fantasy an active and subjective dimension, the psychic realm no longer functioned as a mirror to objective reality. Freud had uncovered, in one stroke, the creative, radical imagination.

Stuck with only one half of the story, however, Freud's critics have downgraded the whole concept of radical imagination, or fantasy, in favour of reality or the event. This is particularly the case in Masson's polemic against Freud, where blame is squarely laid at the master's door as regards the suppression of abusive events. In his determinist conception of seduction, where trauma is reduced to the unproblematic remembering of incest and abuse and also where the present and the future are fully shaped in advance by such destructive events of the past, Masson evades the complex issue of how happenings of life are invested with, and subjectively reworked through, fantasy and affect. That is, he limits seduction to the factual and altogether erases the fantasmatic, emotional and temporal aspects of Freud's theory. Freud's own conceptual interest in the way interpersonal happenings become invested with fantasy developed out of his work with patients demonstrating hysterical and obsessional symptoms, which he at first thought stemmed back to repressed memories of abusive sexual scenes in early childhood. But, *pace* Masson, Freud did not deny or suppress the existence of abusive memories; Freud, in fact, worked overtime – from wrestling with the reconstruction of patients' painful memories to the elaboration of theoretical constructs such as 'primal scene' – to convince his medical colleagues of the emotional and interpersonal consequences of seductive trauma (Schimek, 1987). Moreover and ironically, in terms of the anti-psychology assault on psychoanalysis, Freud continued throughout his career to stress the traumatic effects of 'seduction' – even while noting that such events were the outcome of a complex process of the retrieval of memory as embedded in the therapeutic reconstruction of sexual scenes. 'Actual seduction', Freud wrote as late as 1931, 'is common enough . . . [and] invariably disturbs the natural course of the developmental processes, and it often leaves behind extensive and lasting consequences'. Hardly the thoughts of one seeking to 'suppress' the harmful emotional consequences of trauma!

Rather than working with a binary divide where priorities must be assigned either to external trauma or the power of the life of the mind, the critical challenge – or so I want to propose – is to locate constructive paths for grasping the intermeshing of psychic fantasy and material experience. Indeed, Lynne Segal has argued that there is no essential contradiction between attributing the vicissitudes of adult symptoms to a mix of actual and fantasized events. Such a conceptual move, says Segal, was evident in Freud's own psychoanalytic sensibilities:

> years after he came to believe that neurotic symptoms and memories of early sexual experience stemmed from psychical realities and unconscious fantasies, rather than from some single (or repeated) traumatic scene,

Freud also accepted his patients' accounts of actual seduction and abuse alongside his own emphasis on the significance of sexual *desires* in childhood.

(1999: 128)

This clearly renders unconscious fantasy a part, perhaps a *sine qua non*, of all happenings. Thus, through the Freudian lens it is not a question of denying the event, but of understanding it otherwise. Psychoanalysis does not deny the extraordinary suffering that trauma can cause, nor the long-term consequences of trauma for emotional and cultural life. But, for Freud, recognition of trauma is only the beginning of the matter. The following, critical step demands an examination of, and reflection upon, the multiplex *psychic representatives* which necessarily underpin any experience of trauma. That is to say, it is crucial to enquire as to the imaginary contours of the experienced traumatic contradictions, so that the individual might come to understand the ways in which the event has been invested with, or drained of, meaning.

What is important in the dimension of the imagination, or fantasy, as concerns the individual is also crucial for society at large – hence the relevance of Freud to the social sciences and humanities. To acknowledge the fundamental and radical creativity of human imagination, whether one considers the disciplines of sociology, political science or cultural studies, is to take up issues about the *psychic orientation of social practices*. In the Freudian frame of reference, questions about the social reproduction of symbolic networks or the cultural transmission of tradition and custom are examined through reference to the imaginary elaboration of significations – that is, the fantasies which underpin any social formation or institutional practice. Every life, every activity, every event, every social or cultural practice is constituted and reproduced through representational and affective modes of psychic processing. In the light of Freud's work, the world is, in the most general sense, at once an imaginative and social-historical project.

Trauma talk and recovered memory: toward a critique of antipsychological psychology

In social-historical terms, modernity is about structures, systems, orders. In psychical terms, it is about identities, projects, constructions. Identity is but the gathering of rules and resources from the structures of modern life (social, economic, cultural, political) in and through which modern men and women attempt to come to terms with the demands of ordinary moral life. Solutions to the balancing act of relating social-historical and psychical forms, as detailed in classical social theory, have for the most part tended to be lop-sided. Indeed, it might be argued that it was only by erasing the subjective self from theoretical consideration that traditional sociological theory managed to direct attention to the complex structures of institutional social life. The liquidation of the self into some supra-individual sociology was, it seems, essential to the formation of the social sciences.

This is not just a matter of saying that the study of the institutional structures of modern living evolved without due reference to changes in the nature of identity and the self. Rather, this omission signals something about our cultural tendency – as a rationalizing expression of ideological interests and desires – to divorce human subjectivity from the surrounding social world itself. 'History', wrote Nietzsche (1983: 86) in 'On the uses and disadvantages of history for life',

> confuses the feelings and sensibilities when these are not strong enough to assess the path by themselves. He who no longer dares to trust himself but involuntarily asks of history 'How ought I to feel about this?' finds that his timidity gradually turns him into an actor and that he is playing a role, usually indeed many roles and therefore playing them badly and superficially.

History for Nietzsche is just the way we take our cue from larger social forces in the editing and organizing of daily life. Personal and social lives contain a multiple number of histories, each which functions according to its own internal logics, composed of crossings and tangles with other historical and institutional forces. And yet, in our own time, personal history is all too easily swamped by History; the subject, increasingly constrained by the powers of the past, tradition and culture, becomes the helplessly determined product of History.

In postmodern conditions, subjectivity remains not so much undertheorized as displaced, over-determined, liquidated. What was referred to as the 'end of the individual' in the critical theory of the Frankfurt school has its counterpart today in much postmodern social theory, in which decentring, fragmentation and dispersal feed into each other to produce that never-ending spectacle known as 'death of the subject'. The postmodern subject, drained of ego strength and maintaining role-performance thanks only to brittle narcissism, is culturally orientated through objectification and externalization. In contemporary media language, this becomes the iron determinism of victimhood. The ubiquity of 'adult survivor groups', 'repressed memory' and other contemporary psychological phenomena that dominate talk shows and self-help manuals testifies to the paths through which many individuals seek to alleviate personal distress and unhappiness via socially encoded processes of pop psychology.

Not that long ago the American sociologist Jeffrey Prager published a remarkable study, *Presenting the Past: Psychoanalysis and the Sociology of Misremembering*, that critically looked at both the psychodynamics and cultural significance of the discourse of trauma – demonstrating the increasing tendency of individuals and groups to appropriate pop psychology categories of media-driven culture in order to gain some minimal understanding, and presumably sought-after psychic protection, from painful emotional states. Such reliance on seemingly 'objective' schemata of understanding – from 'repressed memory' to 'post-traumatic stress disorder' – is, according to Prager, in the process of being intensified. 'We live', writes Prager (1998: 140), 'in an age that, though profoundly psychological in its talk about the influence of traumatic pasts on the present, has created a particularly antipsychological psychology. It is an age that externalises the self and, in so doing, subdues subjectivity.'

Prager's diagnosis of 'antipsychological psychology' captures nicely the emotional climate of our fluid era of modernity and postmodernization, and offers important clues for rethinking the pressures and perils of identity-construction and identity-maintenance today. Taking up Nietzsche's critique of the subordination of individuals to history, Prager sees recent debates over recovered memory as symptomatic of how contemporary social practice and dialogue encourages people towards external explanations for their psychic problems and distress.

> Trauma talk has come to dominate understanding of the self, its past and the relation to its earlier experiences to present-day unhappiness. Such talk now extends far beyond the circumstances in which this objectivistic psychology was pioneer. We have become a society of trauma survivors, as we each describe, think and feel the past traumatically and understand the present in relation to it.
>
> (Prager, 1988)

This recasting of memory as accurate historical record of events is viewed by Prager as profoundly damaging to the individual, not to mention stifling to society's recognition of its own self-production. At the same time, such cultural tendencies make it all the more difficult to pursue a more constructivist angle on the remembering mind – as represented in, say, psychoanalysis, which emphasizes the status of the subject in relation to the interpreting present. Memory, for Prager as for Freud, is embedded in the present and thus insepa-rable from the environment in which remembering occurs. In other words, what we remember about our past is always shot through with a range of cognitive and affective factors, in and through which memory is reproduced in relation to changing interpersonal and cultural contexts. As Prager (1988: 215) aptly puts it:

> Memory is best understood as after-the-fact representation of the past, reworked as it is made meaningful for the present. Memories may be the result of many transcriptions over time, but at any given time the remem-berer typically experiences them as unproblematic structures or as facts, and as external to the rememberer. But despite seeming 'objective', memory nonetheless is stimulated by current needs, desires, and defences and organised by available schemata of understanding.

The idea that the agency of an individual can be compromised or constrained by happenings of the internal world, according to Prager, demands a conception of the 'virtuality of memory'. Memory, he says, is identical neither to the past which is invoked through recall nor to the remembering individual subject. In the psychoanalytic frame of reference, memory is always representation, the product of many psychical transcriptions over time. As Prager observes (1998: 215):

> Once we understand memory as a post-hoc *representation* of the past and not a *return* to the past itself, we can better appreciate the dangers of a literalist conception of memory that does not consider the contribution to time and the current interests of the interpreter to the remembering of the past.

Such an understanding of the relation between memory, time and history is hardly likely to win a sympathetic hearing in the courts of Freud-bashers and warriors of the Culture Wars. Yet to cast memory as representation and not as fact is, most fittingly, a move towards social critique: from the culturally dominant, determinant conception of memory, in which the present is fully moulded by the past, to a critical conception of memory, in which the past is conceived as *constructions* and *reconstructions* of remembering subjects attempting to situate themselves in the present and orientate themselves to the future.

In drawing out the personal and political ramifications of his theoretical construct, Prager offers a detailed case study, threaded throughout the book, of a female patient who – during the course of psychoanalytic treatment with Prager – came to remember that her father had abused her sexually during her childhood. The patient – Prager's Ms A – was an intelligent graduate student, exploring in therapy her perceived gap between the appearance she gave off to others (supremely confident, competent and successful) and a more troubling, negative and often depressed sense of self. Having recalled scenes of her own childhood sexual abuse, Ms A confronted her father, as well as other members of her family, with these rememberings; the failure of family members to corroborate her claims led her, in turn, to break off relations with the family for a period. Above all, Ms A's rememberings also dramatically intensified the emotionally charged relations between patient and analyst. Prager notes that he was initially unpursuaded of Ms A's suspicions. He writes:

> For my part, I was quite surprised to hear of Ms A's suspicions. Little in the preceding year and a half of treatment had prepared me for this direction in our work together. And having heard only her assertion that she had been abused, unsupported by any specific recollections of incidents of abuse, I found myself unpersuaded, and neither granted her permission nor forbade her to attend a survivors' group. At the same time, I was not confident in my own skepticism about her memories. I wavered between feeling that my uncertainty sprang from my professional integrity, which demanded that 'truth prevailed', and worrying that I was discovering the limits of my capacity to empathise with a woman's experience.
>
> (1998: 10)

The recovery of some of Ms A's feelings, if not actual memories, about abuse led her into voracious reading about 'adult survivors' of childhood incest. She in time started recommending such reading matter to her analyst, Prager, who further details his own scepticism in personal and therapeutic terms thus:

> I was feeling vulnerable to the cultural critique that had been levelled not only at analysts but at men in general as being unwilling to enter women's 'psychic reality' and to appreciate the degree of oppression and subordi-nation of women in this patriarchal society . . . my 'analytic stance' seemed more and more like a defensive posture in which I was withdrawing from genuine involvement with my patient's pain so as to protect myself. I couldn't help wondering whether I was also defending the status quo, denying women's reality and affirming a logico-rational, male order of which I had long been a beneficiary. Had sexual politics – hers and mine – overwhelmed psychoanalysis?

Prager writes with remarkable insight of the reflexivity of psychoanalysis, especially of the necessity to keep open an emotional and dialogical space for his patient to explore further distressing memories of early childhood experi-ences. As it happens, Prager's Ms A came in time to question whether the trauma she remembered as childhood sexual abuse might instead have been an emotional violation. 'By the end of the analysis', writes Prager (1998: 10),

> Ms A views had changed. . . . She no longer maintained that the abuse had occurred, and, moreover, she believed that the 'memories' had been products of current psychic conflict both with me and with her father. 'Remembering' trauma, she concluded, had been her unconscious attempt to defend against painful, embarrassing and seemingly dangerous emotions. Recalling her father as evil, she came to believe, had been a defensive denial of strong positive feelings toward him that had recently resurfaced.

Such a short summary of this case-study can convey only a minimal sense of the emotional difficulties of Prager's patient who 'fails to remember', then 'remembers', and finally 'unremembers' her past. Yet summarization remains useful at this point, if only because I want to use Prager's Ms A as a foil for criti-cally examining some of the assumptions about memory which were embodied in recent Culture War discussions and debates. For the manner in which psychoanalysis has been drawn into a reductive understanding of memory in recent Freud-bashing adds a particular twist or irony to the Culture Wars. The revisionist anti-psychoanalysis movement, represented by Masson and Crews amongst others, has constructed an extreme, and thus unrepresentative, version of Freudian theory in which either (a) the individual is fully responsible for his or her own unhappiness, or (b) the recovery of traumatic memory functions as a prelude to the trial and condemnation of those responsible (read: parents) for inflicted damage. But such a dichotomization of Freud only holds memory hostage, leaving the human subject split between a reductive individualism on the one hand, and sociological objectivism on the other.

Now we cannot best explicate what memory and remembering are without looking at how the individual subject fits into interpersonal relationships and the social world more generally. Recent research in psychoanalysis is of key importance in this respect. In contemporary psychoanalytic accounts of memory, there has been a sharp critique of the notion that trauma – as a kind of external force – causes personal distress or crisis in any deterministic sense. Jean Laplanche, in his magisterial tracing of Freud's abandoned seduction theory and its materials, and whose work I want to look at in some detail in what follows, comes to the conclusion that the traumatic power of seductive events is neither stored away in a preconscious apparatus or container (as if simply awaiting personal recall) nor repressed in a mechanical sense (as if bubbling away in the psyche and awaiting an explosive return of the repressed). Rather, Laplanche makes the link in Freud between the intrusive impact of the adult Other on the one hand, and the traumatic registration, representation or inscription of the Other's presence (a message or image which, in turn, is displaced and isolated) on the other hand. As is common in contemporary psychoanalytic theory, Laplanche rejects the idea that analysts and patients are seeking to excavate or unlock the past 'as it really happened'. Nor does he have much sympathy for the narrative turn in recent psychoanalytic theorizing, where access to memories of the past is understood as a matter of current stories and constructions arising in the present. Laplanche instead attempts to delineate a 'realism of the unconscious', arguing that the notions of Otherness and translation are central for grasping the nature of repression and thus of the repressed. Rejecting as too simplistic the idea of the unconscious as repressed memory or displaced historical record, he instead conceptualizes the unconscious as *excluded fragments of enigmatic messages implanted by the Other*. Laplanche develops this standpoint explicitly in contrast to approaches emphasizing narritavization of the psychological past:

> Even if we concentrate all our attention on the retroactive temporal directions, in the sense that someone reinterprets their past, this past cannot be a purely factual one, an unprocessed or raw 'given'. It contains rather in an immanent fashion something that comes before – a message from the other.
>
> (Laplanche, 1999: 265)

In differentiating his conception of the unconscious from approaches that fix repressed desire as a kind of copying of past events, Laplanche emphasizes the unintegrated aspects – the waste arising from all attempts at translation – of deposits by the Other. Such unconscious remainders are for Laplanche at the core of anxiety and phobic reaction: the passage from seductive intrusions of the Other to unintegrated enigmatic and exciting fantasy-constructions is constitutive of the unconscious. In theorizing these unconscious deposits that resist binding and symbolization, yet continually demand expenditures of psychic energy in the form of attempts at translation and retranslation, Laplanche turns to the Freudian notion of 'deferred action', or *Nachträglichkeit*. Freud used this term to refer to the strange, multiplex ways in which the past works upon the present, highlighting that the human subject is always self-divided in the sense of being at once behind and ahead of itself in experiences and expressions of representational desire. According to Freud, the sexual nature of early childhood experience, especially memory traces, can be revived and recast in the light of subsequent experiences or fantasies; what is fundamental, says Freud, is the *delay* between infantile experiences and the subsequent release of sexual feeling from sometime after puberty. The emotional consequences of traumatic *Nachträglichkeit* stems from the individual retrospectively attributing sexual meanings to an earlier experience, even though such sexual thoughts, imaginings and feelings did not occur at the time of the earlier experience. 'Our psychical mechanism', as Freud wrote in 1896, 'has come into being by a process of stratification: the material presence in the form of memory-tracing being subject from time to time to a *re-arrangement* in accordance with fresh circumstances – to a *re-transcription*' (quoted in Segal, 1999: 139).

Laplanche takes up Freud's speculations, though he cautions against the dangers of a deterministic temporal perspective (the notion that seduction determines subsequent trauma) as well as a hermeneutic temporal perspective (of seductive trauma grasped retrospectively). According to Laplanche, the traumatic acquisition of sexual representation as mediated through a scene that was for the individual neither traumatic nor sexual as an experienced event arises as a consequence of the Other's implantation of a scrambled or compromised message. Thus, a process of inscription (of intrusive and enigmatic intimacies of the Other) in the first moment, and the individual's subsequent attempt to work out the deposited inscriptions through binding, repression, translation and transcription in the second and all subsequent moments.

Laplanche's critical reading of Freud's notion of afterwardness, or *Nachträglichkeit*, indicates plainly the shortcomings of both determinist and hermeneutic or relativist conceptions of memory. His work is thus useful for contextualizing the foregoing discussion of Prager's Ms A. For Ms A's painful recollections and psychic conflicts were not simply the products of past external traumas, but nor were they the outcome of a retrospective construction of the past from her present situation alone. Rather, it might be argued – following Laplanche's conceptual innovations – that some remainder or waste-product, something certainly resistant to symbolization, was deposited by Ms A's father during her early years – something that was afterwards reinterpreted, retranslated and retranscribed. Prager argues that this 'something' was an emotional violation; he argues, convincingly in my view, that this deposited violation left Ms A feeling unable to defend herself psychically against seemingly dangerous, embarrassing and painful feelings. Neither 'the past' (as a recovery of what really happened in childhood) nor merely a rewriting from the standpoint of the present, what perhaps is most striking here is Ms A's attempt to turn passivity into activity – that is, to make something of the message (the father's emotional violation) in the here-and-now. And in trying to make meaning of, to decipher, the perplexing messages of the father, Ms A became caught up with – in Prager's rendition – the power of cultural externalities and ideological forces. In effect, she turned to core cultural controversies over sexual abuse and trauma as *the* 'something deposited' and as thus determinant of her emotional suffering.

Significantly, the concepts of seductive trauma, afterwardness and translation developed by Laplanche can be contextualized in relation to wider social and political forces. For Laplanche's conceptualization of the subject's psychic activity of translation, binding and repression is a picture, too, of the seductive power of enigmatic signifiers or messages within whole societies, of certain kinds of inscription institutionalized. Laplanche's stress on the subject's attempts from infancy onwards to translate, transpose, bind or displace the seductive and perplexing messages of the Other means, appropriately contextualized in terms of social critique, it is always worth wondering about cultural responses to those alien, foreign or disowned parts of identity – the elements that cannot be easily contained within the dominant matrix of political repression and its after-effects. Racism, for example, might at least indicate something about the otherness of the unconscious, of sexuality and of that fearful erotization of our own strangeness, foreignness, alieness. We might even see that there is a retrospective but curious silent reversal in the denigration of the racialized Other, such that what is strange or foreign within ourselves becomes sealed off from those traumatic and enigmatic inscriptions of the Other. In this context, the psychic processes underpinning racism – projection, repudiation, foreclosure – necessarily contain implantations of the Other.

It is where attempts at translation stall, or where binding fails, that the power of stereotypical, alienating consumerist messages takes hold – as a kind of regressive substitute for the psychic work of imaginative symbolization. Our present-day menu of cultural tropes deployed to assist in this evacuation of enigmatic and exciting registration of social differences are vast and varied, whether they be immigrants, asylum seekers, single mothers, the poor, or others excluded from the economic gains of globalization.

Opening and closing Freud: modern constructions, postmodern revisions

Theorists like Laplanche who give prominence to the Other, conceptualized as the implantation of a message on an unconscious plane, are sometimes associated with the perspective of objectivism. It is perhaps not too difficult to see why, and in the next chapter I shall detail some of the ways in which I think that Laplanche's conceptualization of imagination is problematic. At any rate the issue now arises as to how to connect categories of memory, imagination and creativity to psychoanalytic interrogations of the individual subject. The relevance of the theme of imagination will be of particular concern for us in subsequent chapters when I turn to critique psychoanalysis in the frame of contemporary feminist and postmodern discourses. In the present context, however, I want to consider the topics of subjectivity, self, identity and finally the duality of inside and outside from the vantage-point of psychoanalysis itself, situating the question of the subject through a reconsideration of the nature of human imagination – in particular, the imaginative processing of emotional experience. In what follows I discuss some grey areas of human subjectivity in psychoanalytic theory. I argue that the question of the subject in psychoanalysis is always a question about the nature and limits of thinking itself (thinking understood here, following Bion (1961), as the processing of affect), or of what can be psychically processed and thus transformed.

The navigation of alternative selves and states of mind is central to the psychoanalytic investigation of subjectivity – what I have previously termed the *subject in question* (see Elliott 1995, 1996, 1999, 2001, 2002). For Freud, psychoanalysis involves an opening out of unconscious psychic life to reflection and deliberation; psychoanalytic methodology involves an engagement with the past, which is accessed through looking at what goes on at the level of conscious and unconscious representatives. It is worth wondering about the structure of our internal world, says Freud, since it is precisely through human imagination – at the levels of language and intersubjectivity – that the internal landscape of the subject opens itself to self-understanding and transformation. In Freud's famous phrase: '*Wo Es war, soll Ich werden*' ('Where Id was, there Ego shall become'). There is a profound connection here between remembering and forgetting – links, available through conscious reflection upon symptoms of unconscious fantasy, between identity and difference which can in turn be transformed through thinking and processing, and/or repressed and forgotten. Certain core questions arise in this respect. What is the project of questioning, psychoanalytically speaking, the realm of subjectivity? In psychoanalysis, what are the limits and transformations of the subject? What is the signification of the subject itself, as theory and as practice? And, crucially, in what ways does the advent of the postmodern transform psychoanalytic accounts of subjectivity?

Let us begin addressing these questions by considering Freud's remarks on the therapeutic action of psychoanalysis. There are three dominant discourses (no doubt, other competing discourses could be mentioned) which have emerged about the aims of analysis, typically labelled post-Freudian, post-Kleinian and post-Lacanian. I have positioned these discourses heuristically on a continuum from the more modern to the more postmodern, although I shall suggest that all three interpretations open and close the implications of psychoanalysis too hastily. The first discourse is essentially a rationalist one. This discourse holds that Freud (as sketched out in his topographic model of the psyche) argues for the possibility of making the unconscious conscious and that Freud (as sketched out in his structural model of the psyche) argues for the possibility of helping the ego sublimate the id. The topographic vision suggests that the paralysing grip of unconscious repression can be undone through reason and self-mastery. The structural vision suggests that the ego can be transformed from primarily defender against destructive and aggressive anxieties to primarily integrator of sexual and aggressive affects. This structural view of the aim of the psychoanalytic process – that the id can become effectively sublimated by the ego – was to become deeply entrenched in American ego-psychology, but significantly it has also been evident in the European social theory and philosophy of Jürgen Habermas, Alfred Lorenzer and others (see Elliott, 1999).

The second discourse on the aims of psychoanalysis radiates from the Fairbairnian notion of ego-splitting and the Kleinian notion of projective identification: splits in the object are followed by splits in the ego and then the split-off ego fragments are fantasmatically experienced as being parts of someone else. This view was developed by Klein, and has been further developed by neo-Kleinians to be a natural extension of Freud's project – since Freud (1924) had amended his overall psychology of conflicted subjectivity with the notion of the ego anxiously trying to avoid either being overwhelmed by or losing contact with the id or the superego 'by deforming itself, by submitting to encroachments on its own unity and even perhaps by effecting a cleavage or division of itself' (Freud, 1924: 152–3).

The third discourse on the aims of psychoanalysis is more critical than the first two (not so much a radical revision as a turning on its head), and is associated with Jacques Lacan's 'return to Freud'. Lacan interpreted Freud's maxim not as a therapeutic injunction to promote conflict-free spheres of self-identity, but as a formula which underlines the primacy of the unconscious. Lacan's critique of American ego-psychology, in particular, rejects the notion that the object of analysis is that 'the ego must dislodge the id' (Lacan, 1977: 45). In outlining a specular theory of subject formation, Lacan argues that the ego is 'an imaginary identification or, to be more accurate, an enveloping series of such identifications' (Lacan, 1966: 8). Accordingly, any attempt to strengthen the ego is simply a reinforcement of the illusions and deceptions of a narcissistic mirage. By contrast, Lacanian and post-Lacanian psychoanalysts argue that the unconscious always-already precedes the 'I', and that the object of analysis involves a radical decentring of the self, such that it is understood that the subject will always remain bound to the Other.

Any theory as innovative and complex as Freud's is bound to open itself to multiple interpretations. But, in contrast to these three dominant discourses surrounding Freud's seminal work, an alternative construction of the transformation of the subject in psychoanalysis is proposed. A combination of free association, the mapping of memory, the intersubjective crossings of transference and countertransference, and reflection upon unconscious fantasy: these are the principle means, I argue, by which the subject is able to become more open to itself and to others. By this open-endedness, I seek to underscore a questioning of the links between identity and non-identity, the turning back of fantasy upon itself in order to glimpse the inner complexity of the different states of mind of which we are capable. This scanning of fantasy and desire lies at the core of the transformation of the relation between conscious and unconscious psychic streams to which Freud refers. In addition, as the Kleinians repeatedly stress, it is through reflection upon disowned parts of the mind that the individual subject achieves an alteration of mental functioning.

In Freudian psychoanalysis, the reflective articulation of the subject's psychic representations occurs in and through language. The dynamics of transference and countertransference, following Lacan's integration of post-Saussurian linguistic into psychoanalysis, are variously characterized as a heterogeneous set of grammatical and logical 'structures' (obsessional, paranoid, hysterical, schizophrenic). In fact, perhaps the most widely recognized aspect of the signifying capacity of the human subject – particularly in contemporary critical theory – concerns 'discourse' and 'speech', at both the individual and interpersonal level. But this zoning of language – or of 'being in language' – captures only one dimension of psychic representation, that of symbolization. The pleasures and restrictions of sublimation are of central concern here: the turning of 'private', unconscious enjoyment into some kind of figuration that is valued as part of the socio-symbolic bond, and which can be communicated and translated within language. But to see this dimension of symbolization as exhausting the question of the subject is, of course, a dramatic over-simplification.

In an important contribution to this debate, Kristeva poses the following question: 'Is the destiny of the speaking being reducible to speech and language, or should even other *systems of representation* be taken into consideration in order to think this being's logical particularities and/or in order to reach the very psychic level, on which sense reveals itself to the subject?' (1994: 18). Kristeva – notwithstanding coming to psychoanalysis from linguistics – argues that it is essential for contemporary psychoanalysts to attend to the heterogeneity and polyvalence of psychic representatives; of the eroticization of lost primary involvements which dislocate the subject's capacity to use words:

> The development of semiology has lead to the conception of different signifying systems (iconic code, musical code, etc.) that are irreducible to language (the latter being envisaged as a structure or a grammar, a language or a discourse, a statement or an utterance). This has shaken 'linguistic imperialism'. Concurrently, a return to Freud, and in particular to the Freudian concept of representation, takes into account a plurality of psychic representatives: thing-representation, word-representation, representation of drives, representation of affects. The ensuing result is a 'laminated' model of the psychic signifying process with heterogeneous *traces* and *signs*.
>
> (1994: 18)

What, exactly, are these psychical traces and signs – radically heterogeneous – of which Kristeva speaks? Kristeva's own response to this question has been to displace the Lacanian emphasis on language and intersubjectivity with the notion of a 'semiotic' signifying process, a realm of pre-discursive experience (including the tone and rhythm of infant utterances, gestures, affects and bodily rhythms) which is necessarily prior to symbolic representation and entry into cultural processes. This semiotic is construed by Kristeva as the most direct appearance in consciousness of the drives. She suggests there is a connecting track between semiotic displacement, or unconscious rupture, of language, and the folding back of repression into a symbolic signifying process through which the eroticization of language perpetuates and normalizes itself.

In pursuing this construction, I seek to draw linkages between human subjectivity and the systems of representation that can be taken into consideration in order to think the limits of psychical processing at a social or cultural level. The ideas of postmodernists are very useful in this context because of the acceptance and underlining of the multiplex, fragmentary and discontinuous nature of systems of representation and signification. Embracing the fragmentation and dislocation inherent in human experience implies much about the character of psychic life and intersubjective relations. Against this backdrop, I wish to underline the importance of the postmodern condition (fragmentation, discontinuity, dislocation and turbulence) for analysing the nature of the unconscious, and especially the systems of representation to which it gives rise. It is true that modernist approaches to the question of representation also give some prominence to the fragmented and divided nature of psychic life and human experience. But whereas modernists propose a tight correspondence between what is being thought (the signified) and the fantasies which circulate around such thoughts (the signifier), postmodernist thinking sees these connections as much more open-ended and creative. One significant upshot of this is that, whereas modernists tend to privilege language or rationality in the framing of systems of representation, postmodernists understand meaning as also rooted in non-verbal or pre-symbolic modes of generating experience. Thus, Winnicott and Bion might be seen as early voices of the postmodern impulse in psychoanalysis.

Various modes of generating experience carry rich implications to the analysis of human subjectivity, and demand a radical rethinking of the dominance of the concept of narcissism as it has been elaborated by theorists such as Lacan, Kohut and Lasch. Narcissism and the ego may be closely paired, but from the viewpoint of postmodernism the question of their precise relationship remains contentious, and it is from this angle that analysts influenced by postmodern theory attempt to prise open a more reflective space for human subjectivity. The problem with Lacan's version of the narcissistic genesis of the ego is that it equates rigidified forms of ego formation with the self as such. The alternative offered by postmodernism is that of a complex, contradictory relationship between the ego and unconscious representation, self and other, autonomy and heteronomy. In postmodern terms, Freud's therapeutic maxim demands, not only that unconscious sources of motivation become the object of conscious self-reflection, but that affects (viewed by Freud as the primary drive-derivative) come to full expression in both the life of the subject and society at large. Ultimately, then, postmodernism underscores the importance of passion and the affects, subjective resources necessary for rethinking the subject in the aftermath of poststructuralist thought.

This strongly suggests that, notwithstanding differences of interpretation among competing traditions of psychoanalysis, the constitution of psychic space demands rethinking as regards the structuration of self, others and the wider world. Before we examine what this might mean for social theory and cultural critique, however, we need to examine in more detail recent psychoanalytic dialogues governing both the nature of repression and the explication of subjectivity.

Pretext

Subjectivity, signification and
writing: Kristeva and the
Barthes system

Postmodernism offers an interesting take on our society's recycling or
repetition of signs. All forms of discourse and culture are made up of
recycled words and images, but this is especially the case in our new age
of consumer and media culture. We live in a world pulsating with signs,
a globalized empire of codes and significations, so that the meaning
of everything we think is another thought, of everything we say the
implication that things might be said otherwise. As Roland Barthes and
others pointed out long ago when they drew upon structural linguistics,
semiological and deconstructive theories to open up an ominous gap
between discourses and images in everyday life, meaning is a matter
of difference. All our language is loose: whatever one means to say, all
words are fill-ins for other words – as any cursory glance at a dictionary
reveals.

If language is always being recycled and translated, this does not
necessarily imply that words are deceptive. To some, the misadventures
of meaning denote not only a polyvalence of signification but also,
fundamentally, repressed desire or the body beneath meaning. In fact,
the symbolic order of language, of writing and of texts, is a recording of
this interplay of culture and the body, discourse and desire. 'Writing',
comments Barthes:

> is always rooted in something beyond language, it develops like a
> seed, not like a line, it manifests an essence and holds the threat of
> a secret, it is an *anti-communication*, it is intimidating. All writing
> will therefore contain the ambiguity of an object which is both
> language and coercion: there exists fundamentally in writing
> a 'circumstance' foreign to language, there is, as it were, the weight
> of a gaze conveying an intention which is no longer linguistic. This
> gaze may well express a passion of language, as in literary modes of

writing; it may also express the threat of retribution, as in political ones. . . . [In] literary modes of writing . . . the unity of the signs is ceaselessly fascinated by zones of infra- or ultra-language.

(Barthes, 1974: 20)

This is Barthes on the space of writing in 1953, in *Writing Degree Zero*. For the early Barthes, writing is regarded as both a linguistic derivation or projection and extra-discursive transformation. He means to say that texts are overdetermined, oversignified, self-referential. Texts overflow. But they also have roots, anchorings, closures. 'There exists fundamentally in writing', notes Barthes, 'a "circumstance" foreign to language.' What it is, exactly, that is foreign to language is not something that the early Barthes delineates with much precision. But he goes on to say he suspects this involves a kind of infra-language or ultra-language.

In many books after *Writing Degree Zero*, on such diverse topics as myth, fashion and love, Barthes went on to detail a breathtaking semiological vision of society. He drew from an eclectic range of theorists, including Saussure, Jakobson, Benveniste, Bakhtin and Lacan. His entire theoretical edifice (less a coherent system than a kind of ongoing conceptual cross-referencing) sought to decode the signs our society generates. This he did through situating writing at the crossroads of the universal and the intimate, language and the body. It was an approach that, in time, made Barthes one of the most important semioticans of the postwar years in Europe. In the mid-1960s in Paris, however, when Barthes was teaching at the Ecole Pratique des Hautes Etudes, his seminars were attended by students mostly researching literature, linguistics or cultural studies. One such student captivated with Barthes's interrogation of the overdetermination of signification was Julia Kristeva.

In late 1965, Kristeva had only recently left Bulgaria; she had arrived in Paris with the aim of conducting doctoral research on the limits of structuralism and the theory of the subject. She quickly became a regular at Barthes's seminars and for the following several years was, in fact, a key contributor to his research group.

As odd as it may be to some unaware of the intricate ties between linguistics and psychoanalysis in postwar France, Barthes's experiment with the apsychological or asubjective roots of writing appealed to Kristeva's dialectical sensibilities. The 'death of the author', in the hands of Barthes, became the deferred effect of writing wrought by the body, drives and passion on the one hand, and by the decentring movements of praxis, including language and history on the other. Across and between the lines of the text, writing is at once inner and outer, libidinal and linguistic, *infra*-language and *ultra*-language. In short, Barthes proposed that what makes writing emerge from linguistic categories and rhetorical tradition is the body in the social-historical world.

There is nothing necessarily psychodynamic or affective in orientation about this doctrine. By whatever reckoning, Barthes's decoding of signs is resolutely semiological with an eye toward sociology. In 'Roland Barthes and Writing as Demystification', Kristeva reflects on how Barthes's writings diverged from psychoanalytic interpretation thus:

> *Writing as negativity* appears as an intermediary between the subject's drives, on the one hand, and social practice in language, on the other.
> Nevertheless, for Barthes, this investigation, no matter how subjective, had very little to do with psychoanalysis, which always seemed to him a science of pathology: neurosis and psychosis. Writing, though placed side by side with these pathologies and hand in hand with drives, was irreducible, according to Barthes, to the psychoanalytical approach. For 'drives', 'biology', 'the body' – again, his terms – are always already objectified through literature and transmuted in a mode of writing, a communication, that is historical.
> (Kristeva 2000a: 193)

Barthes was surely right to invert Saussure's assertion that linguistics is part of the broader discipline of semiology, insisting as he did that semiology is, in fact, part of the more general field of linguistics. In doing so, he helped to create an awareness that language always overflows with meaning, exhausts itself; that while at the same time writing communicates an idea it also calls into question its own economy, its own positioning as discourse. But, just as in *Writing Degree Zero* writing operates as a kind of translanguage, then, beginning with his inaugural lecture at the College de France in 1977 and subsequently in *A Lover's Discourse* and *Camera Lucida*, the otherness of language – its strangeness, recasting, introversion – becomes increasingly central to Barthes's interrogation of the subject of writing. For the late Barthes, speaking at his 1977 inaugural lecture,

> Semiology collects the impurity of language, the waste of linguistics, the immediate corruption of the message: nothing less than the fears,

the appearances, the intimidations, the advances, the blandishments, the protests, the excuses, the aggression, the various kinds of music out of which active language is made.

(Calvet 1994: 218)

Twenty-odd years later on, it is this very theme of the musicality of language – the force-field of semiotic pulsations and unconscious eruptions – that Kristeva becomes internationally renowned for in psychoanalytical and feminist circles. Her thinking on this was initially framed many years earlier, when attending Barthes's seminar, when taking in his idiosyncratic way of looking at things, his provocative mixings of language and discourse. This cannot be taken to mean, of course, that Barthes's thinking simply became that of Kristeva. For notwithstanding Kristeva's notion of intertextuality – that every text is a parody and a plagiarism of prior texts – her thinking on the musicality of poetic language ('the semiotic', 'thetic', 'subject-in-process') departs substantially from his intuitions. And yet Kristeva's theory of the subject is, in some key respects, a facilitation of Barthes's approach. 'Every discourse is fictional', Barthes once commented, 'even the most serious discourse' (Calvet 1994: 234). Transpose discourse for subject, and fictional for fantasy, and these lines could have been written by Kristeva.

3   The psychic constitution of the subject

Imagination, identification, primary repression

The subject can begin to sketch out the elements of the real, the object and the human other, only starting with and under the exclusive control of its own imaginary schemata.

(Cornelius Castoriadis, *The Imaginary Institution of Society*)

The 'subject' identifies himself with/in an almost material consistency that finds everything abhorrent.

(Luce Irigary, *Speculum of the Other Woman*)

The more we understand about primitive mentality, which constitutes a deep layer of advanced mentality, the harder it becomes to escape the idea that its implicit sense of and quest for irrational nondifferentiation of subject and object contains a truth of its own, granted that this other truth fits badly with our rational world view and quest for objectivity.

(Hans Loewald, 'The Waning of the Oedipus complex')

In an article commissioned for the *Encyclopedia Britannica*, Freud (1926: 265) explained that psychoanalysis derived

> all mental processes (apart from the reception of external stimuli) from the interplay of forces, which assist or inhibit one another, combine with one another, enter into compromises with one another, etc. All of these forces are originally in the nature of drives; thus they have an organic origin. They are characterized by possessing an immense (somatic) store of power ('*the compulsion to repeat*'); and they are represented mentally as images or ideas with an affective charge.

Forces, inhibitions, compromises, drives, compulsions, representations, imagos, affects: these are many of Freud's most central theoretical categories, all powerfully condensed to a few sentences, capturing as they do the core psychoanalytic demystification of the subject as inherently affective and symbolic, a mix of intense bodily sensations and baroque imaginings. The core of all psychical productions for Freud, as Castoriadis (1987) has pointed out, is the radical imagination – which indicates that the form of the psyche is made up essentially of representations. Freud's rigorous aestheticization of the unconscious is power-fully underscored by his formulation 'ideational representative of drives' (*Vorstellungsreprasentunz des Triebes*) in his paper 'Repression' (1915b), where both ideational and affective elements of the 'psychical representative' are explored. There has been considerable debate for some years now over Freud's theory of psychical representation, particularly as regards terminological issues arising from Freud's differentiation between 'psychical representative', 'ideational representative' and 'instinctual representative' (see Delrieu, 1977; Bourguignon *et al.*, 1989) as well as discriminations between representation and affect in the unconscious (Green, 1995). I shall not comment on these debates, but wish to raise some other, related issues stemming from Freud's account of the primordial psychic world. The Freudian interplay of drive and representation, of affect and fantasy – on the reading I am proposing – short-circuits what we might call the question of ontological construction – that is of how, in psychoanalytic terms, the infant begins life from this completely self-centred mode. Imagination, in other words, is to some degree in contradiction with the world conjured up and thus subjectivized through the subject's representational activity. How can this be? That is, how can the nascent subject's self-enclosed representational flux open up to otherness, difference and the external world?

Toward the end of his career, in fact as late as 1938, Freud still pondered how the initial, radically unconscious 'identifications' or 'investments' of the infant became the very seal of subjectivity. Reflecting on the infant's fantasmatic representational activity, in the frame of what he had previously termed 'primary repression', Freud wrote 'I am the Breast' ('*Ich bin die Brust*'). The sentence was no more than a note, perhaps a jotting intended to inspire future research. As it happens, he did not have the energy, or time, to pursue this idea further. Leaving that to one side, though, Freud's 'I am the Breast' is interesting not only because it is an attempt to get at how the individual subject is initially completely self-centred, but because it is a formulation that outstrips the conceptual terrain of the Freudian unconscious. Displacing the interlock of representation and affect, and yet as resistant to symbolization as the Lacanian Real, Freud's 'I am the Breast' implicitly recognizes the body is already imagination, the transformation of external substance into the stuff of psychical reality.

What follows is an attempt to refine and extend these speculations of Freud on imagination and primary repression. Throughout the chapter, I offer some critical reflections on the state of the self in its unconscious relational world. The principal issue I shall be concerned with is that of connecting a conception of the human subject as self-representing, self-symbolizing and self-reflective with socio-symbolic, intersubjective explanation in psychoanalysis. The forging of such a connection, I argue, involves attention to the following: the ques-tion of unconscious representation; the nature of intersubjectivity; and their mutual imbrication with the structuring properties of modern institutions and culture. In the first section, the chapter unpacks a variety of psychoanalytical assumptions or understandings concerning the developmental genesis of unconscious representation. It is suggested that there are a number of important problems with traditional psychoanalytic accounts of the representational psychic space of the human subject. It is also suggested that we need to probe further in order to understand the crucial links between the unconscious and creativity, representation and the human imagination. Throughout, it will be one of my objectives to trace the rapprochements and realignments between Anglo-American and continental traditions of psychoanalysis that now appear to be taking place. In the second section, I examine the structuration of representation with reference to primary repression and identification. It is argued that primary repression is not merely a preparatory step for the negotiation of Oedipal identity, but is rather essential to the establishment of an elementary form of subjectivity itself. In this connection, the recent psychoanalytical work of Kristeva and Laplanche on primary repression is examined, and subjected to critical analysis. The final sections of the chapter are more reconstructive and innovative in character. For existing psychoanalytical accounts I suggest we should substitute the concept of *rolling identification*, the psychical basis of the shift from self-referential representational activity to an elementary form of intersubjectivity. Rolling identifications are defined as a representational flux that permits human subjects to create a relation to the self-as-object and pre-object relations. Such primal identification, it is suggested, operates through a *representational wrapping of self and others*. The chapter concludes with a consideration of the significance of primary repression, and the politicization of identification.

Rethinking representation: fantasy, creation, imagination

First, then, the question of unconscious representation. This relates directly to some of the deepest problematics of subjectivity.

In *The Interpretation of Dreams*, Freud boldly proclaims that 'nothing but a wish can set our mental apparatus at work' (1900: 567). From the perspective of classical Freudian theory, the work of the psyche functions via the pleasure principle, a principle established through a repetition of desired fantasies. What kind of fantasies lead to psychical pleasure? Freud argued that they might be sexual, or destructive, or derived from self-preservative needs for security. For Freud, representation, drive and affect are the fundamental conditions structuring unconscious fantasy (1915a: 177; 1915b: 148). Unconscious fantasy, to be sure, is constituted as representation, and is the moment of creation *par excellence* of the psyche (on the creative nature of the unconscious see Ricoeur, 1970; Castoriadis, 1984; and Elliott, 1992). This is expressed in Freud's formulation that the psyche must submit the drive to a delegation through representation (*Vorstellungsrepräsentanz des Triebes*). What this means is that psychical functioning depends upon somatic drives passing into psychic representational space, which in turn constitutes itself as a *fantasy fulfilment through a forming of images.* Freud makes clear that he regards representation as the 'most general and the most striking' characteristic of the unconscious, through which 'a thought, and as a rule a thought of something that is wished, is objectified . . . is represented as a scene, or, as it seems to us, is experienced' (1900: 37).

Freud's thinking about unconscious representation takes us to the heart of some of the most crucial questions about self and object formation. Yet, as Greenberg and Mitchell (1983) point out, there are fundamental inconsistencies in Freud's doctrines. On the one hand, Freud can be said to uncover the constitutive imaginary dimensions of self-organization and unconscious relational experience (Castoriadis, 1987; Elliott, 1999). Fantasy, hallucination, omnipotence of thought: these are, for Freud, central unconscious dimensions of the human imagination. From this angle, creation for Freud is understood in terms of the fantasy registration of drives. On the other hand, however, Freud (at various points in his work) displaces these profoundly imaginary dimensions of self-organization. These displacements range from attempts to locate the 'real', objective events of trauma to the search for an original, collective Oedipus complex (1913).

Many psychoanalytic theorists in recent times have recognized, though they have not forcefully acknowledged, the problem of unconscious representation. In Anglo-American psychoanalysis, one general approach focuses upon representation in *developmental* terms. In this perspective, self and object representations are understood as emerging across time and, through intersecting with the interpersonal field, develop into richer, more complex impressions of the external world. Broadly speaking, Anglo-American post-Freudian theories have underscored the role of interpersonal relations in the constitution of psychical structure and the self. From this perspective it is *human relatedness* that generates a sense of selfhood, with relational processes being understood as lying at the heart of self-organization and development. In object relations theory and related variants, the psychic economy is never merely an internal affair, the regulation of unconscious drive conflict alone. Instead, the gratifications and frustrations of psychical life are seen as fundamentally structured by the dynamics of human interaction. Significantly, such recognition of the intersubjective foundation of the self has led psychoanalytic debate away from issues of Oedipal conflict and sexual repression to a concern with the earlier pre-Oedipal period and disturbances in ego-formation.

In a detailed elaboration of Freudian theory, Greenberg (1991) argues that the representational world of the self grows out of a complex interplay of desires for safety and capability. Greenberg suggests that feelings of certainty and excitement are forged and reproduced through acting on the world, through productivity and industry. Similarly in contemporary object relations theory, Sandler (1989), echoing Ferenczi, contends that representation is primarily propelled by engagement with early attachment figures especially via maternal responsiveness – which in turn generates feelings of safety. And so too, Benjamin's (1988) intersubjective psychoanalysis posits the erotic component of unconscious representation as bound up with the dialectic of dependence and interdependence.

However, the problem with all of these gradualist perspectives is that they bypass the question of representation – and its affective driveness – altogether. We find here a generality about psychic representation and a lack of detail as to how the unconscious intersects with the self's relational landscape.

If object relational theorists have too narrowly defined representational forms, they have compounded the problem by failing to examine the self-instituting, material conditions of fantasy itself. This is certainly true of the Kleinian tradition, which divides the internal world between paranoid anger and personal despair. From the Kleinian standpoint, internal fantasy processes generate fundamental contradictions and deformations of intersubjectivity – with such processes being installed in the external world through projective identification and thus institutionalized. However, the view that social life is distorted by fantasy leaves the question of what is being 'distorted' here entirely open. How does fantasy distort the social world in the act of constructing it? How might political conditions affect and determine the systematic distortion of fantasy formations that underpin social life? What seems to happen to the concept of fantasy in Kleinian theory is that, while it is correctly seen as the crucial psychic underpinning of all social activity, it is not recognized as being inseparably bound up with the material conditions of its making (see Elliott, 1994). Instead, fantasy as the ground of intersubjective distortion is closed off from the social world and rounded back upon the human subject itself.

French psychoanalysis offers another perspective on the structuring conditions of self-organization and unconscious representation. In Lacan's theory, the concept of the unconscious is tied directly to organized signifiers, it is conceived as a language, but it relates the organization of desire only to secondary repression as symbolic law (see Castoriadis, 1984; Macey, 1988; and Elliott, 1999 for critical discussions of Lacan's linguistic reconceptualization of Freudian psychoanalysis). More significant, for our purposes, is Lacan's dramatization of self-constitution as a primary relationship to otherness. 'The human ego', says Lacan, 'establishes itself on the basis of the imaginary relation' (1975: 133). Yet the imaginary in Lacan's work refers only to the specular. Lacan's 'mirror stage' is a kind of archaic realm of distorted and alienating images, a spatial world of indistinction between self and other, from which primary narcissism and aggressivity are drawn as key building blocks in the formation of self. Lacan's account of specular self-formation, however, does not stand up to close examination. The argument that the mirror distorts fails to specify the psychic processes interior to the individual subject which makes such misrecognition possible. For example, what is it that leads the subject to (mis)recognize itself from its mirror image? How, exactly, does the individual cash in on this conferring of selfhood, however deformed or brittle? The problem is that surely for an individual to begin to recognize itself in the 'mirror' she or he must already possess a more rudimentary sense of subjectivity. For to take up a reflected image as one's own must no doubt require some general capacity for affective response. I have discussed these problems of Lacan's doctrine in some detail in *Social Theory and Psychoanalysis in Transition* (Elliott, 1999: 138–58).

In French theory, the general response to this impasse in Lacanianism involved a return to the issue of fantasy itself. Imaginary misrecognition as the basis for Oedipal repression was displaced in favour of a thoroughgoing investigation into the pre-history of the subject, notably the question of primal fantasies and inherited memory traces. Among analysts, Laplanche and Pontalis (1968) directly addressed the issue of primal fantasy and repression as the condition for unconscious psychical productions. Laplanche and Pontalis argued that Freud's notion of primal fantasies – seduction, castration, primal scene – refers to the symbolic transmission of the conditions of possibility for unconscious representation.

Echoing Lacan's structuralist tendencies, Laplanche and Pontalis contend that Freud's postulation of an external event in subjective pre-history grants a determining role to a symbolic reality that has 'an autonomous and structural status with regard to the subject who is totally dependent upon it'. Significantly, the question of the origin of representation is thus raised. This symbolic reality, as a force outside and other, acts as a template for the fantasy world of the individual subject. Yet fantasy, Laplanche and Pontalis caution, cannot be reduced to a mere hallucination of the object of desire. On the contrary, fantasy is itself a realm of interchangeable places, plural identifications, multiple entry points. As Laplanche and Pontalis put it:

> Fantasy is not the object of desire, but its setting. In fantasy the subject does not pursue the object or its sign: he appears caught up himself in the sequence of images. He forms no representation of the desired object, but is himself represented as participating in the scene.
>
> (1968: 16)

Such representational multiplication is therefore one of the central dimensions of unconscious fantasy, and Laplanche and Pontalis offer a series of important specifications in this respect. A number of questions, however, are prompted by their formulation of primal fantasy, that is, unconscious representation. What are the conditions for the *emergence* of fantasy? What emergent capacities should be attributed to the psyche in this respect? How are unconscious fantasies elaborated?

The difficulty in pursuing these issues, as Borch-Jacobsen (1988) points out, is that the human subject has been cast principally outside of the domain of representation in most versions of psychoanalysis. That is, while unconscious representation is seen as a necessary condition for the development of subjectivity, it has been reduced to little more than a 'stage' or 'screen' for disguising the functioning of desire. As Borch-Jacobsen notes:

> we are left viewing fantasy as a spectacle represented to a subject who remains outside the drama, outside representation. . . . [However] we have

to leave the visible (the imaginary, the specular) behind and dismantle the theatre, we have to stop placing the subject in a position of exteriority (*sub-jacence*) with respect to representation.

(1988: 44)

A plausible position on the status of unconscious representation, I believe, can be found in the writings of Castoriadis. Castoriadis argues that Freud's 'primal fantasies' are not genuinely originary fantasies because they involve a relatively developed articulation of 'contents' and 'relations' between the self and others. Originary fantasy for Castoriadis, by contrast, involves a *'lack of distinction between the subject and the non-subject'* (1987: 286). Originary fantas-matization, or what Castoriadis terms the 'radical imaginary', is a primal architecture of representations, drives and passions in and through which the subject creates a world for itself. 'The originary psychical subject', says Castoriadis, 'is this primordial 'fantasy': at once the representation and the investment of a Self that is All' (1987: 287). Unconscious representation, according to Castoriadis, is creation *ex nihilo*. Human imagination is pure creation, the making and remaking of images and forms as self-production. This does not mean, absurdly, that human beings are unconstrained in their representational activity, that is, the making of self and object representations. On the contrary, Castoriadis argues that the self-creating nature of repre-sentation 'leans on' biological properties of the individual, and is bound up with the symbolically structured character of the social-historical world.

To speak of 'originary representation' is certainly at odds with the bulk of contemporary theory; from Saussure to Derrida, contemporary theory develops by way of a shift from ideas of 'representation' and 'mentation' and from the notion that the mind 'represents' the world and thereofre provides a foundation for knowledge, and toward the study of language and the analysis of discursive practices. This move away from representational theories of the subject might, at first glance, seem to render Castoriadis's stress on imagination and the imaginary outdated or redundant. Certainly critics have argued that the whole concept of representation, the idea that some transcendental signified automatically assigns a set of stable meanings to the subject, has seriously come to grief since the linguistic turn in modern philosophy. This kind of criticism, however, reflects a fundamental misunderstanding of what Castoriadis means by 'originary fantasmatization'. The concept of unconscious representation for Castoriadis does not denote an organic bond between image and thing, idea and object; it does not mean the 'imitation' or 'copying' of a world in the mind of the subject. Rather, Castoriadis suggests that the unconscious comprises a fantasmatic flux, a representational magma of significations, which is strictly unthinkable within the confines of Western rationality and logic. He defines the imaginary as the capacity to posit that which is not. Against the reductive scopic account of the imaginary posited by Lacan, Castoriadis defines the radical/social imaginary not as the creation of images in the mind or in society, but rather in terms of the signifiable.

Castoriadis (1989), following Freud, further reminds us that originary fantasy and representation underlies the capacity of the subject for critical self-reflection and autonomy. As he says of psychoanalysis itself: 'the possibility of representing *oneself as* representational activity and of putting oneself in question as such is not just a philosophical subtlety; it corresponds to the *minimum* we require of every patient when we try to lead him/her to discover that X is not Y but that it is very much so for *his/her* own representational activity and that there may be reasons for this' (1989: 27). Representation, unconscious flux, originary fantasmatization: these are, says Castoriadis, necessary conditions for the possibility of reflectiveness in the individual human subject.

This focus on representational activity, as an essential source for explicating subjectivity, has also received attention in recent Anglo-American psychoanalysis. Many accounts stress the representational and affective driveness of subjectivity, highlighting that the individual subject generates a sense of personal agency in and through the medium of unconscious forms (Schafer, 1983; Mitchell, 1988). Here the individual subject is understood as constituting and reconstituting agency in the course of imaging itself and other people. Such a focus suggests attention to the nature of unconscious early representations and internalizations, the meshing of these representational forms with object-relatedness, experiences of personal continuity and fragmentation, and also the level of a person's felt agency. Lear (1991) has argued that human autonomy depends upon the individual reflecting upon unconscious feelings and representations as the product of *their own creation and elaboration*. Similarly, Spezzano contends that psychoanalysis aims at 'translating the vocabulary of blame into a vocabulary of responsibility for disturbing and painful affective experience' (1993: 123).

Let me sum up so far. I think it necessary that psychoanalysis and contemporary theory accept this underlining of the profoundly imaginary dimensions of human subjectivity. The imaginary tribulations of the self, it is suggested, are rooted in the relations between originary representation, unconscious flux, fantasy, and affect. That is to say, the 'subject' begins life as representation, no more and no less.

Freud and his followers: on the concepts of repression and identification

The psyche, then, as representational flux, is closed in upon itself, an initial self-sufficiency. This is the psyche's original monadic or auto-erotic organization (see Castoriadis, 1987; Elliott, 1999). As Freud writes of this psychical state:

> It will rightly be objected that an organization which was a slave to the pleasure principle and neglected the reality of the external world could not maintain itself alive for the shortest time, so that it could not have come into existence at all. The employment of a fiction like this is, however, justified when one considers that the infant – provided one includes with

it the care it receives from its mother – does almost realize a psychical system of this kind.

(1911: 220n)

Yet the following questions immediately suggest themselves: what is it that breaks up the self-sufficiency of this psychical state? How does the psyche open itself to a world of structured intersubjectivity? Where does this psychical capacity come from?

Freud thought that the creation of the human subject occurs in and through repression. Primary repression, Freud wrote, 'consists in the psychical (ideational) representative of the drive being denied entrance into the conscious' (1915b: 148). The outcome of primary repression, which arises from the non-satisfaction of infantile needs, is the bonding or fixing of drives to representations (see Elliott, 1999: 27–9). But Freud stops short of spelling out the precise implications of primary repression for the structuration of subjectivity. Instead, his own theoretical and clinical accounts of the development of subjectivity centre upon the concept of secondary repression, or 'repression proper', as formulated in the Oedipus and castration complexes. In Freud's scheme, it is the paternal break-up of the imaginary child/mother dyad which initiates 'repression proper', and constitutes the development of identity and culture.

However, Freud's construction of Oedipal repression as constitutive of identity obscures as much as it illuminates. The view that the small infant (re)presents or discovers *itself* through Oedipal identifications implies that subjectivity is a given, and not a phenomenon to be explicated. The inconsistency here is that the infant surely cannot identify with Oedipal presentations unless it already has a more rudimentary sense of subjectivity. Moreover, it seems that this problem is only compounded if we reverse the logic in operation here, as Lacan does, and trace the imaginary ego as modelling and misrecognizing itself in specular images. For, as previously noted, the specular relation is only constituted as a *relation* to the extent that it is shaped by psychic space itself. And in Lacan's account, this (mis)copying is linked to further alienation through the constitution of the subject via a phallocentrically organized structure of language and culture.

By contrast, the psychoanalytic direction of contemporary theory involves a renewed emphasis upon primary repression and identification. Kristeva (1987, 1989) and Laplanche (1987) provide detailed treatments of the topic. Here it is suggested that the dynamics of primary repression and identification involve an elementary gap between self and other, a gap which is the very condition for the arising of the subject. Primary repression is thus not merely a preparatory step for the constitution of Oedipal identity. Rather, primary repression is considered as elementary to the establishment of subjectivity itself. In what follows, I shall critically examine some of the central theoretical issues on primary repression as discussed by Kristeva and Laplanche. Following this, I shall attempt to sketch an alternative account of primary repression as linked to the dynamics of subjectivity and intersubjectivity.

Primary repression and the loss of the thing: Kristeva's exploration of the imaginary father

For several decades, Kristeva has focused on recasting the relations between subjectivity and society in a series of works situated at the intersection of psychoanalysis, feminism and modern European thought, including *Tales of Love* (1987), *In the Beginning was Love* (1988), *Strangers to Ourselves* (1991), and *New Maladies of the Soul* (1993). Her work blends linguistic and psychoanalytical theory to advance a novel account of how pre-verbal experience – maternal, infantile, poetic – enters into, shapes, distorts and disrupts language through processes of art, literature and psychoanalysis. The result has been a radical opening of the intersections between psychoanalysis and critical social theory, which in turn has provided a transformative political and feminist dimension to Freudian thought and an enhanced psychoanalytical dimension to critical social theory.

Kristeva's various discussions of the constitution of repressed desire demonstrate a persistent concern with human imagination and the creativity of action. Her provocative thesis that the semiotic, poetical dimension of repressed desire cannot be articulated in the conventional language of everyday life or culture was briefly sketched in Chapter 1. However, in order to adequately grasp Kristeva's contribution to psychoanalytic theory, it is necessary now to situate her work in the context of Lacan's 'return to Freud'. Having undertaken her psychoanalytic training with Lacan, it is perhaps not surprising that Kristeva's early writings should emphasize the ordering power of the Symbolic, of language as such. In Lacan's rewriting of Freud, the human subject comes to language, and adopts a position of speaker, from a devastating primordial loss. The pain of this loss leads to a repression that at once buries memories of fulfilment experienced through contact with the phallic mother on the one hand, and catapults the subject-to-be into a Symbolic order of individuation, differentiation and cultural signification on the other. This account of how the human subject is radically split off from its own desire by the bar of repression, represented by the signifier of the phallus, was described by Lacan in the following terms:

> All these propositions merely veil over the fact that the phallus can only play its role as veiled, that is, as in itself the sign of the latency with which everything signifiable is struck as soon as it is raised (*ausgehoben*) to the function of signifier.
>
> The phallus is the signifier of this *Aushebueng* itself which it inaugurates (initiates) by its own disappearance.
>
> (Lacan quoted in Mitchell and Rose, 1985: 82)

In her early work Kristeva accepts these basic tenets of Lacanian theory, but as noted she contrasts Lacan's account of the Symbolic order with a revaluation of the persistence and force of repressed libidinal desires, somatic dispositions and affects – a kind of unconscious rhythm that Kristeva terms 'the semiotic'. Prose and poetry are symbolic forms that Kristeva has psychoanalytically decon-structed to try to capture something of 'the semiotic' or 'maternal body' that remains truly inexpressible. She finds in acts of artistic expression that press language to its limits – that is, in the ruins of the symbolic – a zone, by definition incommunicable, in which desire bursts forth. Is this zone a set of organized subjective meanings, a language, or is it pre-linguistic, and hence indescribable? Not so much pre-linguisitic according Kristeva, as an expression of the pro-linguistic: affects, bodily dispositions, silences, rhythms.

A powerful indication of how far Kristeva has moved away from Lacan can be gleaned from her more recent work, especially *The Sense and Non-Sense of Revolt* (2000). In a remarkably lucid, eloquent, lethal critique of the linguis-tification of French psychoanalysis, Kristeva traces and recontextualizes the radical impulse of Freudian thought. Kristeva brands Lacan's 'return to Freud' rigorous in developing the insights of continental philosophy and linguistics, yet narrow (and, in fact, un-Freudian) in dismantling the dualist drive/conscious vision. Lacan himself, she points out, was a pseudo-mathematician of the unconscious, who structuralized psychoanalysis in the wake of the model of language worked out in *The Interpretation of Dreams*, and who was either unaware or uninterested in how a linguistic interpretation of the unconscious violates Freud's preanalytical studies on the relation between the sexual and the verbal or the master's post-1910 thought on identification, idealization and sub-limation. Neo-Lacanian thought also fares badly, and is accused by Kristeva of fatally confusing psychical representations, or formations, with structuring conscious identifications. 'If we harden the Lacanian line as I have traced it', writes Kristeva (2000: 42–3),

> we end up getting rid of what still constituted Freudian dualism at the heart of this second model, a dualism that situates language between the conscious and unconscious while at the same time maintaining the dualist drive/conscious vision. We thus liquidate the instinctual domain as well as the primary processes. This is the tendency of a certain current in French Lacanian and post-Lacanian psychoanalysis that considers the notion of the drive useless.

In her recent work, Kristeva has become especially interested in Kleinian psychoanalysis, or more specifically Klein's elaboration of Freud's theory of representation or the proto-fantasy. A close reading of Klein, argues Kristeva, demonstrates that the child, from the very beginning of life, is consumed with anxiety. 'No matter how far back Klein reaches into childhood', writes Kristeva (2001a: 137),

> she always discovers a fantasizing ego. A sundry entity made up of verbal and non-verbal representations, sensations, affects, emotions, movements, actions and even concretizations, the Kleinian phantasy is a wholly impure theoretical construct that defies the purists as much as it fascinates

clinicians, particularly those who specialize in children, psychosis, or the psychosomatic disorders.

Moreover, the fantasy-like omnipotent construction of the primary object – the breast – is first and foremost a construction from within, that is, of unstable representational distinctions between *inside* and *outside*, between *inner* and *outer*. 'From the outset', writes Kristeva (2001a: 63) 'the primal object of the paranoid-schizoid position emerges, in Klein's view, if and only if it is an *internal object* constructed through a fantasy of omnipotence.' As Kristeva notes, rightly in my view, Klein's notion of the internal object is entirely distinct from Lacan's order of the imaginary, for Lacan primarily stressed the visual side of fantasy. Lacan's account of spectral distortion – that narcissism is constituted through the intermediary of the object as a function of the subject's absorption in a reflecting surface – underscores the role of the scopic function in the structuration of the ego and the object. Yet what of transverbal representations, affects, emotions, sensations? Here – and make no mistake about it – Kristeva, a 'post-Lacanian', speaks up for Klein's understanding of the internal object, primarily since the Kleinian approach offers a fruitful conceptual map for grasping heterogeneous psychic representations that are altogether missing in Lacan's 'return to Freud'.

As with her previous work, especially *Tales of Love, Black Sun* and *New Maladies*, Kristeva repositions Klein's clinical and conceptual approach to ask: what is psychic representation? Here Kristeva applauds Klein for uncovering *diverse domains of representation* – not only verbal or symbolic representations, but affects, sensations, gestures, and even 'concretizations' to which fantasies are sometimes reduced in psychotic suffering. In Klein's theory, says Kristeva, the centrality of wish and fantasy to human subjectivity is borne of sensation and affect. The movement of the Kleinian investigation, rooted in clinical experience with children and which contributes significantly to our under-standing of both psychosis and autism, is fundamental for grasping the richness and multi-layered creativity of the psyche. In exploring the transverbal archaic realm, a realm that belies visual representation, Klein went beyond the 'secondary imagination' which runs throughout the whole tradition of Western thought to the primary fantasy or constitutive imagination. Kristeva makes an interesting case for the contemporary relevance of Klein's hypothesis of a proto-fantasy, or the instituting fantasy. The correctness of Klein's psycho-analytic theory is confirmed, she argues, by more recent studies that portray the psyche, lodged between anxiety and language, in the form of 'pre-narrative envelopes' (Daniel Stern), 'nameless dreads' (Wilfred Bion) and 'life narcissisms' (Andre Green). Such a focus on the psychic representative prior to representation also connects strongly with Kristeva's own theoretical account of semiotic articulations, defined as a heterogeneous play of unconscious forces – of drives and desires – which exert a pulsional pressure within language itself, and which may be discerned in the rhythm, tone and disruption of speech.

Kristeva is thus out to rescue the notion of drive or affect as potentially radical or subversive. Even so, the tension between psychic repression and unconscious anxiety remains acute. Freud considered that the repression of pleasure, under-stood in terms of the castration ordeal, generates our distress. This anxiety that can tear us apart, however, is for Kristeva rooted in a much earlier period of psychic development, and so connects directly with the maternal function. Orientating the psychic life of the subject around the pre-Oedipal period and the function of the mother are keys for grasping not only the new-born's psychic pain and its manifold trajectories throughout life, but also the origins of creativity and the capacity for symbolization and thinking. The maternal archaic fantasy, for Kristeva as for Klein, puts flesh on the bones of Freud's theory of the unconscious, as the new-born's drives are directed from the outset toward an object (the mother, or, more accurately, her breast).

This brings us to an important aspect of Kristeva's interpretation of Freud, an aspect I want to concentrate on in some detail. In her recent writing, Kristeva connects the constitution of subjectivity to the imaginary tribulations of the pre-Oedipal phase rather than to the Oedipal symbolic process alone. According to Kristeva, the primary identifications of narcissism already represent an advancement over the affective, representational flux of auto-eroticism. She describes primary identification as the 'zero degree' that shapes psychic space itself, and links this arising of the subject to Freud's notion of a 'father in individual prehistory'. In this 'prehistory', the child forges an initial iden-tification, prior to sexual division, with a maternal–paternal container. As Kristeva explains this *pre-Oedipal* identification:

> Freud has described the One with whom I fulfil the identification (this 'most primitive aspect of affective binding to an object') as a Father. Although he did not elaborate what he meant by 'primary identification', he made it clear that this father is a 'father in individual prehistory'. . . . Identification with that 'father in prehistory', that Imaginary Father, is called 'immediate', 'direct', and Freud emphasizes again, 'previous to any concentration on any object whatsoever. . . . The whole symbolic matrix sheltering emptiness is thus set in place in an elaboration that precedes the Oedipus complex.
>
> (1987: 267)

And again, on the sexual indistinction of primary identification:

> The archaeology of such an identifying possibility with an other is provided by the huge place taken up within narcissistic structure by the vortex of primary identification with what Freud called a 'father of personal prehistory'. Endowed with the sexual attributes of both parents, and by that very token a totalizing, phallic figure, it provides satisfactions that are already psychic and not simply immediate, existential requests; that archaic vortex of idealization is immediately an other who gives rise to a powerful, already psychic transference of the previous semiotic body in the process of becoming a narcissistic Ego.
>
> (1987: 33)

Note here that the reference to an *other* ties the emergence of identity to the intersubjective field. Note too that this identification with the imaginary father (which is less a partial object than a pre-object) *constitutes* primary repression; it 'bends the drive toward the symbolic of the other' (Kristeva, 1987: 31).

Kristeva argues that primary identification arises, not from the child's desire for the pre-Oedipal mother, but from an affective tie with the *mother's desire for the phallus*. Echoing Lacan, she contends that the child comes to realize that the mother herself is lacking, incomplete. In this connection, the child encounters the desire of the other: that the mother's desire is invested elsewhere, in the imaginary phallus. For Kristeva, identification with the imaginary father functions as support for the loss of the maternal object, and provides an imaginary lining to subjectivity which guards against depression and melancholia. Thus:

> 'primary identification' with the 'father in individual prehistory' would be the means, the link that might enable one to become reconciled with the loss of the Thing. Primary identification initiates a compensation for the Thing and at the same time secures the subject to another dimension, that of imaginary adherence, reminding one of the bond of faith, which is just what disintegrates in the depressed person.
>
> (1989: 13–14)

Yet, because the investment in this imaginary father comes from the inside, the emergence of identity is itself a precarious, fragile process.

Enigmatic messages: Laplanche

Like Kristeva, Laplanche is also concerned with reconceptualizing the conditions of primal identification and repression, with the purpose of mapping the inaccessible, unconscious significations between the individual subject and the intersubjective realm. Laplanche suggests that an elementary form of subjectivity is constituted when the small infant enters into an identification with certain 'enigmatic signifiers' in the pre-Oedipal phase, a phase which initiates the binding of unconscious drives through primal repression. Though highly technical in formulation, what Laplanche means by the notion of enigmatic signifier, roughly speaking, is the uncanny decentring influence of the Other upon our psychical life. This process of decentring, says Laplanche, occurs at the crossroads of language, body and desire – wherever another's 'message' (Laplanche's term) implants itself as a perplexing question or foreign body in the human subject's psyche. Subjectively speaking, the role of enigmatic signifiers is one always at work in the emotional life of the subject, and yet the sort of specific enigmas or perplexing messages that tend to dominate a person's experience of self derive, by and large, from childhood. According to Laplanche, enigmatic messages conveyed by parents (at first by the mother) are especially consequential for the development of subjectivity since such implantations arise prior to the establishment proper of the signifying character of the symbolic order. As Laplanche puts this: 'The *enigma* is in itself a *seduction* and its mechanisms are unconscious. . . . The 'attentions of a mother' or the 'aggression of a father' are seductive only because they are not transparent. They are seductive because they are opaque, because they convey something enigmatic' (1987: 128).

If the enigmatic message is integral to the psychic origins of the unconscious, it is equally central to human subjectivity itself, so that Laplanche is able to develop a neo-Lacanian critique of the trajectory of both psycho-sexuality and identity. He outlines the foundational force of an opaque, impossibly paradoxical Otherness – the result of intrusive and exciting adult enigmas – so that the human subject can never get to the heart of family secrets or sexual researches but must live nevertheless with these enigmas through the continual emotional work of translation, reconstruction and binding. In any case, this is so since adult messages always already outstrip the small infant's capacity for emotional processing and affective response. Laplanche calls this the 'fundamental anthropological situation' of humans, the fact that the infant wouldn't survive without the care and nurture provided by the adult, a situation that locates the infant as struggling to comprehend the adult's expressions of feeling, gestures of care and conveyances of relatedness. For try as the infant might to comprehend elements of the adult's communication – attempting a kind of 'proto-understanding' through the primitive translation and binding of adult enigmas – there is always a left-over or residue, which for Laplanche constitutes the unconscious and primal repressions.

More than merely perplexing, however, enigmatic messages are completely mysterious. For the enigmatic message is itself, in an uncanny sort of way, always scrambled, overloaded with signification, impenetrable. Laplanche's account of all this might perhaps be likened to the sense of strangeness an adult might feel when, having entered a room, he or she discovered people talking a highly specialized language, like the discourse of nuclear physics, nanotechnology or deconstruction. For Laplanche, messages are enigmatic because they are compromised by the repressed unconscious lodged inside us: a contradictory condensation of unconscious desires invades the enigmatic signifiers, such that the adult does not know what it wants of the infant in any case. This is a version of the classic psychoanalytic doctrine that the small infant's unconscious is formed with reference to the parental unconscious. From one angle, then, Laplanche is simply making the Freudian point that parents have an unconscious. But, in another sense, he goes further than Freud, underscoring that it is the messages parents do not understand or even know about (due to the dynamic impact of unconscious wishes and the ego's resistance to them) that transfers as a repressed residue within the child's psyche. From this angle, what is on the outside, parental or adult (sexual) messages, constitutes an inaccessible field of significations on the inside, the repressed unconscious. In the words of Laplanche, the implication of this is that there 'is no initial or natural opposition between the instinctual and the intersubjective, or between the instinctual and the cultural' (1987: 137).

Laplanche's favourite stage of infant development appears to lie with the earliest transactions between mother and child, the pre-Oedipal realm where floating needs and appetites meet with scrambled and mysterious adult messages, which he uses to illustrate the paradox of primal seduction. Returning the Freud's discussion of maternal care and devotion as central to the origins of the infant's psychic life, Laplanche argues that the breast is a carrier of maternal fantasy which transmits opaque sexual significations within the mother–child relation. As Laplanche puts this:

> Can analytic theory afford to go on ignoring the extent women uncon-
> sciously and sexually cathect the breast, which appears to be the natural
> organ for lactation? It is inconceivable that the infant does not notice this
> sexual cathexis, which might be said to be perverse in the same sense in
> which that term is defined in the *Three Essays*. It is impossible to imagine
> that the infant does not suspect that this cathexis is the source of a nagging
> question: what does the breast want from me, apart from wanting to suckle
> me, and come to that, why does it want to suckle me?
>
> (1987: 126)

The child thus receives a sexually distorted message from mother, a message which the child is emotionally unable to comprehend.

Primary repression rethought: rolling identifications and representational wrappings of self and other

There is, I believe, much that is of interest in Kristeva and Laplanche on the constitution of the unconscious through primary repression. Both Kristeva and Laplanche, in differing theoretical ways, underline the importance of primary repression as the support for the arising of an elementary form of subjectivity, which is subsequently secured through the Oedipus and castration complexes. However, there are also serious theoretical difficulties arising from their work. Kristeva has been much criticized, in both psychoanalytic and feminist circles, for linking the moment of identification with the imaginary father. For feminists such as Cornell (1991: 68–71), this has the effect of reinscribing gender stereotypes within the pre-Oedipal phase, resulting in a denial of woman's imaginary. As Cornell (1991: 68) develops this:

> The later Kristeva, like Lacan, insists that the very condition for the *arising*
> of the subject is identification of the phallus. This identification results not
> from the desire for the mother, but the reading of the desire *of* the mother
> which the child interprets as the mother's desire for the phallus.

Cornell's critique of Kristeva interestingly stresses that it is from a reading of the desire of desire, the desire of the Other, that primary identification arises and grants the subject's assent to identity in the symbolic order. From a feminist angle, Cornell is especially attuned to the abjection of the mother that this moment of identification involves, though she is also to some degree aware of the positioning of desire as an external, impersonal force (the desire of desire) rather than as emanating from the child's desire *for* the mother. From a related but distinct perspective, Laplanche's work has also been criticized for its neglect of the more creative dimensions of sexual subjectivity. As Jacqueline Rose has pointed out, Laplanche's reinterpretation of primary repression means that the 'child receives everything from the outside', desire being inscribed within the repressed unconscious via the deformations of parental sexuality itself (Laplanche, 1992: 61). In my view, these criticisms are indeed valid. The stand-points of Kristeva and Laplanche are flawed in respect of the power accorded to the other (imaginary father/seduction) over psychic interiority, or the outside as constitutive of desire itself. By contrast, I suggest that we must develop a psychoanalytic account of subjectivity and intersubjectivity which breaks with this inside/outside boundary.

For these accounts I suggest we should substitute the delineation of an elementary dimension of subjectivity formed in and through primary inter-subjectivity – a mode dependent upon the fixation of primal repression and identification. In the constitution of primary intersubjectivity, the small infant actively enters into the push-and-pull of object – or, more accurately, pre-object – relations. This is less a phenomenon of the other 'breaking in' from the outside than one of ordering psychic interiority within intersubjective boundaries of shared, unconscious experience. The organizing of shared, uncon-scious experience occurs through a process that I call *rolling identification*. Derived from the representational flux of the unconscious, rolling identifications provide for the insertion of subjectivity into a complex interplay between self-as-object and pre-object relations. Rolling identifications literally spill out across libidinal space, with representational flux passing into objects, and objects into psychical life, in a ceaseless exchange. Here the rudimentary beginnings of pre-self experience arises from factors such as sensory impressions of autistic shapes and objects (Tustin, 1980, 1984; Ogden, 1989b), which form feelings of warmth, hardness, coldness, texture and the like; a primitive relation to bounded surfaces (Ogden, 1989b), such as the child's own body, the body of the mother as well as non-human substances; and from maternal rhythmicity (Kristeva, 1984), including tone, breath and silences.

There is a proto-symbolic as well as a sensory poetics at work here. Persons and things may not yet be objects, but the small infant constantly invests and assimilates what is outside itself – though, once again, it must be stressed that the monadic core of the subject as it functions during this elemental form of intersubjective experience is, in fact, diametrically opposed to all that we under-stand by the terms 'inside' and 'outside'. 'Here', as Castoriadis (1987: 294) says, 'there is no way of separating representation and "perception" or "sensation". The maternal breast or what takes its place, is a part without being a distinct part, of what will later become the "own body" and which is, obviously, not yet a "body".' There is thus something of an infinite regress operating here, such that a primitive psychological organization of experience is constituted by identificatory incorporations of the (m)other that structure relations to self, others and the object-world in an ongoing way. Does the other, in some way, transport the infant to the heart of reality, a mix of proto-subject and proto-world? How can the libidinal articulations of the babbling child become somehow 'organized' within the uncontrollability that otherness necessarily brings?

Because the monadic core of the psyche is representationally diffuse, it is free-floating – such that rolling identifications bring together sensory experience and pre-objects, reconciling affective flux and the other within. To return to Castoriadis (1987: 294) once more:

> The libido circulating between the *infans* and the breast is a libido of auto-cathexis. It is preferable not to speak of 'narcissism' in this regard, not even of 'primary' narcissism, for this refers to a libido fixed upon itself to the *exclusion* of all the rest, whereas what is in question here is a totalitarian *inclusion*. Instead we should use Bleuler's term of autism which was explicitly approved by Freud in the same context and with respect to the very same problem. This autism is *'undivided'*: not the autism of representation, of the affect and of the intention as separate, but a single affect which *is* immediately (self-)representation and the intention of the atemporal permanence of this 'state'.

Now as regards the psychoanalytic notion of primary repression, it can be said that all individuals develop a framework for reworkings of psychical organization, based on sensory modes of organizing experience which remain undivided at the level of psychic reality. The analysis of the sensory core of the primal subject worked out by Thomas Ogden, rather than that of Castoriadis himself, is very useful here. Reaching back to the earliest days of the pre-Oedipal, Ogden theorizes what he terms an 'autistic-contiguous position', described by him (1989b: 31) as 'a sensory-dominated mode in which the most inchoate sense of self is built upon the rhythm of sensation, particularly the sensations of the skin surface'. Such autistic-contiguous experience is not a biological or pre-psychological phase of development, but is rather psycho-dynamically operative from birth and functions in the life of the subject in large part from connections and relations of a sensory kind. Like Castoriadis, Ogden stresses that the infant's earliest relations with objects come from contact with the caretaking other in a pre-symbolic, sensory-dominated mode. Theorizing the autistic or undivided nature of such experience in neo-Kleinian terms, Ogden notes that the infant's relationship to the object is quite different to the depressive position (where there is a relationship between subjects) and also to the paranoid-schizoid position (where both self and other are treated as objects). Rather, the nascent subject's undivided or autistic 'experience' or 'state' is that of non-reflective sensory being, the first imaginative elaboration of bodily needs.

In one sense, Ogden aestheticizes imagination, so that – thanks to the autistic-contiguous valorization of bodily experience – subject and object, sensation and representation pass fluently into each other so as to ensure the possibility of a pre-symbolic break-up of the psychical monad. The neo-Kleinian Ogden thus adds particular insight and intriguing depth to Castoriadis's paradoxical claim that the 'autism is undivided', in the sense that he details the small infant's or proto-subject's relationship to the object in the autistic-contiguous position. As Ogden (1989b: 32) writes:

> It is a relationship of shape to the feeling of enclosure, of beat to the feeling of rhythm, of hardness to the feeling of edgedness. Sequences, symmetries, periodicity, skin-to-skin 'moulding' are all examples of contiguities that are the ingredients out of which the beginnings of rudimentary self-experience arise.

Ogden, together with Castoriadis, stand out among psychoanalysts who have preserved certain universal elements of Freud's original account of the psychic origins of the human subject, while at the same time expanding and refining it in a systematic manner to account for the primary force of representation and repression in the constitution of the unconscious. In what follows, I shall draw – although selectively and critically – upon their ideas. On the basis of both his clinical work and the reconstruction of diverse traditions in contemporary psychoanalysis, Ogden has identified the forms of object-relation – or, more accurately, relations to the pre-object – that derives from autistic-contiguous modes of experience. The nursing experience, the experience of being held, of being rocked to sleep, sung to as well as caressed by the mother: Ogden's discussion of rhythmicity and experiences of sensory contiguity that make up a person's earliest relations with objects is highly persuasive. But I do not think that he unearths sufficiently the essential nature of such primary, autistic or what I term rolling identifications as a constructive process, one in which the internalized attributes of pre-objects and part-objects are employed in the service of a transformation or working through of the psyche.

The contradictions of experiences of sensory contiguity are a familiar motif of the pre-Oedipal realm. For as with the writings of other psychoanalysts who have tracked the earliest forms of psychological organization, Ogden notes that the autistic-contiguous mode of generating experience is almost impossible to capture in words. What Ogden means by this is less that psychoanalysis is methodologically incapable of theorizing such experience, and rather that pre-Oedipal loves and loathings are discernible only through their effects, conceptualized backward after the event. For Ogden, it is in this altercation between the paranoid-schizoid and depressive modes that the autistic-contiguous mode takes on tangible embodiment, marking the space in which the intersubjectivity of self and other plays out. And yet Ogden's rendering of autistic identifications, and of how such incorporations survive within us as the hard core of the unconscious, remains tantalizingly obscure.

Ogden sees us all as permanently producing and reproducing primitive representations of pre-objects or proto-objects in our dealings with things and other people, drawing upon elementary identifications from the autistic-contiguous mode to bolster the shape and content of our more mature, multiple identifications with self and others in daily life. Yet of what does this radically imaginary positing of elementary identifications consist? Ogden posits the existence of basic mechanisms whereby external experiences are taken in, of primitive identificatory processes by which contiguity of surfaces may be introjected. But he does not provide a satisfactory account of the imaginary constitution of sensory surfaces, the elements of creation in the subject's constitution of a sensory world, nor the initial unmediated identity of the infant, sensation, affect and representational flux. Ogden says that autistic identifications provide a kind of 'sensory floor' to psychic experience. And yet if we reflect on the pre-Oedipal tie of infant (proto-subject) and breast (proto-object), it can be said that the making of fluid identifications from experiences of rhythmic rocking or sucking involves more than the constitution of the breast as an object, as separate or different from the subject. From the angle of the monadic core of the psyche, what is important about rhythm, texture, boundedness, warmth, coldness and the like is the undifferentiated, unmediated quality of identification as a process. Before experiences of hardness or softness are located as representations of what the proto-subject finds in interpersonal contact, the proto-subject just *is* hardness or softness. But, *pace* Ogden, I argue that there must be some minimal representational colouring involved here – which I seek to delineate with reference to Freud's concept of primary repression and also the representative prior to representation, of which more shortly.

Rolling identifications veer away in erratic directions, and their elaboration is plural, multiple, discontinuous. An elementary form of identification, the pre-identification presupposed by internalization, rolling identification saturates libidinal space. This mode of identification flows, continually *rolls* out anew. Before the differentiation proper of self and other, this modality of psychic organization is basic to the wealth of images, fantasies and feelings that circulate within intersubjective communication. To capture the nature of rolling identification, we must connect the auto-erotic indistinction between the self and the non-self of which Castoriadis speaks with the concept of primary repression. Now primal repression, as expressed by Freud, involves the fixation of the drive to a representation, the registration (*Niederschrift*) of which constitutes the repressed unconscious. Such a relation, the fixation or bonding of libidinal drive and psychic representation, is closely bound up with primary identification, the 'original form of emotional tie with an object' (Freud, 1935–74: 107). My argument is that, pursuing Freud's logic concerning primal repression and identification, it is possible to establish dialectically related connections between basic aspects of self-organization and intersubjective settings. That is, the experience of subjectivity and intersubjectivity presuppose one another. In this respect, rolling identifications are an imaginary anchor connecting subjectivity and the object world.

Now primary identification 'does not wait upon an object-relationship proper' (Laplanche and Pontalis, 1985: 336). It is constituted, rather, through a process of incorporating a pre-object; or, as Kristeva says, primary identification 'bends the drive toward the symbolic of the other' (Kristeva, 1987: 31). But how, exactly, is the drive 'bent' in the direction of the other? How does the subject make this shift from self-referential representational fulfilment to primary intersubjectivity? How, in any case, does the presentation of otherness enter into the construction of the psyche? Several factors suggest themselves on the basis of the foregoing observations. To begin with, the infant's subjectivity – marked by representational flux – can be thought of as becoming *internally split* once the emergent relation to the pre-object is established. Primary identification, and the general narcissism which it ushers in, is therefore closely bound up with loss. Loss here is understood as a result of the preliminary dissolution of basic representational self-sufficiency. As Castoriadis expresses this:

> Once the psyche has suffered the break up of its monadic 'state' imposed upon it by the 'object', the other and its own body, it is forever thrown off-centre in relation to itself, orientated in terms of that which it is no longer and can no longer be. *The psyche is its own lost object.*
>
> (1987: 296–7)

The subject, simply, suffers the loss of self-referential representational fulfilment, and it substitutes a relation to pre-objects and self-as-object as the basis for creating 'a place where one lives' (Winnicott, 1971).

To be sure, the possible adaptive reactions must register basic relational connections. Indeed, this is the outlook described by Kristeva and Laplanche – the subject is referred beyond itself via an imaginary anchor in parental significations. This standpoint, while more sophisticated than most, is still inadequate however, since its conception of the subject and the unconscious is too simple. In my view, the relation between the rudimentary beginnings of subjectivity and primary intersubjectivity – the psychical registration of self-as-object and pre-object relations – cannot be understood outside of the representational dynamics of desire itself. Now in Freud's account of the nascent subject's fall from pre-Oedipal Eden, basic relational connections are established in the psyche through the arising of the affect of unpleasure associated with hunger. The nascent subject creates a hallucinatory representation of the breast in an attempt to avoid the terrors of reality, which in Freud's theorization involves a primordial wound incurred by the absence of the mother. Through hallucinatory wish fulfilment, the nascent subject imagines the mother present in fantasy, even though she is in fact missing in actuality. Originary fantasmatic representation for Freud is thus the prototype of all further representations, fantasy and dream formation in the psyche. The 'original representation' is what cannot be included within any self-grasping or self-reflexivity of the subject's imaginary productions, but whose very absence marks the stratified and intercommunicating elaborations of our imaginary worlds, as a kind of vortex around which desire circulates.

As far as a foundational myth of the psychic constitution of the subject goes, Freud's narrative is, one might claim, at once too subject-centred and not focused enough on the imaginary domain. His treatment of how unpleasurable affect, drawing on traces of reality, triggers the creation of the hallucinated breast contains rich insight, with its subtle examination of the origins of imaginary creation. Certainly when Freud speaks of the pre-Oedipal infant as having 'created an object out of the mother' (1926: 170) he captures with original insight the breathtakingly innovative and creative dimensions of the imaginary domain. For the most part, however, Freud's speculations fail to do justice to the lucidity of his concepts. For what allows the nascent subject's originary representation to become the prototype of all further representations is conceptualized by Freud only at the level of the hallucinated breast as 'object'. Yet, as Castoriadis notes, this supposedly 'original' hallucination is, in fact, a secondary formation – based on the elaboration of quite complex connections between subjectivity, part-objects and objects. As Castoriadis sees it, it is not hallucinatory wish fulfilment (a secondary figuration) which shapes the paradox of representation. For Castoriadis, the roots of our unconscious lives develop out of the creation of an *Ur-Vorstellung*, an instituting fantasy or proto-representation which must be absent from the unconscious if, paradoxically, we are to function as 'subjects of the unconscious'. Perhaps the most striking feature of Castoriadis's interrogation of the pre-history of the subject is his elaboration of the nascent subject as a 'unitary subjective circuit' (1987: 298). It is just this representa-tional self-circuitry which allows the nascent subject to operate as a 'fantasmatic scene', an 'infinitely plastic hallucination', in which the pre-object or part-object is but a segment of the subject.

Just as Castoriadis would have us concentrate on the monadic core of the psyche (the nascent subject as 'unitary subjective circuit') and accordingly refashions the psychoanalytic doctrine of *anaclisis* ('leaning-on') to elucidate how the psyche 'lends itself to socialization', Ogden would have us concentrate on the presymbolic, sensory mode in which surface contiguity cements a person's earliest relations with objects. As Ogden (1989b: 33) puts this: 'These sensory experiences with 'objects' (which only an outside observer would be aware of as objects) are the media through which the earliest forms of organised and organising experience are created'. But even if we recognize that radically imaginary processes and experiences of sensory contiguity contribute to the earliest 'structure' of psychological organization, we are still confronted with the dilemma of how the nascent subject encounters shared experience. There is also the further problem of determining exactly what facilitating factors are necessary for primary or rolling identification to unfold.

Now contemporary research concerning human subjectivity suggests that the psyche's capacity to produce unconscious representations from the earliest days of life is not separated off from the time/space environments of other persons in the manner that classical Freudian theory supposes, and for which

Castoriadis (and in some senses Ogden too) provides a challenging justification. In recent research, work has focused on the earliest and most primitive phases of psychic functioning, emphasizing the role of the mother in a very different manner from Freud and Castoriadis. The relation between the nascent subject (infant) and other (mother) is revalued as essentially creative, and the constitution of psychic structure is held to depend upon various affective exchanges and communicative dialogues. Feminist psychoanalysts (see, for example, Irigray, 1993), in particular, have stressed that the maternal body plays a constitutive role in emotional life and the structuring of the psyche. As Jessica Benjamin explains in *Shadow of the Other*:

> The idea that self–other dialogue is the fundamental basis for the development of mind has evolved in tandem with our revaluing of the early maternal dyad, its affective and communicative possibilities. In the classical psychoanalytic emphasis on the father, the mother's work in maintaining and producing life was taken for granted, rather than represented, and so the alienation of the subject from that which created and maintained 'his' life was reproduced. In psychoanalytic terms, maternal work is above all that of representing, reflecting, and containing the child's mind.
>
> (1998: xv)

From this perspective, it is possible to rethink the psychic underpinnings of representation and the web of identifications that connect the subject-to-be to imaginary and symbolic worlds. The use of the symbolic father or phallus to conceptualize the emergence of individuation in the Freudian and Lacanian standpoints is shown to rest on a masculinist inability to envision the mother as both a containing and a sexual subject within the child's psychic world. As Irigaray has argued, the failure to represent the umbilicus – in psychoanalytic theory as well as in cultural life more generally – as a symbol of connection with, and separation from, the mother has led to the continuing dominance of the phallus in contemporary theory.

This revaluing of the intersubjective sphere as it concerns the development of the psyche also incorporates a recognition that the creative play of subjectivities structures a potential space within which a web of psychic and socio-symbolic identifications can unfold.[1] Various theorists emphasize how psychic space and the location of otherness are interwoven in the constitution of subjectivity and the frame of intersubjectivity. In the work of Irigaray, this investigation emerges as part of an attempt to rework the psychoanalytic conceptualization of the child/mother dyad, giving special attention to bodily flows and to experiences of fluidity itself as other. Anzieu (1989) discusses the archaeology of a 'skin ego', a preverbal writing made up of traces upon the skin. Hélène Cixous similarly seeks to explore the repudiation of the body in the nascent subject's imaginary relationship to the phallic mother. There is also research in psychology suggesting that interaction between the psyche and its environment starts in the womb, and that from the moment of birth the infant is engaged in creative and active communications with the world (see Stern, 1985; Chamberlain, 1987).

The general characteristics I outlined in the foregoing discussion regarding primary or rolling identification, if they are valid, are also relevant for describing how the psyche opens up to externality (otherness, difference) in a predominantly imaginary mode. Now Ogden's account of the earliest experiences of sensory contiguity, I have suggested, comes close to filling out in detail Castoriadis's philosophical construction of the radically imaginary as genuine psychic creation. Yet if we return to Odgen and his discussion of how the earliest sensory experiences with 'objects' are the media through which psychical production is created, we see that, although his discussion is subtle and intricate, he does not in fact specify the facilitating conditions necessary for the structuration of such primitive psychic organization. Indeed, there is a passage in Ogden where he appears to rule out the necessity of considerations of representation in the autistic-contiguous mode altogether. 'The rudiments of the sensory experience itself in an autistic-contiguous mode', writes Ogden (1989b: 35), 'have nothing to do with the representation of one's affective states, either idiographically or symbolically'.

However, and here I return to threads of my argument concerning primary or rolling identification, Ogden's assertion cannot stand without some explanation of the status of the *representative prior to representation*. According to the view I am proposing, there is a *representational wrapping of self and other* achieved through primary repression and identification. By this I mean that the subject establishes a preliminary ordering, to use a kind of shorthand, of pre-self experience, otherness and difference as the basis for the elaboration of psychic space itself. Such representational wrapping does not just 'register' other persons and the object world, but is the central mechanism which makes their humanization possible. *Representational wrapping spirals in and out of intersubjective life, ordering and reordering both psychical imagination and the social process of which it is part.* What I am suggesting is that the status of the representative prior to representation, though never explicity theorized by Freud as such, is turned from the outset towards otherness and sociality. I say 'turned towards' in the sense not of a representational incorporation of difference (as the psyche functions here in a pre-symbolic mode), but rather as the minimal capacity for the registration of pre-self and pre-object experience in the productive imagination.

We can explore some possible connections here by means of an example. Let me briefly concentrate on the dream of Irma's injection, the dream that Freud takes in *The Interpretation of Dreams* as a paradigm for his thesis that dreams are wish-fulfilments:

> *A large hall – numerous guests, whom we are receiving. – Among them was Irma. I at once took her on one side as though to answer her letter and to reproach her for not having accepted my 'solution' yet. I said to her: 'If you still get pains, it's really your own fault.' She replied: 'If you only knew what pains I've got now in my throat*

and stomach and abdomen – it's choking me' – I was alarmed and looked at her. She looked pale and puffy. I thought to myself that after all I must be missing some organic trouble. I took her to the window and looked down her throat, and she showed signs of recalcitrance, like women with artificial dentures. I thought to myself that there was really no need for her to do that. – She then opened her mouth properly and on the right side I found a big white patch; at an other place I saw extensive whitish grey scabs upon some remarkable curly structures which were evidently modelled on the turbinal bones of the nose. – I at once called in Dr M., and he repeated the examination and confirmed it. . . . Dr M. looked quite different from usual; he was very pale, he walked with a limp and his chin was clean-shaven . . . . My friend Otto was now standing beside her as well, and my friend Leopold was percussing her through her bodice and saying: 'She has a dull area low down on the left. 'He also indicated that a portion of the skin on the left shoulder was infiltrated. (I noticed this, just as he did, in spite of her dress.) . . . M. said: 'There's no doubt it's an infection, but no matter; dysentery will supervene and the toxin will be eliminated'. . . . We were directly aware, too, of the origin of the infection. Not long before, when she was feeling unwell, my friend Otto had given her an injection of a preparation of propyl, propyls . . . propionic acid . . . trimethylamin (and I saw before me the formula for this printed in heavy type). . . . Injections of that sort ought not to be made so thoughtlessly. . . . And probably the syringe had not been clean.

(Freud, 1900, S.E. 4: 107)

The Irma dream, among other things, bears directly on the place and role of representations in unconscious wish-fulfilment. Indeed, Freud's 'specimen dream' powerfully underlines the representational constitution and structuring of unconscious pleasure itself. What is the pleasure represented in this dream? According to Freud, the dream released him from 'responsibility for Irma's condition by showing that it was due to other factors' (Freud, 1900, S.E. 4: 118). The representational architecture of the dream casts Dr M., Leopold and Otto at fault; a responsibility issuing from their medical incompetence (the thoughtless injection, the dirty syringe and so on). Significantly, the dream also transfers responsibility to the patient herself. Interpreting the dream as a wish-fulfilment of 'professional conscientiousness', Freud says of this fantasy scenario: 'I was not to blame for Irma's pains, since she herself was to blame for them by refusing to accept my solution. I was not concerned with Irma's pains, since they were of an organic nature and quite incurable by psychological treatment' (Freud, 1900, S.E. 4: 119).

But this is only the tip of the iceberg. The Irma dream, being Freud's own dream, has been continually revised and transformed within psychoanalytic lore: a dream problematic, a lesson in the limits of self-analysis, a source for speculation about Freud himself. Significantly, in this way, the articulated representations – Irma's resistance to opening her mouth, her injection with a dirty syringe, and the like – have been read as symptomatic of Freud's sexual fantasies (see Gay, 1988: 83).

Undoubtedly the dream of Irma's injection reveals much about Freud's fantasy world, but the point that calls for our attention is somewhat different. The representational space of the dream, and of Freud's associations to the dream, can best be grasped only in the movement of its own production. This dream, for example, figures in Lacan's thought as underscoring the imaginary deceptions at the heart of identification.

> The ego is the sum of the identifications of the subject, with all that that implies as to its radical contingency. If you allow me to give an image of it, the ego is like the superimposition of various coats borrowed from what I will call the bric-a-brac of its props department.
>
> (Lacan, 1991: 155)

Lacan's idea of a 'superimposition' of various props is interesting in this connection, but we need to press further into the representational architecture of the dream itself. We plunge, at this point, into the representational flux – the rolling identifications and wrappings of self and other – of fantasy itself. It is possible to trace the indistinction and reversibility which characterizes Freud's fantasy scenario at a number of levels, of which I can only mention one or two here. First, behind Irma, as many commentators have argued, we find Emma Eckstein, a central figure in the origins of psychoanalysis itself. Emma Eckstein offers a particularly clear instance of Freud's alarm at the thought of male medical practitioners maltreating their female patients. In December 1894, Freud arranged for his friend and medical mentor, Wilhelm Fliess, to operate on Emma's nose in order to alleviate her distressing hysterical symptoms. The operation backfired: Fliess had left a half-metre of gauze in Emma's nasal cavity which, when later extracted, led to a massive haemorrhage and the near death of the patient. The dream of Irma's injection is rife with the guilt that Freud experienced over Fliess's bungled operation upon Emma Eckstein. As Freud notes of Fliess in his self-analysis of the Irma dream: 'Should not this friend, who plays such a large role in my life, appear further in the dream's context of thought?' It is certainly arguable that Fliess did play a larger role in the dream than Freud imagined. Indeed, the dream of Irma's injection is itself a massive displacement of Freud's anxiety about Fliess himself; and thus, by extension, of Freud's wish to be absolved from medically irresponsible behaviour. As Peter Gay (1988: 82) writes:

> The dream scene grows crowded with physician-friends of Freud's, all of them in suitable disguise: Oscar Rie, paediatrician to Freud's children; Breuer, that eminence in Vienna's medical circles; and Fliess, too, in the garb of a knowledgeable specialist with whom Freud is on the best of terms. Somehow these doctors – all but Fliess! – prove to have been responsible for Irma's persistent pains.

Second, this collapsing of self–other boundaries and representational recycling of primary intersubjectivity is perhaps even clearer in the feminine identifications registered in the Irma dream. For the women who figure in the dream are women after whom Freud's own daughters were named. (While there has been considerable debate over the 'composite' identities that make up the dream, it seems clear that Freud's Irma is Anna Hammerschlag-Lichtheim; her friend is Sophie Schwab-Paneth; and the third woman, who Freud associates with his wife Martha, is Mathilde Breuer.) As Freud commented to Abraham about the dream: 'Mathilde, Sophie and Anna . . . my daughters' three god-mothers, and I have them all!' (quoted in Appignanesi and Forrester, 1992: 127). It could be argued that Freud's sense of surprise – 'I have them all!' – goes to the heart of glimpsing, not only sexual megalomania, but the representational depth of wish-fulfilment itself. There is a kind of infinite regress here: sexual desire leads to a falling into the 'other', which reactivates the unending nature of unconscious desire. Rolling identifications thus fall, not only within the self–other split, but within the familial, social network itself. As Appignanesi and Forrester comment: 'It is not sexual megalomania in the sense of quantity that is most striking in this dream, but the different sorts of women who are possessed. Not three, so much, as patient, widow, godmother, friend – and daughter' (1992: 129). Significantly, the fantasy staged in and through the dream permits the obtaining of pleasure; desires which deconstruct identity and differentiation, which realize the rolling indistinction between self and other, which repeat 'what occurred and what continues to occur in the manufacture of the so-called primal phantasm' (Lyotard, 1989: 19).

Summary: the representational dynamics of subjectivity and intersubjectivity

We are now in a position to sum up the argument thus far. I have suggested that there is a connecting track between the representational activity of the subject on the one hand and the dynamics of intersubjectivity on the other. These connections are forged, I suggested, through rolling identifications and representational wrappings of self and other. The emergence of subjectivity, according to this view, can be represented as follows:

1   In the shift from self-referential representational fulfilment to primary intersubjectivity, the infant's subjectivity is organized through *rolling identifications*. In this context, *representational wrappings of self and other* are the constitutive means for the child's sense of 'going on being' (Winnicott, 1956).

2   These mechanisms provide the ontological backdrop for psychic space itself and the ordering of imaginary experience. To the extent that represen-tational wrappings are articulated, the subject can negotiate the imaginary tribulations of 'potential space' (Winnicott, 1971) and the 'semiotic' (Kristeva, 1974).

3   What puts an end to the child's fantasied world without differentiation is the constitution of the individual as subject through the impact of 'social

imaginary significations' (Castoriadis, 1987). The intertwining of representational wrapping, imaginary and socio-symbolic forms is the means through which human beings establish a psychical relation to the self, others, received social meanings, society and culture.

The significance of primary repression, and the politicization of identification

How far does the notion of primary repression lead us to rethink the constitution and/or positioning of the subject in terms of socio-symbolic signification? Does the concept of rolling identification help to unlock the prison of identity, a prison in which (according to Lacan) imaginary misrecognition renders the ego itself 'specious'? Does the notion of representational wrappings of self and other offer a non-violative relation to otherness and difference? Does my argument concerning the complex patterns of primary repression and the arising of the subject through representational forms and wrappings offer any kind of release from the constraint of identity, gender and power in their current institutionalized forms?

The insights of Freud, and of contemporary psychoanalysis more generally, should of course lead us to caution in this respect. Whatever the radicalizing possibilities of this more differentiated rendering of repression and identification that I've presented, identity requires meaning, and therefore symbolic law, which constitutes subjectivity in its socio-cultural dimensions. The transition from a fantasy world of representation to socio-symbolic signification refers the individual subject beyond itself. The break-up of the psychical monad, and crucially the socialization of the psyche, are the medium through which a relation to the Other is established, and therefore to broader cultural, historical and political chains of signification. The entry of the subject into socially constituted representations secures the repetition of signification, of law. Thus, imaginary representations are, at least on one level, pressed into the service of the current social order, gender hierarchy, power relations and the like. For these reasons it makes little sense to understand the psychical processes organized through primal repression as signalling a 'beyond' to symbolic law. The signifying process of any given social order depends upon the repetition of common, symbolic forms – a phenomenon which in part explains the relative closure of social systems and modern institutions.

However, none of this means that human subjects can be reduced to mere 'supports' of symbolic law. Contrary to Lacanian and related deterministic theories, 'history' is not fixed once and for all, and offers no guarantees with regard to the organization of power. Thus the connection between law and desire, ideology and the affective, is not a fixed reality instituted by the symbolic. Freud's account of Oedipus, as Kristeva comments, 'was not, as he has been too easily accused of, to respect the paternal law of taboos that sketch our social interplay . . . [but rather] to sort out the types of representations of which a subject is capable' (1987: 9–10). In this respect, representational forms, I have suggested, are shaped to their core in and through pre-Oedipal processes of repression and identification. As an elementary elaboration of pre-self experience and pre-object relations, primal repression permits the *representational splitting of the subject*, which is bound up with pleasures and traumas of the intersubjective network itself. This elementary organization of psychical space will be repressed with entry to the socio-symbolic order, thus cementing the reproduction of 'social imaginary significations'. However, these elementary, representational wrappings of self and other are never entirely repressed. Pre-Oedipal represen- tations, at the outer limit of our symbolism and discourse, cannot be shut off from identity and culture, and continually burst forth anew within any of our symbolic systems.

The argument I am developing here is closely linked to that of Kristeva, who sees us all as permanently swept along by semiotic forces, bearing at the very core of our identity something intrinsically resistant to symbolic articulation yet always-already derailing or overriding our interpersonal dialogue. Kristeva, who is very much taken with Freud's notion of a 'father in prehistory', is divided in her more recent work as to the possibilities for transforming the symbolic order through the semiotic on the one hand, and the necessity of identification with the imaginary father for the production of individual identity on the other. Some critics, like Cornell (1991, 1993), interpret this as a turn from the semiotic to an idealized relation to the paternal function. Even if this is so, however, it is surely possible to step back from Kristeva's inflation of the paternal function and instead stress, as I try to do, more creative possibilities arising from the fluid, rolling and multiple identifications stemming from the imaginary constitution of sensory experience. From this angle, then, what is the socio-cultural sig- nificance of primary repression and rolling identification? What is at issue here is the interlacing of representational wrapping of pre-self and pre-object connections on the one hand and socially instituted representations on the other hand. If we understand that social significations are taken up and invested by subjects within the matrix of former pre-Oedipal modes of generating experi- ence, we can see that there are a wealth of fantasies, identifications, contiguities and rhythmicities available to the subject as she or he creatively engages with cultural forms. Such early, pre-Oedipal modes of generating experience provide not only a support for identity, but also the identificatory basis from which to re-imagine our world. Representational wrappings of self and other – constituted in and through primal repression – infuse the power of the radical imagination and help to contest, question and destabilize our relation to the symbolic order. Let me return to the troubled relation between psychoanalysis and feminism once more to draw out these conceptual points, primarily by focusing on current debates about sexed identities and gender hierarchy.

I noted in the opening chapter that a dominant strand in psychoanalytically- orientated feminist theory has, for the most part, been unable to engage with the multiple possibilities for gender identity that must arise – at a conceptual level at the very least – as a result of contemporary work on the imaginary constitution of psychic space. For all its undoubted insights into the prison of gender hierarchy, such mainstream accounts of sexed identities have tended to adopt the classic view of identification as filtered through the Oedipus complex: that is, that Oedipal patterns of identification involve incorporating one gender and repudiating another. However, such a view of gender hierarchy has not only entered into a significant contradiction with the lived experience of sexualities in the postmodern West, but has also come under mounting question as a result of recent research on gender identifications. In this work, the consolidation of gender identity is built out of multiple identifications, fluid incorporations and repudiations, the flow of affect and fantasy, continuities and connectedness. The American feminist psychoanalyst, Jessica Benjamin, captures well the centrality of identification to the framing of all experiences of relationship when she writes:

> Identificatory love is a specific formation, it is the love that wants to be recognised by the other as like. Identification is not merely a matter of incorporating the other as ideal, but of loving and having a relationship with the person who embodies the ideal.
>
> (1998: 61)

In terms of patterns of gender identification, Benjamin wishes to speak up for what she terms 'complementarity' over exclusivity of identity positions. She sees, rightly in my view, that the flow of the individual subject's multiple gender identifications can only be framed upon connectedness to the other's existence as a subject. Making the person with whom we identify our own, without destroying the other in fantasy through this process, is central in Benjamin's view to the development of the child's internal differentiations of mind. Yet, tellingly, Benjamin closes down discussion of what psychodynamics underpin such identificatory investments just before consideration of the concept of primary repression manoeuvres her into a version of psychoanalytic subjectivism – or so she seems to fear as a result of her allegiance to inter-subjective theory. However, it is precisely the evocation of identificatory love in the subject that rests upon primary repression and its operations: the imaginary constitution of sensory experience in the autistic mode, the psychical break-up of the monad through primal identification with pre-self and pre-object contiguities, and on and on.

Applied to the field of social difference and sexual identity, recognition of the imaginary valorization of sensory experience becomes a vision of alternative meanings and desires positioned against closure in the name of socio-symbolic reproduction. Developing upon the work of Castoriadis, Kristeva, Laplanche and Ogden, I argue that the autistic-sensory forms the imaginary basis for the constitution of the subject. In the pursuit of radical imagination, there are meanings and values embedded in this domain of the pre-Oedipal which are of vital importance. Representational wrappings of pre-self and pre-object connections, as an ongoing unconscious process of identification, are resilient enough to always threaten or destabilize the hierarchical closure imposed on meaning and language in the socio-symbolic order. The dream of radical imagination is thus, in part, the dream of retracing the shared representational and affective modes of generating experience which link us ineluctably together.

The politics of difference require creativity, innovation, reflectiveness, in order to enact the different itself. In pursuit of the new, the different, beyond the constraint and domination of the current social order, there are values and affects embedded in the subject's relation to primal identification which are of vital importance. Primal identification, and the repression which consolidates it, opens a preliminary distance between the self and others, and is thus a foundation for personal and collective autonomy. For this link to the other, prior to mirror asymmetry and the imprint of social significations, can offer a prefigurative image of a cultural condition in which relatedness, fulfilment and creativity are more fully realized. The role of unconscious representation in dreaming the new lies precisely in this connection to the other, primary intersubjectivity, a condition from which we might imagine self, society, politics and ethics anew.

Pretext
On the adventures of difference

Psychoanalysis, as the late Cornelius Castoriadis once forecast, shall be eclipsed as therapy but will prosper as theory. The Culture Wars and recent Freud-bashing tend to confirm he was right on the first count. The current fascination in the social sciences and humanities with all things Freudian, from fantasy to fetish, also suggest the accuracy of his punditry on the second. I argue that it is primarily in our fluid, globalized and postmodern world that the potentially reflexive and freeing impact of psychoanalysis on the way we think, theorise, as well as process information at an emotional level, might best be approached. For the legacy of Freud when filtered through the lens of the postmodern, at least at the hands of its more innovative practitioners, allows us to glimpse what a *psychoanalysis of psychoanalysis* might look like at the level of culture and politics.

This is not to say that the postmodern rendition of psychoanalysis is everywhere supreme. Far from it. Psychoanalysis in its postmodern recasting does certainly not enter into an alliance with either psychology (a discipline which, at any rate, has now almost dispensed with Freud entirely) or sociology (a discipline which, for the most part, still struggles with modernist readings of Freud as represented in the theoretical departures of, say, Talcott Parsons or Nancy Chodorow). Nor does it fare much better within the psychoanalytic profession itself. For the psycho-analytic establishment, roughly speaking, manipulates the reception of Freudian theory through the activity of training (read: drilling) of candidates into analysts eligible to pronounce on the pathologiza-tion of human subjects and daily life. That a strong modernist desire for identifying, classifying, drawing boundaries and dividing people into psychological categories is at work here is surely all too evident. As Douglas Kirsner (2000) notes of the undemocratic spirit of psychoanalytic institutes the world over in his eye-opening study *Unfree Associations*, the profession reproduces itself through the imposition of a clear hierarchy, an authoritarian ideology, a rigid conception of truth and contempt for conceptual innovations or departures as threatening or 'non-analytic'. Far-fetched? Well, maybe. But even if Kirsner overstates his case, the modernist zeal of psychoanalytic institutes is beyond doubt, and perhaps repair.

Julia Kristeva has recently argued that present-day modernist anchorings of desire for certitude are increasingly evident in the practice of psychoanalysis itself. As Kristeva observes, 'Today, and still more in the future, I think psychoanalysis is the art – I admit the conceit – of allowing men and women who inhabit modern, arrogant, polished, expensive and exciting cities, to safeguard a way of life' (2002: 67). Having shed the heavy Freudian lenses she wears when interpreting various artistic processes and cultural activities, Kristeva's concern is that psychoanalytic therapy seems to do so little for the reflective and democratic aspirations of its subjects. In practice, it is as if the modernist regulating frame of psychoanalysis keeps subjects of analysis held in check, preventing men and women from moving forward; and certainly at some distance from changing the self, let alone the world.

Psychoanalysis calls such a limiting of the powers of critical self-reflection 'repetition': that which we cannot process at the levels of consciousness and the unconscious, to paraphrase Freud, we are destined to repeat. That the practice of modernist psychoanalysis has been, ironically, caught in its own logics of repetition is something not lost on other traditions of critical thought – especially constructivist approaches. For what psychoanalysts term repetition is, for some authors, nothing less than a process of social normalization. Nikolas Rose, who argues in Foucauldian vein that the act of confession constitutes subjectivity of the self as well as identity as an object for inspection and interrogation – sees the normalising impact of psychoanalysis in terms of an attempt to stop difference and thus kill a desire for otherness.

> Psychotherapeutics is linked at a profound level to the socio-political obligation of the modern self. The self it seeks to liberate or restore is the entity able to steer its individual path through life by means of the act of personal decision and the assumption of personal responsibility.
>
> (Rose, 1989: 253–4)

Another way of putting this point is to say that it is through the repetitive art of self-confession and self-interrogation that difference and otherness are brought low, leaving the self with nothing else, as it were, than an oppressive technique for monitoring subjectivity. Rose takes his cue from Foucault's account of the 'psy-complex' – the idea that psychologists, psychotherapists, psychiatrists, psychoanalysists and counsellors of all kinds are fundamentally preoccupied with the monitoring, regulation and normalization of individual psychic functioning. In our own time, the cultural logic of the psy-complex has been shifted up a gear. We now live, contends Rose, in a confessional society. The dominance of the therapeutic has come to infiltrate most aspects of social life, especially at the micro-level of the most common and trivial aspects of human encounter. As Rose develops this point:

> Psychotherapeutic language and advice extends beyond the consultation, the interview, the appointment: it has become a part of the staple fare of the mass media of communication, in the magazine advice columns and in documentaries and discussions on television. No financial exchange need be involved, for on live radio phone-in programmes we may confess our most intimate problems for free and have them instantly analysed – or eavesdrop on the difficulties that so many of our fellow citizens appear to have conducting the business of their lives.
>
> (1989: 193)

In one fell swoop the therapeutic, it seems, has become a cure for cultural difference and our desire for otherness.

So, we live now in a society where therapeutic vocabularies rule. From the worried-well in psychotherapy to TV talk-shows and celebrity-tell-all interviews, ours is the era of a confessional revolution. Yet it still may be worth wondering why the modernist impulse to confess – especially the public confession of things privately experienced – is thought to define subjectivity in its entirety. Whether confessional culture, that is to say, is the apotheosis or the death of deliberative and reflective subjectivity?

There are indeed profound reasons for not thinking it is the death of subjectivity. In a sharp critique of the social constructionist position, Vivien Burr and Trevor Butt argue that social theorists such as Foucault and Rose are unable to confront the issue of the psychological experience of socially constructed identities. 'We may agree', they write, that the myriad of syndromes, pathologies and neuroses affecting us are socially constructed, and that the therapist and counsellors to whom we appeal for help are the, albeit unwitting, figureheads of an extensive system of social control through disciplinary power. Nevertheless, the distress and misery experienced by people, framed though it is in terms of personal inadequacy and pathology, cannot, morally or empirically, be ignored.

(2000: 194)

Social constructionist arguments thus abolish the human experience it intends to illuminate. The passion to unearth social construction, in other words, leads in the end to a mere construction of passion. Again, let me quote Burr and Butt: 'Writers such as Foucault and Rose have not broached the issue of what our response, if any, should be at the level of the individual. Indeed, poststructuralist analyses have tended to regard the level of the social or of 'discourse' as the only appropriate one' (2000: 194).

All this raises the question of whether psychoanalysis enables the human subject to explore and tolerate alternative constructions of self – the kind of imaginative wanderings that Freud unearthed in the process of 'free association' – or simply exchanges one socially constructed identity for another that is, at least on one reckoning, equally pernicious. Now, interestingly, what distinguishes Kristeva's critique of psychotherapy from that of social constructivist theorists is her strong emphasis on *affective investments underpinning psychotherapy as ritual* in order to 'safeguard a way of life'. It is worth wondering, says Kristeva, what kind of affective resistance it requires to undergo psychotherapy or psychoanalysis in order to fashion a freezing of critical self-interrogation and self-reflection. This critique, let me repeat, Kristeva actually launches from the vantage point of psychoanalytic theory itself: a kind of psychoanalysis of the limits or dead-ends of psychotherapeutical practice and of psychoanalysis as ritual. As such, this critique can be used to confront Burr and Butt's concern with 'psychological experience of socially constructed identities'. There may of course be little point in insisting on the conceptual advantages of such an approach – social constructivists, to be sure, can always make the retort that 'affective investments in identity' are just further constructions, and on and on in an infinite regress – and yet I do believe that close engagement with the ongoing affective dimensions of our personal and social lives is a crucial task of social theory. And it is a task that leads us to confront some of the core social dilemmas of the age – of the search for rearticulating identity in the global frame of interpersonal interconnections and dependencies, of postmodern hungering for cultural difference and otherness, and of individual and collective desires for human autonomy.

One of the defining characteristics of contemporary culture has been a longing for cultural difference, for a sufficient sense of otherness – in the way we define individual freedom, in ideals of creativity, beauty and art, in the desire for and demands of multicultural communities and in the pursuit of spontaneous living. One of the most interesting developments in much cultural theory at the present time is its underscoring of the degree to which the pursuit of difference and otherness infiltrates a whole range of psychological and political vocabularies, and of how these vocabularies are necessarily transforming our relationships to both the past and the present. The idea of cultural difference moves on the frontier between identity and non-identity, and is thus preoccupied among other things with the relation between self and other, homogeneity and fragmentation, consensus and plurality. What has happened to the fabric of everyday life and social relations of late, or at least this is so according to one influential version of postmodern cultural theory, is not only that this pursuit of difference has become locked in an ongoing battle with more traditionalist, structured identities and identity structures – ranging from family values to religious fundamentalism to neo-fascism. It is rather that difference is now promoted as a markedly contradictory psychological and political aim in itself, to which individuals and groups can only do sufficient justice through incessant self-critique, repeated reflexive mappings and the transgressive tracking of both identity and geopolitical axes on which the field of culture plays out. Even so, the politics of difference is clearly a risky undertaking – both at the level of self-identity, where otherness is located as regards the psyche and interpersonal relationships, and at the level of radical politics, where otherness is addressed in terms of the whole society. Too much toleration for difference and you run the risk of fragmentation; too little and you are left with a spurious (modernist) homogeneity.

If the pursuit of difference as a political goal captures the contemporary social imagination then this tells us as much about the modern as it does about the postmodern condition. And one thing it tells us, I think, is that there is – now, for many people – a kind of cultural benchmark against which the excesses and eccentricities of modernism and modernity can be measured. There is, I argue, a deep fear of enforced uniformity and uniform sameness, of not having enough psychic and cultural space to develop the uniqueness of self, or repression of idiosyncrasy in the name of security and safety. To put it in a nutshell: people are increasingly suspicious today of the fates of those who believe themselves identical to the images they have of themselves – for postmodern men and women of today's polished, expensive cities, it's recognised that the desire to make others in the image of oneself involves a destructive and debilitating denial of difference and otherness. From our experiences, or indeed from our inherited or acquired knowledge, of traditional family arrangements, of patriarchal gender codes, of bureaucratic hierarchies and rigid work routines and of deadening institutional party politics – we are fearful of modernist compulsions, summed up elegantly by Zygmunt Bauman as the desire for 'clean order and orderly cleanliness' as well as 'reason-dictated rules and regulations'.

From a psychoanalytic point of view, such self-reflective attempts to grasp the creative powers of difference, otherness, pleasure and transgression depend, in turn, upon profound emotional transformations. When cast in a suitably expansive, heterogeneous and other-directed cast of mind, the postmodern imaginary can be seen as one open to multiple perspectives, coupled with high tolerance of ambiguity and ambivalence. By 'postmodern', I refer, in the most general terms, to the contemporary philosophical standpoint which rejects epic narratives, solid metaphysical foundations to knowledge and everyday life, universal values, self-identical subjects and on and on. Postmodernism has been among other things a way of linking the personal and the global at a time in which the texture of everyday life is being profoundly reshaped by the activities of transnational corporations, the culture industry and communications sectors. Yet from within this philosophical tradition, postmodern theorists have had remarkably little which is original or compelling to say of the transformed psychic experiences of human subjects, nor for that matter of the altered dynamics of interpersonal relationships. It is, of course, true that there remain general pointers. Jacques Derrida thought that deconstructive concepts of difference and dissemination were not limited only to the interpretation of texts and that a widening appreciation of diversity was on the rise everywhere. Jean-François Lyotard, by contrast, highlighted the breakdown of modernist encodings of human strivings or unconscious drives and conducted inquiries into the open structures of libidinal economy. Nonetheless, these remain highly abstract critiques. Ways of feeling and forms of psychic representation are largely divorced from questions of culture and politics in postmodern conditions.

Enter the relevance of psychoanalysis, which has had a great deal to say about the production of human meaning and emotion in a postmodern world preoccupied with conspicuous consumption, global economic shifts and new information technologies. In fact, a number of innovative psychoanalysts and psychoanalytic critics have produced work of incomparable value on the nature of contemporary living and our postmodern emotional dilemmas. The pioneering insights of psychoanalysts including Thomas Ogden, Jessica Benjamin, Christopher Bollas, Charles Spezzano, Julia Kristeva and Jean Laplanche are of major importance in this respect. So are the path-breaking psychoanalytically-informed works of cultural critique of Judith Butler, Slavoj Žižek, Jacqueline Rose, Stephen Frosh, Lynne Segal, Joel Whitebook and Jane Flax. Many of the ideas of these psychoanalysts and critics have deepened and enriched the debate over postmodernism, partly due to the insights offered on the transformed emotional characteristics of 'post-individual identities' or 'postmodern nomads'. Certainly, where contemporary psychoanalysis has been most arrestingly original – at least in terms of the discourse of postmodernism – lies in its stress on the emotional contradictions of attaching meaning to experience in a world which revolves increasingly on image, information and consumption.

In one sense, psychoanalysis has put flesh on the bones of the postmodern recasting of identity. Contemporary psychoanalysis has given us valuable insights into the emotional transformations which underpin everyday life in a postmodern world of fragmentation and fracture. One could thus attempt to deepen the postmodernist emphasis on difference, diversity and otherness by drawing upon a range of concepts in contemporary psychoanalysis that underscore the profoundly imaginary and creative capacities of the psyche in its traffic with culture, from Kristeva's evocation of 'open psychic systems' to Castoriadis's spontaneous 'radical imaginary'. Yet while this critical excavation of enlarged emotional capacities for processing social differences in current cultural conditions has undeniably been a useful supplement to postmodernism, perhaps the more enduring contribution of psychoanalysis to contemporary theory will be its insights into the intriguing new emotional dilemmas of individuals attempting to process information in a world overburdened with soundbites and telecommunications. From this angle, the postmodern celebration of a world that ushers in hyper-reality, cyborgs and the post-human condition looks decidedly uncritical or apolitical: such is the aversion of much of this discourse to considering the emotional consequences of transformations in culture, communication and capitalism.

4 Sexuality, complexity, anxiety

The encounter between psychoanalysis, feminism and postmodernism

Something of the consummation of sexual difference has still not been articulated or transmitted. Is there not still something held in reserve within the silence of female history: an energy, morphology, growth or blossoming still to come from the female realm? Such a flowering keeps the future open. The world remains uncertain in the fact of this strange advent.

(Luce Irigaray, *An Ethics of Sexual Difference*)

By 'woman' I understand what cannot be represented, what is not said, what remains above nomenclatures and ideologies.

(Julia Kristeva, 'Woman cannot be defined')

What's a desire originating from lack? A pretty meagre desire.

(Hélène Cixous, 'The laugh of the Medusa')

Is the repressed unconscious, in some sense or another, the key to unlocking gender oppression? The question is, of course, at the heart of the feminist debate over Freud. Many, including such authors as Simone de Beauvoir, Betty Friedan, Germaine Greer and Kate Millet, have given an answer in the negative. Always it was the phallocentrism of Freudian psychoanalysis that doomed it to failure in the eyes of such feminists. Freud's theories were seen as conceptually legitimating woman's social subordination. Indeed, Freud's accounts of 'penis envy' and his account of feminine sexuality as supplementary and derivative (the little girl as castrated and stunted) were upheld as definitive both of Freud's private fear of women, and the reactionary nature of psychoanalytic theory. Sometime later, feminists adapted Freud's ideas to radical political ends. Juliet Mitchell's bold claim in 1974 that 'a rejection of psychoanalysis and of Freud's works is fatal for feminism' signalled this sea-change. A sharp division subsequently developed between the work of feminists influenced by Jacques Lacan's 'return to Freud', and those more committed to object-relational or Kleinian approaches. This division in psychoanalytic feminism remains important. However, the rise of post-structuralism and postmodernism in universities throughout the West has led to an explosion of interest in Lacan's Freud within feminist circles.

My purpose in this chapter is not to map the engagements with, and attacks on, Freud in feminist theory. Rather, I shall restrict myself to a consideration of some of the more theoretically reflective claims of contemporary feminism, which will direct us further to the theories of post-structuralism and post-modernism. I want to use these current theoretical controversies as a foil against which to examine, and thus elucidate, some of the functions of Freud in the frame of feminism. Given the two-way traffic between psychoanalysis and politics, I want to consider some discursive paths opened by these discourses in contemporary theoretical debate. This is less a matter of trying to judge how well, and in what ways, psychoanalysis has been linked to feminism than it is a matter of deploying Freud to think the advances and deadlocks of new feminist discourses. Needless to say, this necessarily involves using Freud to assess the limits of what psychoanalysis both permits and prohibits in terms of political critique itself.

Feminism, post-structuralism and postmodernism

Imagine, if you will, a society in the not too distant past, before the eclipse of Reason, possibly before the rise of the Unconscious, and certainly before the arrival of deconstruction and post-structuralism, when sexuality was connected unproblematically to gender hierarchy. A society, that is to say, in which sexuality maps sharply and cleanly onto gender differences. A society in which the categories 'women' and 'men' simply loop back upon themselves in an infinite regress. A social world in which the scientific knowledge of gender, regarded as more real than the Real, unearthed the sexuality of men as active and assertive, and the desire of women as passive and submissive; a kind of deadlocked opposition that puts the sexes securely in place to perform the business of social and sexual reproduction. And a world in which sexuality is treated as co-terminous with heterosexual genital sexuality, an equation that either banishes or subsumes all non-heterosexual organizations of desire just as surely as it naturalizes 'woman' as a thoroughly sexualized category of Otherness.

That moment of society might be further imagined as a moment in which the women's movement comes to develop a form of social-historical knowledge that, somewhat paradoxically, transcends this ruthless and oppressive gender division; a kind of knowledge that not only outstrips existing historical constructions that serve to naturalize sexuality, but one that also espouses a creative agenda for political transformation and revolution. This figuration of knowledge of which we are speaking is itself part and parcel of the modernist urge to unmask asymmetrical relations of power, especially distorted gender relations. For modernist feminism, this unmasking is to be performed through a problematization and dismantling of dominant dualisms which underpin Western ways of thinking about and organizing gender relations. Dualisms of self/other, mind/body, reason/emotion, nature/culture, private/public and science/ideology have been central to feminist critiques of epistemology, and also the analysis of sexually oppressive political relations. From problematizing the political processes involved in the naturalization of gender relations, and equipped with the maxim that 'the personal is the political', modernist feminism installs itself precisely within some imagined liberatory space beyond the reaches of sexual domination.

All this takes place in the name feminism, but that is not to say that the discursive field of the women's movement unfolds without contradiction or ambivalence. For to acknowledge the phallocentrism of modern culture is also to implicitly acknowledge a range of conceptual vocabularies that unmask regimes of gender power. This amounts to saying that feminism, in its modernist moment, initiated a number of conceptual raids on fields of knowledge such as anthropology, psychoanalysis and sociology in order to bring low the institutional regulation of sexuality and its systems of gender representation. For example Freud, that patriarchal father of the normalizing discourse of psychoanalysis, was put to use against himself, from which a psychoanalytically-informed feminism could then reveal all circuits of desire as an outcrop of Oedipal repetition, and in which Woman functions as that prohibited signifier between men which secures the phallocentric social contract. Similarly, Lévi-Strauss's account of kinship systems was drawn upon to designate Woman as an object of exchange that founds the moment of masculinist culture itself. (The classic text here is Mitchell, 1974.) But the significant point here, in all of these feminist responses, is that the unmasking of sexual oppression is pitted against an apparently wholly structured, rationalized, universal system of gender division. Bring down gender, so the rallying cry went, and you'll bring down the repressive social system in which sexuality is encoded, if not today then at least in the supremely positive utopianism of tomorrow. But the cost of this global perspective was great indeed, wiping out the specifics of difference in particular and the ambiguities of sexual power relations in general. Consequently, the sexual in modernist feminism simply became more and more the by-product of all social dialectics, from the laws of cultural exchange to the laws of capitalist modernization.

That such a conceptual and political understanding of sexuality was bound to go awry seems self-evident today, not only from any rigorous reading of, say, psychoanalysis or post-structuralism, but also from the range of social-historical institutional transformations which have profoundly altered the stakes of sexual knowledge itself. For sexuality is no longer exclusively tied to the ideological regulations of gender in recent rewritings of social and cultural theory; rather the sexual in recent social theory has increasingly come to signify an excess or supplementarity, from which it might be re-imagined as occupying a semi-autonomous space. Dislodging the fetishized unity of sexuality and gender polarity, this semi-autonomous realm of desire – or, more specifically in Althusserian terms, this 'relative autonomy' – is at once linked to, and detached from, the solid structures of material institutions. This amounts to saying that the libidinal-sexual is sealed off into its own realm and yet constantly bursts out of this self-enclosure to dislocate the matrix of social-historical meanings. The doubleness of the libidinal-sexual is that it is at once narcissistically self-referential and experientially other-directed: A kind of 'subjectless subject', to borrow from Adorno. Or perhaps simply a jack-in-the-box which always threatens to unmask the contingency of gender foundations.

If all of this sounds a little too much like a replay of previous developments in radical critique – think, for instance, of Herbert Marcuse's utopian forecast of an emergent 'libidinal rationality' in the 1950s – it is worth bearing in mind that the transgressive potential of the libidinal-sexual in contemporary feminist theory has as its target not only discourses and practices but also the body and its pleasures. That is to say, the libidinal-sexual becomes characterized as a force that reverberates endlessly around all sites of human communication, fracturing conventional distinctions between rationality and desire, masculinity and femininity, the cognitive and affective, the linguistic and non-linguistic. From this angle, the post-structuralism of Foucault, Lacan, Derrida, Lyotard, Deleuze and others outstrips traditional feminist thought, with its profound questioning of rational knowledge, its displacing of determinable truth, its flamboyant debunking of all major hierarchies, its privileging of the signifier and dislocation of symbolic meaning with libidinal intensities. In post-structuralist feminism this will be translated into a fully-blown dismantling of ideological closure in the field of gender relations, and matters relating to the ways in which the women's movement has proceeded to define its own goals through the marginal-ization and exclusion of sexualities has come to be understood increasingly in this light. Post-structuralist feminism then understands that the relation between sexuality and gender is not identical; they are certainly mutually imbricated, but their relation is not one of mere equivalence. Gender is always sexualized, and sexuality is shot through with gender power; but from a radical viewpoint it can be argued that sexuality and gender are mutually dislocating, conflicting, fracturing.

This dislocation brings us directly into highly contested and heterogeneous practices of contemporary feminist theorizing, or of what Fredric Jameson would call the 'post-contemporary cognitive mapping' of sexuality/gender rela-tions (Jameson, 1991). In this context, the modernist search for an underlying disease which deforms autonomous gender relations gives way to a postmodern multiplication of conceptual and political interests such that, from one angle, contemporary feminism becomes every bit as dispersed and fragmented in its theoretical operations as the very structure and matrix of meanings it is seeking to understand. In this respect, a core political fear registered by many people is that, lost in the libidinal ecstasies of indeterminacy and erotic possibilities of sexual signification, feminism is in danger of losing the plot altogether. Contemporary feminist thought, in this view, seems to have fallen for the sterile political discourse of the academy, a conceptual move that in one stroke disconnects its interests and aims from the actual practice of gender struggle and transformation. All of this current feminist talk about the gap or lag between social practice and theoretical reflection is thus considered as extraneous academic noise; and it is from this understanding of the contem-porary critical climate that a number of feminists continue to hanker after a revolutionary political position that would somehow be magically identical-to-itself. This reaction, in other words, continues to dream of certitude and transparency: if only feminism could get back to basics – perhaps in the manner that John Lennon condensed the spirit of the 1960s into the slogan, 'All we are saying is give peace a chance' – then surely it could dispense with the elitist and pretentious jargon of post-structuralism and postmodernism.

From another angle, however, the framing of matters in this way becomes possible only if one is still out to colonize, or perhaps even master, existing knowledge of oppressive patriarchal practices in line with the degrading demands of an instrumental rationality. Thus, postmodernist feminism proclaims: forget the Law of the Father – the problem of institutionalization is simply depressing and a dead end anyway – and try to glimpse the repressed stain of difference inscribed within the categories of opposition that perpetuate gender hierarchy. The interpretative strategies that emerge in recent works by Jacqueline Rose, Gayatri Spivak, Judith Butler, Drucilla Cornell, Rosi Bradotti, Lynne Segal and Elizabeth Grosz seek, in the broadest outlines, to unhinge our psychic and cultural identification of gender with core sex identity, to destabilize foundational understandings of sex and gender in favour of enacted, fantasized or contingent discourses of gender, and to attempt to turn the logic of sexual difference back upon itself to show how it reaches into the operations of desire itself (see Rose, 1996; Butler, 1993; Cornell, 1992; Bradotti, 1992; Grosz, 1995; the best recent psychoanalytic critique of sexuality in contemporary theory is Stephen Frosh, 1994). This brand of feminist politics, basing its theoretical operations on a blending of post-structuralism, psycho-analysis and postmodernism, deals another powerful blow to patriarchal ideologies therefore by refusing to accept the requirements for formalization – psychic, social, cultural and political – at face value. And once again feminism seeks to imagine a path of sexual development beyond the dead weight of masculinist rationality, but this time without needing to submit its strategic blueprints to the terroristic pressures of Reason and totality.

It is this pluralization of the field of sexual difference – the dispersal of selves, bodies, sexualities, pleasures and fantasies – that has been politically under-written as of core importance by contemporary currents of post-structuralist and postmodernist feminism. And one significant result of this rethinking of the cultural possibilities of sexuality as a utopic medium has been a recovery of vital political issues, such as the body and the problem of unconscious desire, which traditional feminism tended to brutally suppress. (The question of the body has been of major importance for feminist theory and politics in recent times, and the key point of convergence between feminism and post-structuralism arises from the work of Michel Foucault. For a comprehensive overview of these developments, see McNay, 1992.) The problem of unconscious desire has also been paramount with regard to normative and political questions raised by some currents of feminist thought, and the key contributors in this area have been Julia Kristeva, Luce Irigaray and Hélène Cixous in French feminist thought, and Nancy Chodorow, Jessica Benjamin and Jane Flax in

Anglo-American feminism. (For a summary of these trends in psychoanalytic feminism, see Elliott, 2002; Flax, 1990.) Notwithstanding the more creative and subversive aspects of these recent political strategies articulated in some currents of feminism, however, many critics have wished to highlight the performative contradiction between asserting the death of the subject and of truth on the one hand, and then of still confidently maintaining that men oppress women on the other. This leads to an absurd political situation, or so many feminist critics have argued: the need to scratch where it should no longer itch. Focusing on the contradictory character of recent feminist writing – the split between the extreme particularism of post-structuralism and the universal claims of collective feminist politics – many critics have argued, in effect, that feminism will only make further political gains if it displaces the difficult ontological and epistemological questions raised by post-structuralism and postmodernism. For in so far as feminist thought influenced by these theories seems to lose contact with the 'realities' of the external world, or merely treats reality as some kind of displaced consequence of fantasy and sexual difference, it is surely better to be without the profound political pessimism of post-structuralist doctrine and return instead to the pressing historical realities of gender hierarchy. So, too, the postmodern critique of difference, sexual and intimate, is at the heart of contemporary anxiety about queer theory. Here there is a deep controversy about changes which link homosexuality to other critical concerns such as representation, desire, positionality, discourse and the body on the one hand, and the downgrading of movement politics and political action on the other. As Dennis Altman writes:

> Much of what has become known as 'queer theory' appears remarkably unaware of the history and writings of gay liberation, which is sometimes depicted as essentialist, despite a body of gay liberation work which explicitly drew on Freudian notions of polymorphous perversity. By 1995 I could read an honours thesis which spoke as if such notions had never occurred to anyone in the gay movement, and were the discovery of French intellectuals writing ten years after the early debates in the sexual liberation movements.
>
> (Altman, 1996)

Clearly, this is more than just a matter of getting our intellectual history right; it has to do instead with that cultural evasion or repression which contemporary critical discourses, from postmodernism to queer theory, have helped usher into existence.

Such a refusal to permit post-structuralism and postmodernism any political role in the crisis of contemporary feminism betrays I think, not only a wish to return to an earlier intellectual period of feminist confidence and surety, but also a radical rejection of complexity itself. This is a rejection of both the complexity of psychic life and of the complex political world of human beliefs, values, sentiments, pleasures and desires. The very complexity of human sexuality, coupled to the uncontainability of the social imagination and cultural process, seems to call forth an overwhelming anxiety in certain currents of contemporary feminism; an anxiety which threatens to dislocate the political coherence of the women's movement itself. From this angle, the rush to take flight into feminist collective action as a resolved project, when premised upon the mindless rejection of other points of view and states of mind, can be viewed as an institutional attempt to keep anxiety and ambivalence at bay.

Sexual difference, or more of the same?

It is one of the sad ironies of the feminist appropriation of psychoanalysis as a theory that it at once serves to unlock the fixity of gender positioning in the socio-symbolic order and also reinscribes desire into the binary logic – or if Derrida is right, the supplementary logic – of sexual difference. This political dilemma is especially acute in Lacanian feminist theory in which the construction of desire in and through language is viewed as co-extensive with the subject's submission to the Law of the Father, a submission which imprisons women and men within the repetitive discourses of phallocentrism. The strength of Lacanian-based feminism lies in its uncovering of the linguistic and sexual codes which perpetuate gender hierarchy; yet its central limitation is that, given its subjective determinism and political pessimism, the possibility of alternative gender relations is done away with in one stroke. From this angle, the emergence of post-Lacanian feminist writing can be seen as a political attempt to find some way out – usually by going further and further back into the subject's pre-Oedipal sexual history – of this deadly impasse.

There is, however, another psychoanalytic view on the intricate connections between imagination and sexuality which potentially transfigures the inner complex of gender. I refer to the Freudian conception of 'unconscious representation', to those continuously moving fantasies of the unconscious imagination, especially as they pertain to emotional experiences of self and other. Freud's account of the psychoanalytical process, to be sure, is preoccupied by the complicity between imagination and repression, desire and defence. For Freud, the unconscious is a representational flux of desire and affect, driving thoughts and associations along a multitude of pathways, displacing and condensing the forced unities of consciousness. This is the aspect of Freud's work that most powerfully underscores the creative workings of the self, and it is an aspect that I think is often insufficiently emphasized in post-Freudian psychoanalytical doctrines, as well as in the application of Freudian ideas to the social sciences and humanities more generally. This is not simply the result of a failure to grasp the 'essence' of Freud's teachings, because (as I have argued at length elsewhere, see Elliott, 1999; Elliott 1996: chapter 2) the founding father of psychoanalysis neglected to explicitly *theorize* the more inventive, creative dimensions of the unconscious imagination. There were, of course, good reasons for such a conceptual neglect or displacement. Given that Freud was preoccupied with human suffering, it is hardly surprising that he dedicated his energies to uncovering the tropes of repression and mechanisms of defence that constitute blockages in the processing of affect – blockages which makes themselves known through symptoms. Yet Freud also continually underscored the inventiveness of the unconscious imagination, pointing out in *The Interpretation of Dreams* that no dream can be fully interpreted because it contains too many trains of thought and complexities of affect. There is always a part of the dream, writes Freud,

> which has to be left obscure; this is because we become aware during the work of interpretation that at that point there is a tangle of dream-thoughts which cannot be unravelled and which moreover adds nothing to our knowledge of the content of the dream. This is the dream's navel, the spot where it reaches down into the unknown. The dream-thoughts to which we are led by interpretation have to, in an entirely universal manner, remain without any definite endings; they are bound to branch out in every direction into the intricate network of our world of thought. It is at some point where this meshwork is particularly close that the dream-wish grows up, like a mushroom out of its mycelium.
>
> (Freud, 1900: 525)

In the writings of contemporary psychoanalysts such as Thomas Ogden, Christopher Bollas, Jessica Benjamin, Charles Spezzano and Stephen Mitchell, there is an explicit concern with the interconnections between desire, imagination, and the notion of sexuality as an open-ended process (see Ogden, 1989b; Bollas, 1995; Benjamin, 1995; Spezzano, 1993; Mitchell, 1993). A combination of desire and imagination, when available for psychic processing and reflective thinking, underpins the scanning of alternative selves and states of mind. The pleasures and dangers of self-experience, and of the self in its dealings with the social world, become available to reflective knowing only after an immersion in experience, in which emotional contact is created between the conscious and unconscious, inside and outside, identity and non-identity. This opening out to reflective knowing is open-ended in the sense that ambivalence and otherness are tolerated and explored in terms of their inner complexity; it can be thought of as a kind of internal celebration of the sheer diversity and plurality of human worlds. Thomas Ogden, for example, speaks of 'the fear of not knowing', a fear which (if not consciously perceived) can lead to the unleashing of destructive fantasy and of attacks on open-ended thinking. Toleration of 'not knowing', says Ogden, is fundamental to a creative engagement with the self, others, and the social world. I have connected this 'fear of not knowing', in my *Subject to Ourselves* (1996), to modernist desires for certitude, order, control and mastery, and have contrasted it with postmodern tolerance of ambiguity, ambivalence, uncertainty, contingency and difference.

From this psychoanalytical recasting of radical imagination, we can begin to raise questions about whether contemporary feminist thought enables the recognition of our inner complexity as sexual, gendered subjects, or about whether it has become a way of closing down on such questions, or at least of keeping that which is disturbing and overwhelming about ourselves at bay. The core issues which arise are these. How does contemporary feminism attempt to think the new and grasp the power of imagination? What kind of processing or remembering is feminism undertaking in its concern with the production and transformation of sexualities? What blockages and disturbances serve to limit or constrain the thinking of feminism afresh? Does feminism simply reiterate itself? How, and in what ways, has feminism become repetitive? Is postmodern feminism always more of the same, simply dressed up in new clothes? Or is the repetition of feminism part and parcel of the logics of sexual difference itself?

In *Social Theory and Psychoanalysis in Transition* (1999), I outlined three levels of analysis with respect to the nature of unconscious desire which could offer a reflective and systematic framework for the study of self and society – namely, the representational flux of individual fantasy, the indeterminacy of imaginary significations, and the socio-symbolic realm of received cultural meanings. Concerning problems of sexual difference and gender complexity, I attempted to underscore the profound role of the imagination and unconscious fantasy in both the perpetuation and transformation of gendered subjectivities. Against the tide of much Lacanian feminist thought, I argued that our fantasized aspects of sexuality and of sexual difference necessarily implies transmutations in the socio-symbolic world of gender hierarchy, and I attempted to document such changes by reference to developments in the women's movement itself. I set out the intricate links between the human imagination and social institutions (in this case, the women's movement) in the following way:

> The imaginary underpinning of women's political mobilization has both influenced social policies and in turn has been reshaped by new institutional resources. That is, women's collective action in society has, among other things, led to the institutional redefinition of the objectives and aims of the women's movement. This is clear, for example, in the shift from the 1970s, when an essential female subjectivity was posited against male domination, to the growing tendency today for the women's movements to support a plurality of female subject positions (such as sexual, work, and political identities). At a theoretical level, then, it can be said that processes of imaginary transformation establish new symbolic possibilities from which a variety of gender issues come to be addressed anew.

In what follows I want to amplify on these connections between imagination and society, fantasy and institution, but I want to do this through a reversal of logics: that is, by considering what happens when there is a loss of imagination and a negation of the freedom to attach meaning to experience in open-ended ways. The task here is to describe some recent self-imposed restrictions on feminist theorizing and politics, and of how the disavowal of imagination is implicated in the destruction of difference, and especially alternative political possibilities implicit in sexual difference. Later in the chapter, I turn to consider a more open and combinatorial feminist approach to the complex linkages between identity, sexuality and society, or, as this can be framed in psycho-analytical terms, the production of psychic space, the making of radical imagination, and the composition of social relations or practices.

From ambivalence to inflexibility: the fear of difference

The rise of the concept of difference, as we have seen, is directly linked to the contemporary currents of postmodernism and post-structuralism, and its political significance is often measured against the linear, bureaucratic, well-ordered administered world of modernity. In contemporary feminism, the political value attributed to the recovery of difference is that it potentially opens the mysteriously repressed realm of sexual division to a kind of thinking that goes beyond modernist categories of opposition that serve to sustain gender hierarchy. Precisely because identity is no longer thought of as a stable entity, its meaning opening onto the problematic realm of ambiguity and indeter-minacy, the discourse on feminist politics moves increasingly to consider what political possibilities arise from the troubled significations of identity and difference. But what kind of love affair, we might ask, is feminism having with difference? Is it, for example, that something that promotes a radical inquiry into the political construction of sexuality and gender? Or is it something that has simply developed into a fixed normativity, as a new kind of political correctness for feminism?

In order to take up these questions, let us turn now to examine Naomi Wolf's *Fire With Fire* (1994; the quotations that follow are from pages xiv and xvi respectively). The follow-up to her international bestseller, *The Beauty Myth*, *Fire With Fire* – which is subtitled 'The New Female Power and How It Will Change the 21st Century' – continues Wolf's preoccupation with developing a feminist discourse which is somehow politically relevant to postmodern culture. Rejecting the idea that feminism can simply pick up pre-existing theories of power and oppression and apply them to our culture of gender inequality, Wolf instead tackles head-on the difficult problem of putting theory securely in the context of women's – and men's – everyday activities in order to think sexual politics afresh. Wolf claims that the urgent priority is to construct a feminist politics which can think positive and negative dimensions of the intricate connections between existing power networks on the one hand, and sexuality and gender hierarchy on the other. Furthermore, she asserts that a practical and useful language, rather than simply more moralizing discourse, is required for the advancement of feminist action.

Wolf begins her discussion of power in *Fire With Fire*, appropriately enough, with the declaration that the 1990s have ushered in a 'genderquake'. Emerging against the backlash years of the 1980s, when women's personal and political gains were under attack everywhere, the new era of the 'genderquake' promises a radical transformation of sexual politics and of the distribution of power between the sexes. As Wolf explains this development:

> The 'genderquake' started in America with the eruption of Oklahoma law professor Anita Hill's charges of sexual harassment, rocked through the 1991–2's famous rape trials, flung into the light of day allegations of Senator Bob Packwood's sexual harassment of colleagues, and of the sexual abuse of US Navy women at the Tailhook Convention; and provided the impetus for 52 new women legislators to take their seats in the House of Representatives and the Senate.

That Wolf's narrative is set securely within recent political developments in the USA is, one might think, a curious opening move for such an 'international feminist' to make – especially given that it is part of her argument that the logics of 'genderquake' are increasingly global in character. But if the geo-political specificity of the case is never adequately questioned, it is more than compensated for in terms of Wolf's bold linkage between historical and sexual/political knowledge. As she provocatively claims,

> we are at what historians of women's progress call 'an open moment'. Twenty-five years of dedicated feminist activism have hauled the political infrastructure into place, enough women in the middle classes have enough money and clout, and most women now have enough desire and determination to begin to balance the imbalance of power between the sexes.

There are, however, dangers and risks here as well; but for Wolf these are less to do with the economic infrastructure governing sexuality and gender hierarchy than with the cultural sphere of human social relationships. Such a focus on the cultural sphere brings into play the politics of feminism itself, and she certainly has damning things to say about the rise of 'victim feminism' – that version of feminism which constructs women as sexually pure and personally altruistic, and only then considers the damage done to women in a world of male oppression. For Wolf, the weakness of this case is that it establishes an identity-politics from the process of victimization it describes. That is to say, it draws all women under the sign of victimization, riding roughshod over major personal, cultural, social and political differences between women; differences of sexual orientation, race, ethnicity and class. The core limitation of this kind of identity-politics for feminism then is that it obscures the differential effects of relations of domination and oppression, including those between women. As such, it is unable to comprehend that economic and cultural inequalities vary considerably among women, in terms of the degree of oppression, exploitation of the body, repression of desire and the like.

Against this backcloth, Wolf argues for expanding the concept of difference to encompass women's and men's everyday activities, and suggests the political urgency of attempting to talk across gender differences in order to break the fixity of our current embattled perspectives. She scornfully rejects the anxiety that an attempt to think power differently – to consider sexual and gender differences between women and also between the sexes – will lead feminism into disarray, into a form of political impotence arising from partial perspectives, in which each viewpoint on gender is considered as good as the next. Those who imagine that truth is absolute in the field of gender relations, says Wolf, are held helplessly in thrall to a fixed, monolithic conception of political change; indeed such rigid determinism is itself part and parcel of the destructive logics of 'political correctness'. Feminism, according to Wolf, if it is to become flexible and creative again, needs to reject, once and for all, the notion of political correctness; it needs to face up to ambivalence and ambiguity, not as some limit to the powers of intellectual clarity and knowledge, but as central to inter-personal relationships and human sexuality; it needs to see that 'worldly power' is complex, ambiguous and indeterminate.

There is, then, another dimension beyond the dominant logic of 'political correctness' which frames the critical feminist capacity, but it does this through trying to *understand* the complexity and ambivalence of unequal gender rela-tions; it does not simply legislate in advance how such dramas and difficulties should be comprehended in the first place. Yet there is a tension in Wolf's work as to how thinking and acting might be related in terms of feminism today. At times, Wolf indicates that it is because of the complexity of the relationship between self and society that feminist theory must resituate itself as a theory in connection to the lived experience of gender, sexuality, bodies, desire and the like. At other times, Wolf seems anxious about the potential deadlocks and dead-ends that may inhibit feminist action if notions of complexity, ambiguity and ambivalence are fully embraced. Here, it might be said, the cognitive and normative elements of her discourse begin to enter into an embarrassing contradiction. In other words, just as Wolf begins to rethink the connections between theory and practice in postmodernist culture, she gets hung up about the interlacing of these domains, deciding in the end it is better to stick with the devil you know than the one you don't.

By the conclusion of *Fire With Fire*, Wolf's discourse fully reflects a flight from the conceptual, as well as from a confrontation with the messiness and ambivalence of human social relationships. In a section entitled 'Psychological strategies', Wolf writes: 'Power feminism cannot work until we try to make changes in the way we treat ourselves and others'. She then offers a kind of 'shopping list' required for putting power feminism into action. The strategies she proposes include (and I quote her, again):

- Avoid generalizations about men that imply that their maleness is the unchangeable source of the problem.
- Never choose to widen the rift between the sexes when the option exists to narrow it, without censoring the truth.
- Resist the idea that sexual orientation is fixed and categorical, or that any one woman's sexual choices are more legitimate than any other's.

- Make it socially acceptable for women to discuss their skills and achievements.
- Remember and take possession of the girlhood will for power and fantasies of grandeur.
- Practice asking for more money, and urge our friends to so.

(Wolf's 'Psychological Strategies' is to be found in chapter 18, 'What We Can Do Now')

By ranking these demands on the same level, as strategies which fit all social relations and institutions, Wolf takes up a reactionary political stance. For the effect of this normative performativity ('never choose', 'practice asking') is to reduce the very operating conditions of ambivalence and ambiguity to nought. Clearly, the pressure to offer some kind of *feminist solution*, however politically maladroit and culturally vacuous, managed to get the upper hand in Wolf's thinking – a psychic reaction which, in psychoanalytic terms, can be described as a 'translation into action'. Wolf's 'shopping list' creates, in effect, a really tight fit between feminist ideology and social action, thereby crowding out the very indeterminacy of the self/society link which she alluded to previously. No space for mind, imagination or fantasy, because the ideology processes the reality to fit the 'psychological strategies' on offer.

Consider, by contrast, the encounter between feminism, psychoanalysis and political theory staged by the British theorist Jacqueline Rose. In her book *Why War?* (1993), Rose takes up the question that so troubled Freud towards the end of his life: the origins or nature of violence in general, and of why violence figures so prominently in contemporary culture in particular (see Rose, 1993). (The title of Rose's book is taken from Freud's essay 'Why War?', which was part of Freud's public exchange with Einstein on the subject of war) (see Freud, 1932). In a Freudian context, the problematic of war is that of a failure in emotional self-knowledge. Rose writes: 'to suggest that war is in some sense the repressed of its conceptualization – that is, of any attempt to think it – might be one way of explaining why we are never prepared for the full horror of war' (see Rose, 1993). War brings us face to face with our own inner darkness, the destructiveness we fear in ourselves. In routine conditions of social life, the irrational and psychotic features of the psyche are held in check by the more constructive and realistic functioning of various cultural groups, dominant authorities and institutionalized expert-systems. In conditions of war, however, individuals and groups are easily overcome with paranoia and megalomania, projecting the destructiveness we fear in ourselves onto the other, the alien. (Rose cites Franco Fornari's classic claim that war is a 'paranoid elaboration of mourning' – 1975: xviii.)

Echoing Freud, Rose argues that violence and war represent the dissolution of society itself. 'War', writes Rose, 'makes the other accountable for a horror we can then wipe out with impunity, precisely because we have located it so firmly in the other's place. This saves us the effort of ambivalence, the hard work of recognizing that we love where we hate, that, in our hearts and minds at least, we kill those to whom we are most closely and intimately attached' (see Rose, 1993). Such an approach to thinking violence and war, it might be noted, has a long psycho-social tradition. Politics, according to the founder of political psychology, Harold Lasswell, is indeed about the regulation of anger and hatred. From the Stone Age to Star Wars, political identities have been made in the service of hate, and especially irrational hate. The key point about hatred is that it is other-directed; the hater is convinced that the source of the problem lies in the person or group or nation which is so despised and denigrated. Accordingly, political subjects can take pleasure in violence as legitimate State force, as war, while always projecting 'real' violence elsewhere: the displacement of repressed rage onto socially sanctioned public enemies. From this angle, the dreaded negative powers of modernity depend upon the continual eruption of repressed feelings of violent anger, of hatred, of nameless dread.

In the concluding part of this chapter, I want to take the work of Rose as a prime example of an attempt to analyse the issue of the complexity of mind from a feminist perspective. Rose's work is of special interest in the present context, not because it is informed by psychoanalytical themes (in fact, Rose's work offers a powerful feminist critique of Freud and psychoanalysis), but because she seeks to keep questions about complexity, ambivalence and indeterminacy open for conceptual reflection and consideration. Rose situates the question of violence in relation to structures of power, and especially structures of gender power; and it is from this angle that her writing makes for a powerful blend-ing of feminist scholarship, psychoanalytic criticism and political theory. Developing upon her feminist and political critique of psychoanalysis in *Sexuality in the Field of Vision* (1986), Rose argues that psychoanalysis elucidates not only the repression of sexual feelings, but, just as important for the women's movement, the repression of hate and destructiveness (see Rose, 1986). Violence, says Rose, is of fundamental significance to contemporary feminism and gender politics. On one level, this is so because of the rise of sexual violence during the 1980s and 1990s (ranging from sexual harassment to rape and body muti-lation), underpinned by the cultural implosion of apocalyptic sexual fantasy. On another level, a level that is perhaps even deeper, Rose suggests that feminism has too often made violence and hatred the curse of male subjectivity alone. Utilizing psychoanalytic theory to destabilize the assurance of a stable, self-identical subject, Rose contends that both men and women fear a destruc-tiveness within, and that therefore much of the rhetoric of feminism needs to be critically revised.

This point is superbly made in Rose's examination of the psychic and historical connections between Margaret Thatcher and Ruth Ellis. The link between these two women is well known: in 1955 Ellis was the last woman to be hanged in England, and Thatcher brought her back to public attention in 1983 in her effort to reintroduce capital punishment in the United Kingdom. Rose notes that this link between Thatcher and Ellis highlights that violence can be used by females in a dramatic fashion. Ellis occupies a location of sexual, physical violence (she shot her lover); Thatcher occupies a location of political violence, the authority of the State to kill. For Rose, the logic of fantasy in which these forms of violence operate are mutually imbricated. Ellis's femininity, says Rose, could only appear as an outrage to society because of the deadly consistency of her premeditation. (Ellis stated in court that 'I had an idea that I wanted to kill him'.) The premeditated rationality of Ellis was deeply problematical precisely because it too closely resembled that violence which the law is founded upon – the violence implicit in objectivism and rationalism. 'Murderers', writes Rose (1993: 60), 'who premeditate are therefore the most dangerous because they too closely resemble the symbolic and psychic structure written into the legal apparatus that comes to meet them.' Rose argues that Thatcher's support for the return of capital punishment was underwritten by a kind of 'super-rationality', the point at which violence secures its own legitimation.

> It is not the irrationality of Thatcher's rhetoric that strikes me as the problem, but its supreme rationalism, the way that it operates according to a protocol of reason elevated to the status of a law. In this case, we cannot counter that ideology with a greater rationality without entering into one of the predominant fantasies of the ideology itself.
>
> (Rose, 1993)

Thatcher and Ellis can then be said to represent different forms of 'reason in excess' – the first State backed, the second of the criminal code.

Rose's theoretical purchase on the contemporary political climate is one that is always at odds with itself. On the one hand, she wants to show that psychoanalytic knowledge is itself essential to the framing of a radical political vision. On the other hand, Rose insists that the more troubling effects of repression are deeply inscribed in everything we do – sexual, cultural and political. The upshot of this is a revised version of the relationship between politics, psychoanalysis and feminism, a version that breaks with the notion of utopian liberation (what would a 'collective liberation' of the unconscious actually look like?) and, instead, embraces the difficult antagonisms between sexuality and aggression, desire and defence, life and death. For if there is ambivalence in the field of identity and sexual life, a similar doubleness can be seen to lie on the side of (conscious) knowledge and politics. That is to say, Rose connects the dynamic unconscious, not only to those broad areas of gender activity with which feminism concerns itself, but to the discourses of knowledge itself, including those of theory and critique. In striving to figure the latent desire of (conscious) knowledge, Rose underlines the sexual and psychic stakes of the political in the strongest sense, capturing not just the fantasy component of aspects of society and history, but also the circuit of unconscious dislocation in the relationship between psychoanalysis and social theory more generally.

As might be expected from this kind of cultural diagnosis, much of the psychoanalytic emphasis centres on negativity and dislocation. Following Lacan's Freud, Rose seeks to analyse, not only our construction in and through the symbolic order of language, but also the ways in which this constitution of subject-positions and psychic locations fails, lapses and dissolves. This is a para-doxical theoretical endeavour, since it involves looking at how the interrelation between psyche and society at once succeeds and fails – or, at least, of how that interrelation is always in the process of redefining and reconstructing itself. It is in this sense that Rose can be said to have followed faithfully Freud's notion of the death drive, a primary aggressiveness in human beings which at once lurks within our narcissistic gratifications and drives the ego toward violent acts of self-undoing. The objectives or strategies of the death drive, carried out through the brutal directives of the superego, is essential for grasping the fantasy dimensions of the dark side of modernity, and it precisely for this reason that Rose devotes much of her psychoanalytic and political attention to war and other terrors of recent history. For it is only by confronting the most painful and distressing aspects of our collective experience, says Rose, that we may come to better understand the psychic and the social-historical forms implicated in the production and formation of destructive political identities. Rose's work, then, represents a kind of applied psychoanalysis of feminist ethics, concerned as it is with the question of autonomy and its forms of realization. For Rose, autonomy is a question of neither rejecting nor appropriating the law, but of fostering an ambivalence that will allow human subjects to withdraw projections based on destructive urges, and thereby strengthen creative social and political relations.

Rose's *Why War?* and Wolf's *Fire With Fire*, though very different versions of feminist theory, attempt to grapple with the place of gender in the further-most reaches of our personal and political lives. Both seek to engage with the increasing complexities of sexual life and identity in the postmodern age, and in a certain sense both have important and troubling things to say about notions of gender and social transformation. Unlike *Why War?*, however, *Fire With Fire* seeks to provide accessible and ready-made solutions for gender transformation, and to that extent Wolf's work can be considered simplistic and deterministic. Rose, by contrast, returns us to Freud's really insightful discoveries about the indeterminacy of the (critical) radical imagination, and of the complexity this carries for considering, as well as trying to enact, alter-native social futures. For Rose, there is no final point of arrival, only interesting questions. Such questions, as I have sought to demonstrate, concern both the operations of psychoanalytic and feminist theory. As Rose (1993: 255) develops this:

> the point at which psychoanalysis as a practice comes up against the limits of its own interpretative process, might be the point at which there could be the strongest dialogue between psychoanalytic practice and the readings of psychoanalysis in the humanities which stress the ultimate failure of controlling interpretative procedures.

Conclusion

In this chapter I have sought to portray the contributions of Freud to feminist and social theory in broad strokes, in order to consider some of the different ways in which psychoanalytic theory can be drawn upon to examine current intellectual discourses on gender, sexuality and intimacy. The connections between psychoanalysis and politics, as I have tried to indicate, involve a two-way traffic. That is, the application of Freud to feminist and social theory has led many authors to discuss problems of human subjectivity, desire, sexuality, fantasy and interpersonal relationships in more reflective ways than was the case before. At the same time, however, feminist and social theory has made important contributions to our understanding of the gains and losses of viewing social relations and cultural processes through a Freudian lens. In response to this intellectual interchange, I have sought to indicate how we might approach contemporary intellectual debates and deadlocks in feminist and social theory from the vantage point of psychoanalysis itself. Not in the sense of applying ready-to-hand formulas or dogma, but rather as a tool for keeping open difficult interpretative issues about those imaginary and symbolic forms implicated in the structuration of self and society in the late modern age.

Pretext
Ethics, psychoanalysis and postmodernity

In *The Life of the Mind*, the political philosopher Hannah Arendt wrote of a 'frailty of human affairs'. Through a powerful extension of Kant's philosophical reflections on judgement, Arendt expanded the terrain of positive rationality and politics to include taste, intuition, aesthetic judgement and imagination. Deeply attuned to the accelerated progress of technology, and with her political theory framed against the backcloth of twentieth-century totalitarianism and death camps, Arendt calls us to reflect seriously upon the precariousness or vulnerability of political communities founded upon pluralities of narrative. Her highly original conception of narration enquired how it is that public space is constituted as political – as self-actualizing sites of power – only when lives can be recounted or narrated and thus shared with others who, through memory, speech and symbolic persuasion, give localized expression to such acts of narration and thus make history into a historically specific, condensed sign – what Arendt terms the revelation of the 'who'. Kristeva, in a powerful psychoanalytic study of Arendt's political thought, conceptualises the location of frailty or vulnerability in human affairs thus:

> Judgement is clearly vulnerable. That vulnerability, however, is precisely what enables it to provide a place for *The Life of the Mind* as the revelation of a 'who' and to avoid getting stuck in a 'system' governed by intrinsically totalitarian values. . . . Seduced and yet bogged down by the 'frailty of human affairs', Arendt gives her attention to the two pitfalls that threaten judgement – pitfalls that appear to coexist with the linear existence of human time in the process of life and, by implication, in the modern practice of politics: irreversibility and unpredictability.
>
> (Kristeva, 2001: 230)

What has long intrigued followers of Arendt's political theory is her unflagging commitment to language, and especially poetry as an indispensable medium for the institution and flowering of civil society. In the hands of Arendt, poetry is no longer defined as the opposite of the political, the discursive or the public: poetry, she argued, is 'the most human of the arts'. Poetic language, symbolism, the aesthetic: such cultural forms permit the public sphere to operate as a discursive space reflecting both shared interests and conflicting agendas. And yet critics of Arendt claim that her various attempts to aestheticize political judgement are a radically contradictory affair, if only because the principle of a general aesthetics of imagination in which an equilibrium of the general and the particular, of the individual body and the plural domain of politics, is not pushed far enough. Kristeva, for example, while affirming the correctness of Arendt's attempt to expand the concept of the political to include aesthetic judgement, taste, intuition and imagination, nonetheless argues that the recovery and flowering of public political life depends on a creative narrativization that cannot but reflect the psychic splitting of the subject – something Arendt's political theory was unable to comprehend due to her failure to theorize the repressed unconscious. As Kristeva develops this critique of Arendt:

> We can simply note that relegating the body to an uninteresting generality, simply because it is biological and is an obstacle to the uniqueness of the 'who', allows Arendt to do away with psychology and psychoanalysis. Compared to medicine and physiology, which are interested in what our organs have in common, as she believes – certainly that's true, but they study more than that! – Arendt condemns them together: 'Psychology, depth psychology or psychoanalysis, [reveals] no more than the ever-changing moods, the ups and downs of our psychic life, and its results and discoveries are neither particularly appealing nor very meaningful in themselves'. The expression 'neither particularly appealing' is undoubtedly the most revealing here: not only is psychoanalysis 'not appealing', it is frightening. It frightens *her*.

> (2001b: 64)

There can be little doubt that Kristeva sympathizes with Arendt's pluralist political position, rooted as it is in concepts such as narrative, language and public space. And yet, more perhaps than Arendt, Kristeva is attuned to the emotional contradictions of frailty, vulnerability, affection, intimacy. From her revised post-Lacanian conceptual standpoint, Kristeva contends that the telling of narratives fractures as much as it unifies identity; she asserts that language is, crucially, an emotional holding operation against the disruptive subjective impact of lost loves, repressed pasts, displaced selves.

What might such 'lost loves, repressed pasts, displaced selves' look like in terms of our contemporary cultural condition? Loved objects lost, cherished cultural ideals eclipsed: modernism, colonialism, imperialism, patriarchy and on and on. Pasts repressed are often enough thought to be buried or destroyed – and yet we see a resurgence of guilt everywhere in the polished, expensive cities of the West, as if the dethronement of European imperialism is at some level shameful, too embarrassing. Thus there is a nostalgia for yesteryear, when identities were solid, durable, built to last. This may be, as Zygmunt Bauman suggests, the reason postmodernism fits hand-in-glove the social and mental habits of contemporary women and men, mesmerized by the prospects of breaking free from an exhausted modernity and yet always harbouring a pathology distinctively modernist in design and compulsion, as though one might just actually bid farewell to modernist impulses for structured order and orderly structures once and for all. Society as factories of meaning, to paraphrase Bauman's designation of the liquid stage of the late modern world, takes on postmodern qualities to the degree modernity turns back on itself, monitoring its cultural conditions and psychological illusions. And yet still we might ask: what might the evocative blend of pluralized narrative or language on the one hand, and the globalization of public political space on the other, look like from the vantage point of a postmodern culture mourning the loss of modernist dreams for orderly structures and certitude?

The postmodern version of psychoanalysis that I have sought to promote in a number of recent books – *Concepts of the Self* (2001), *Psychoanalytic Theory: An Introduction* (2002), *Critical Visions* (2003), *Subject to Ourselves* (2004) and in this book – is one more committed to the emotional processing of cultural difference and affective celebration of otherness than to cognitive certitude or rational mastery. In the pursuit of political demands for appreciation of cultural differences and otherness, there are values embedded in psychoanalytic theory which are of vital importance – especially as regards the unique particularities of individuals and also regarding our equal rights to participate in the self-shaping of the future direction of society. For psychoanalysis starts from the premise that people have to learn to take into account their own emotional limits and dependencies – not simply as a kind of brake on narcissism and omnipotent thought, but for creative engagement with others and for the prospects of human autonomy. To genuinely recognize another's difference and autonomy thus requires acknowledgement of the contingent ground of social things, of biological structure, of human need, of emotional desire, of Eros and sexuality in various forms of social association. Such an ethics of self-constitution, as Arendt and Kristeva after her affirm, is one concerned with human frailties and vulnerabilities.

The incessant search for some kind of balance in personal and social life between creative self-making and imaginative cultural production on the one hand, and recognition of the profound ontological implications of frailty and vulnerability on the other, lies at the heart of desires for human autonomy. Where there are demands for autonomous society, to return to Castoriadis once more, these are the fruits of action undertaken by individuals seeking *ontological opening*. The pleasure of finding such openings beyond the highly regulated informational, cognitive and organizational closures of the late modern epoch lies precisely in engaging with self and world in a fundamental way, beyond instrumentally orientated fantasies of technoscientific control. Engagement with a cluster of basic moral and biological issues of human life – the nature of love and passion, the impact of illness, human existence and death – can allow individuals to become deeply aware of the self-making of their world, of the role of imaginary constructions in their interpersonal relationships and of the contingency of social things more generally.

> Autonomous society is that society which self-institutes itself explicitly and lucidly, the one that knows that it itself posits its institutions and significations, [and] this means that it knows as well that they have no source other than its own instituting and signification-giving activity, no extrasocial 'guarantee'.
>
> (Castoriadis)

Self-reflexivity of such a state of social affairs – that there is, contrary to the ideological proclamations of modernity, 'no extrasocial guarantee' – is precisely the promise of the postmodern: the splitting of meaning, representation and signification into deconstructed and reconstructed objects of reflection. Postmodern dismantling of the self-institution of meaning or signifcation is, of course, a radically ambiguous affair – as it is as difficult to truly grasp one's 'own instituting and signification-giving activity' as it might be to imagine an alternative to it. All in all, if the postmodern declaration of autonomy involves a radical dismantling or deconstruction of the social world itself, this is because postmodernity (as a series of global transformations in institutions, sociality and culture) nurtures in some sense the existence of individuals with rationally and emotionally articulated capacities for self-interrogation and self-reflection. The achievement of such a state of mind, it might be added, raises in turn the thorny issue of what kind of good it might do us – individually and collectively – to emotionally grasp, tolerate and reflect on the loss of a modernist 'extrasocial guarantee' (illusions of omnipotence generated and sustained by Enlightenment rationality, technoscience, religion and so on).

'Postmodernity', writes Bauman, 'perhaps more than anything else is a *state of mind*. More precisely a state of those minds who have the habit (or is it a compulsion?) to reflect on themselves, to search their own contents and report what they found' (2001). In pursuit of the postmodern celebration of reflexivity, difference, otherness and autonomy, there are values inherent in the tradition of psychoanalysis which are of vital importance. The psychoanalytic aesthetic – ranging from free association through reverie to toleration of the depressive position – is in this sense a proto-postmodern cultural theory, one that both deconstructs and reconstructs modernist discourses of subjectivity, truth, reason and freedom. Equally valuable, psychoanalytic theory underscores the powerful emotional pressures and limits of the mind that threaten and potentially defeat the goal of autonomy, and therefore offers insights into the corporatist strategies of instrumental rationality which must be challenged and contested.

5 Psychoanalysis at its limits

Navigating the postmodern turn

with Charles Spezzano

> Postmodernity does not necessarily mean the end, the discreditation of the rejection of modernity. Postmodernity is no more (but no less either) than the modern mind taking a long, attentive and sober look at itself, at its condition and its past works, not fully liking what it sees and sensing the urge to change.
>
> (Zygmunt Bauman, *Modernity and Ambivalence*)

> The point is that we are *within* the culture of postmodernism to the point where its facile repudiation is as impossible as any equally facile celebration of it is complacent and corrupt.
>
> (Fredric Jameson, *Postmodernism: or, The Cultural Logic of Late Capitalism*)

In a 1929 essay, T. S. Eliot wrote about Dante that 'he not only thought in a way in which every man of his culture in the whole of Europe then thought, but he employed a method which was common and commonly understood throughout Europe' (cited in Trachtenberg, 1979: 1). Dante may have been the last writer to enjoy this guaranteed rapport with his audience. Certainly no psychoanalytic author can expect anything like it. Quite the contrary, it is guaranteed that all psychoanalysts writing for their 'colleagues' today will encounter, among at least some readers, disbelief at their failure to grasp basic principles, headshaking over their hubris in imagining that what they have written contains new ideas, or lack of interest from readers not of their 'school' because they talk 'another language' that is too 'old fashioned' or 'not really psychoanalysis'.

Further, in the theorizing and clinical reports contained in contemporary analytic journals one does not only find authors whose work is intended to advance (or fits neatly into) a project called ego analysis, self psychology, object relational theory, or Kleinian analysis. One also finds authors whose work seems harder to pigeonhole; but, as philosopher Iris Murdoch (1993: 1–2) has suggested: 'We fear plurality, diffusion, senseless accident, chaos, we want to transform what we cannot dominate or understand into something reassuring and familiar, into ordinary being, into history, art, religion, science.' We want to say: 'That is classical analysis, self psychology, relational psychoanalysis. The author is an element of one of our reassuring unities.'

As the individual voices in psychoanalysis proliferate, we need more unifying labels to maintain order and ward off chaos. 'Postmodernism' is the most recent. As with other labels, it relies for its appearance of usefulness and validity on the availability of a contrary perspective: 'modernism'. In this case, for the first time in the history of psychoanalysis, the duelling labels have been imported from other disciplines. This has tended to increase the confusion about their usage beyond the level that has beset the use of other psychoanalytic dichotomies. The aim of this chapter is not so ambitious as to clear up this confusion, but rather simply to describe it. It will be argued, in fact, that it might be a good idea to allow it to remain confusing.

Modernism and postmodernism: the alleged dichotomy

The 'thing' against which postmodernism is most often described as setting itself – the thing called modernism – was midwifed into existence by Kant's angry reaction to the blindness of metaphysics and the emptiness of empiricism. Although he championed it with some qualifications, what Kant offered in place of these pretenders was that most precious child of the Enlightenment: reason. Through reason (and only through reason) 'could the universal, eternal, and the immutable qualities of all humanity be revealed' (Harvey, 1990: 12). As such knowledge accumulated, 'rational modes of thought promised liberation from the irrationalities of myth, religion, superstition,' and, especially, 'release from the arbitrary use of power as well as from the dark side of our own human natures' (ibid.).

As might be expected, once such a monolithic entity as modernism has been constituted, it becomes convenient and compelling to write as if everything that is not it is one other thing, in this case postmodernism. If modernism has been a quest for truth and reality and if its modus operandi has been positivism or objectivism, then everything that is not positivistic and objectivist is assumed to be thoroughly antagonistic to truth and reality. If, however, modernism itself was a cubist painting – with ambiguously related surfaces of reason, truth, certainty, objectivity, and positivism made to look like a unified whole – then a contemporary theorist who takes issue with one of these points might not take issue with all of them. This, it turns out, might well be the messy truth of postmodern thinking in psychoanalysis and other disciplines. Consider the following epistemologies.

British philosopher **Roger Scruton** (1994) argues that Kant's take on human beings knowing the world is not the final word, but it is the best one. We cannot look at the world from outside our concepts and know the world as it is. We cannot see it from no particular point of view, as God might. In fact, we could not even begin to think about the world if we did not believe that we were viewing it through concepts of objectivity and that our judgements of it would represent reality.

German critical theorist **Jürgen Habermas** argues that all human beings possess the same faculty of reason. We experience the results of reason's successful application when we find ourselves with dialogical consensus or in coordinated action with others. 'The intersubjectivity of the validity of communication rules is confirmed in the reciprocity of actions and expectations. Whether this reciprocity occurs or fails to occur can be discovered only by the parties involved; but they make this discovery intersubjectively' (1970: 141).

In his highly readable introduction to postmodernism, **John McGowan** (1991: ix) uses the term 'to designate a specific form of cultural critique that has become increasingly conspicuous in the academy since about 1975'. He understands postmodernism as referring to an antifoundationalist critique, but adds to this a positive dimension: a search for freedom and pluralism that accepts the necessity, if not the virtue, of norms to which people, institutions and practices are responsive.

American philosopher **Simon Blackburn** (1993: 4) takes what he calls a 'quasi-realist' position: 'that truth is the aim of judgment; that our disciplines make us better able to appreciate it, that it is, however, independent of us, and that we are fallible in our grasp of it'.

Jacques Derrida suggests that we read all texts deconstructively. We must 'work through the structured genealogy of its concepts in the most scrupulous and immanent fashion, but at the same time to determine from a certain external perspective that it cannot name or describe what this history may have concealed or excluded' (1981: 6). We might paraphrase Norris (1987), in his excellent account of Derrida's philosophical project, and say that the effect of Derrida's philosophy is to render 'intensely problematic' much of what passes for 'rigorous thought in psychoanalysis (as well as in philosophy and literary theory). 'But this effect is not achieved by dispensing with the protocols of detailed, meticulous argument, or by simply abandoning the conceptual ground on which such arguments have hitherto been conducted' (Norris, 1987: 20).

Barnaby Barratt (1993), in his book *Psychoanalysis and the Postmodern Impulse*, offers a vision of psychoanalysis as a process of free-associative deconstruction – 'deconstructive and negatively dialectical in a subversively postmodern sense' rather than 'insight establishing and reflective in the modern philosophical sense' (Barratt, 1993: xiv).

Italian philosopher **Gianni Vattimo** (1980: 43), during a discussion of Nietzsche's reduction of truth to morality, takes the following position:

> Whenever a proposition seems evident, there operates a series of historical premises and predispositions towards acceptance or rejection on the part of the subject, and these predispositions are guided by an overriding interest

in the preservation and development not simply of 'life' as such, but of a particular form of life.

Neopragmatist philosopher **Richard Rorty** (1982: 92) argues that there 'are two ways of thinking about various things'. We can think of truth 'as a vertical relationship between representations and what is represented'. We can also think of truth 'horizontally – as the culminating reinterpretation of our predecessors' reinterpretation'. He adds: 'It is the difference between regarding truth, goodness, and beauty as eternal objects which we try to locate and reveal, and regarding them as artifacts whose fundamental design we often have to alter' (ibid.).

In *The Postmodern Condition: A Report on Knowledge*, **Jean-François Lyotard** (1984: xxv) writes: 'I define postmodern as incredulity toward metanarratives.' For Lyotard, the postmodern world is made up of Wittgensteinian language games and 'the social subject itself seems to dissolve in this dissemination of language games' (ibid.). Even science needs to have rules that prescribe what moves are admissible into its language game. These prescriptions are the same sorts of presuppositions that form the foundation of any language game.

Where would one draw a line, on this roughly arranged continuum of perspectives, to separate modern from postmodern given the blend of continuities and breaks that simultaneously link and separate each one from its neighbours? 'Modernism' and 'postmodernism' are not homogeneous or unambiguous facts, but only partially successful attempts to locate and define intellectual centres of gravity. Psychoanalysts looking to this epistemological debate, in their effort to assess their attitudes toward their own interpretations, must tolerate greater heterogeneity than they might have hoped to find.

Three faces of postmodernism

The modernity/postmodernity debate can be seen to fall into three realms, each of which must be fully considered when tracing the impact of postmodernity upon psychoanalytic theory and practice. First, there is the aesthetic debate over modernism and postmodernism, which concerns above all the nature of representation in the contemporary epoch. Postmodernism, in this particular sense, concerns a particular set of aesthetic or cultural values which were first given expression in the domains of architecture, the plastic and visual arts, poetry and literature. In contrast to the high modernist ambitions of uncovering an inner truth behind surface appearances, postmodernism exhibits a new playfulness, a mixing of previous aesthetic distinctions of content and form, high and low culture, the personal and public realms. The modernist attempt to discover a 'deeper' reality is abandoned in the postmodern in favour of the celebration of style and surface. The preoccupation of modernism with principles of meaning and rationality is replaced with a tolerance for diversity and difference, the characteristics of which are reflected in a postmodern criticism which values irony, cynicism, pastiche, commercialism and, in some cases, relativism (see Jameson, 1991). To portray the complexity of aesthetic surfaces and signs in the postmodern, Deleuze and Guattari (1977) invoke the metaphor of 'rhizome': a peculiar rootstock that is multidirectional, chaotic and random in its expansion. In this new aesthetic experience, postmodernism is a self-constituting world, determined by its own internal movement and process.

The second area of debate has focused on the philosophical and cultural concepts of modernity and postmodernity. Here it has been argued that a postmodern approach is necessary to avoid the realist assumptions of the Cartesian–Kantian–Hegelian tradition. Perhaps no other text has marked the intellectual terms of reference here as much as Lyotard's (1984) short treatise *The Postmodern Condition: A Report on Knowledge*. Postmodernism, writes Lyotard, 'designates the state of our culture following the transformations which, since the end of the nineteenth century, have altered the game rules for science, literature and the arts' (1984: xxv). The 'game rules' to which Lyotard refers involve a letting go of the grand narratives of traditional philosophy and science and an acceptance of the 'heteromorphous nature of language games'. Reason comes in many varieties. Two groups applying it effectively and adaptively to the same situation might well end up inventing, and living in, different Wittgensteinian language games without common ground rules. Here, the emphasis is away from forms of thought that promote uniformity and universality, and toward an appreciation of particularity, especially as regards the holding in mind of ambiguity and difference. Lyotard's position on postmodernism has been described as extreme in so far as it presents a radical separation of the nature of language games from their sociocultural context, and, as such, is said to threaten a complete fragmentation of subjectivity (see Norris (1993) and Eagleton (1990) for critical appraisals of Lyotard's late work).

As a result of postmodern theories of knowledge, there has been a profound questioning of foundationalism. Derrida (1978) argues that Western metaphysics is haunted by impossible dreams of certitude and transparency. Derrida, and the deconstructionism that his work has promoted, draws attention to the binary oppositions of textual practices and rhetorical strategies, using a poststructuralist conception of language as a differential play of signifiers to uncouple language from the world it seeks to colonize through acts of description. There will be in everything a writer writes or a patient says a contradiction that the author of the statement cannot acknowledge. As Stanley Fish (1989: 215) sums up the goals of a Derridean deconstructive reading, it will 'surface those contradictions and expose those suppressions'. As a result, such a reading will expose those ideas or feelings which have been suppressed (repressed or dissociated, we might add). These exposures 'trouble' the apparent unity of the text. We say that this unity has been defensively constructed. Deconstructivists say that such a unity was achieved in the first place 'only by covering over all the excluded emphases and interests that might threaten it'. According to Fish, Derridean deconstruction does not uncover these contradictions and dialectic hiding operations of rhetoric in order to reach 'the Truth; rather it continually uncovers the truth of rhetorical operations, the truth that all operations, including the operation of deconstruction itself, are rhetorical' (1989: 215). From this standpoint, there is no philosophical or ideological position that is able to claim *ultimate* authority or justification. On the contrary, the justification of knowledge, as the postmodern pragmatist Richard Rorty has argued, is always a matter of argumentation from different positions and perspectives, such that our beliefs about the world are necessarily local, provisional and contingent.

The third area of debate is concerned more explicitly with the personal, social and cultural aspects of postmodern society. Here the issue concerns the way in which postmodernity affects the world of human selves and of interpersonal relationships. And it is at the level of our personal and cultural worlds, we suggest, that postmodernism most forcefully breaks its links with the ontological premises of modernity. Here attention is focused on contemporary culture and its technologies, in particular the ways in which globalization and instantaneous communication is transforming self-identity and interpersonal relationships. Globalization, transnational communication systems, new information technologies, the industrialization of war, universal consumerism: these are core institutional dimensions of contemporary societies, and most students of contemporary culture agree that such transformations carry immense implications as regards selfhood, self-identity, and subjectivity (Frosh, 1991; Giddens, 1991; Thompson, 1990; Bauman, 1995; Elliott, 2001; Lemert, 1997). The transformation of personal experience that postmodernity ushers into existence concerns, among other things, a compression of space and mutation of time, rapid and at times cataclysmic forms of change, an exponential increase in the dynamism of social and economic life, as well as a growing sense of fragmentation and dislocation. Such transformations, to repeat, are not only social in character; on the contrary, they penetrate to the core of psychic experience and restructure unconscious transactions between human subjects in new, and often dramatic, ways.

It is from this flux and turmoil of contemporary social life that many commentators have branded postmodernity as anti-historical, relativist and disordered. Postmodernism, in this reading, represents the dislocation of meaning and logic, whether of society or of the mind. It is possible to hold a more optimistic view of this apparent cultural disorientation, however, once the irreducibility of the plurality of human worlds is accepted. The social theorist Zygmunt Bauman (1990, 1991, 1992, 1993, 2000, 2001), for example, argues that postmodernity represents a new dawning, rather than a twilight, for the generation of meaning. 'Postmodernity,' Bauman (1991: 35) writes, 'is marked by a view of the human world as irreducibly and irrevocably pluralistic, split into a multitude of sovereign units and sites of authority, with no horizontal or vertical order, either in actuality or in potency.' This emphasis on plurality and multiplicity highlights that postmodernity involves a rejection of the typically modernist search for foundations, absolutes and universals. Postmodernity is a self-constituting and self-propelling culture, a culture which is increasingly self-referential in direction. From cable TV to the information superhighway: postmodern culture is a culture turned back upon itself, generated in and through reflexive systems of technological knowledge.

The strength of Bauman's interpretation is that it demonstrates that modernity and postmodernity are not dichotomous. Culturally, we have not transcended modernity, nor have we entered a postmodern society writ large. Instead, it can be said that contemporary Western societies deploy modern and postmodern cultural forms simultaneously. Postmodernity, Bauman argues, is better understood as 'modernity without illusions'. It is a form of life, or indeed a state of mind, in which the messiness of life is directly embraced and dealt with as challenge. Pluralism, contingency, ambiguity, ambivalence, uncertainty: these features of social life were assigned a negative value – they were seen as pathologies to be eradicated – in the modern era. For Bauman, however, these are not distortions to be overcome, but are the distinctive features of a mode of social experience which has broken with the disabling hold of objectivity, necessity, law.

Thus, the picture that is being presented is that modernity and postmodernity are not homogeneous or unambiguous facts; nor are they dichotomous entities. Rather, as modes of contemporary experience, modernity and postmodernity locate and define cognitive-affective centres of gravity for individuals seeking to come to terms with the difficulties of day-to-day life. As a result, psychoanalysts looking to this epistemological debate, in their effort to assess their attitudes toward their own interpretations, must tolerate greater heterogeneity than they might have hoped to find.

In the following section of this chapter, two typically reductive critiques of the postmodern turn in psychoanalysis are considered. They are reductive in the sense that postmodernism is reduced to a single meaning, and thus the complexity of postmodernity is screened from view. It is argued, in contrast to much recent thinking on the subject, that there are indeed alliances between certain thinkers known in their own fields as postmodern and some contemporary psychoanalysts. It is also argued that, contrary to dominant assumptions concerning the inescapability of fragmentation, all but the most extreme forms of postmodernity permit an 'opening out' to reflective psychical activity, a space for the thinking or processing of uncertainty, ambivalence, otherness and difference. Similarly, although some postmodern thinking is relativistic, it is perspectivism and not relativism that is essential to postmodernism. Acknowledging the viability and plausibility of multiple perspectives does not consign one to accepting that any interpretation is as good as any other.

Postmodern psychoanalysis: two recent views

James Glass's critique of postmodern theorizing

In *Shattered Selves: Multiple Personality in a Postmodern World*, James Glass (1993) accepts that many of the objectivist ambitions of modernity should be renounced. He supports the postmodern critique of all-inclusive and dominating metanarratives, and he underscores the importance of recent French psychoanalytic feminist critiques of the phallocentric values and assumptions of modernity in promoting personal and political change in the contemporary epoch.

Glass, however, also sees a costly price tag on this postmodern agenda. If the identity of the self, as some postmodernists assert, following the French psychoanalyst Jacques Lacan, is imaginary – a kind of papering over of the indeterminacy of desire itself – then the human subject is fully desubjectivized. Such a brand of postmodernism, says Glass, isolates the self; he argues that in postmodernism there is nothing hidden or split off in psychological experience, nothing inaccessible to ideological explanation. This is perhaps a reasonable concern about Lacanian and similar brands of postmodernism, but since Glass assumes that postmodernism is homogeneous, he believes that all postmodernists carry this subject-destroying virus:

> In their insistence on freeing the self from any historical or structural conception of what the self is, the postmodernists reject, in coming to an understanding of what identity 'is,' the influence of infancy, the psychoanalytic notion of the preoedipal, the Freudian conception of the unconscious (drive theory), and the idea that actions of the self may be represented in severe forms of internal psychological conflict whose origins lie in primitive emotional symbolization.
>
> (1993: 5)

Postmodernist theories, in this reading, are not only attempting to destabilize modernist conceptions of subjectivity, meaning and truth, they are out to do away with the basic tensions or contradictions of self and world altogether. As a result they must all end up criticizing and rejecting everything modern in Freudian psychoanalysis: 'multiplicity of self' will lead to the psychological repudiation of difference and of language; the fragmentation idealized in the postmodernity discourse is really multiple personality disorder and schizophrenia; flux threatens the self, subjectivity and identity.

Finally, we are presented with a list of postmodern theorists, a list which includes Derrida, Lyotard, Baudrillard, Cixous, Irigaray and others (all quite different) who are all said to be indifferent to the harm or injury of psychological fragmentation as well as ignorant of the post-Freudian stress on relationality and intersubjectivity. (That some of these theorists have produced some of the most important critiques of psychoanalysis in France since the Second World

War is something that seems to have escaped Glass's attention, not to mention that some of them are practicing analysts.)

Kimberlyn Leary's critique of postmodern theorizing

For most clinicians questions about selves, subjects and truth become important insofar as they suggest options to be considered and decisions to be made in the analytic situation. Kimberlyn Leary, in her essay 'Psychoanalytic "Problems" and Postmodern "Solutions"' (1994), argued that 'postmodern solutions' suggest illusory answers to real clinical problems. She used the writings of Hoffman and Schafer as examples of postmodernism.

The 'implication that follows' from postmodern writings, Leary argues, 'is that we can, at will, assume a self that suits us if the proper audience can be assembled' (1994: 454). This is a hyperbolic rendering of the postmodern argument that, given a different social context, we might imagine people coming to have other senses of what it means to be a self than the sense they now have in our culture. This is especially the case, in that the postmodern deconstruction of subjectivity is precisely an attempt to criticize and rethink modernist notions of the will, intention, agency, and the like. Leary, however, argues that there is no difference between imagining that one might be whomever one wants to be if only the right audience could be assembled (or that one is only stuck being who one is because one has always had the wrong audience) and being diagnosable as borderline or narcissistic.

Before considering whether Schafer or Hoffman might be construed, from anything either has written, to have ever embraced a 'choose your own self' position, it is noted that, as many readers might have noticed, Leary's marriage of Hoffman and Schafer is itself problematic. She recognizes that there are significant differences between the various positions they take in their writings, and she details some of these. Yet, she cannot resist the temptation to conclude, after all, that, despite these differences, their theoretical projects are variations on the postmodern theme of relativism about truth and fragmentation of the self.

This lumping together of Hoffman and Schafer under the postmodern label glosses over the unique features of their quite different theories that are crucial if one wants to use them as examples of postmodern theorizing in psychoanalysis (and it also buries the modernist features of both men's work). Hoffman sees analysts' participation as a function of their subjectivity (countertransference, in the broadest sense). They will neither be aware nor want to be aware of every aspect of this unconscious subjectivity. Thus, they ought to remain (or realize that they are) more uncertain of what they mean and what they are doing than many analysts – of all the major schools – have been. If a patient claims to know or suspect something about the analyst's personality or experience, then the analyst does not necessarily affirm or deny, but shows interest in the patient's observations and wonders what conclusions the patient might draw from them.

Schafer, by contrast, emphasizes that the way in which the analyst understands and interprets is always partly a manifestation of the analyst's theory. He says little or nothing about the analyst's unconscious psychology. For example, Schafer (1992: 52) writes of a teacher, S. M., who 'derives pleasure from regularly treating his students cruelly'. In Freud's psychosexual language, the patient is sadistic. 'He, however, thinks that he treats his students fairly, dispassionately, professionally.' As Schafer points out, we, as analysts, along with many other observers, might conclude that he is deceiving himself. 'The attribution of self-deception is, however,' Schafer argues – and here is where he becomes postmodern – 'based on a number of unstated assumptions, interpretations, and evidential claims.'

> Far from this deception being an unmediated perception by an 'objective' observer of what S. M. is 'really' doing, it is a rather elaborate construction.
>
> (1992: 52)

> . . . it is the storylines that establish the facts of the case, which of these facts are to be taken as significant (for example, as evidence of sadism), and how these facts are to be situated. . . . The case of S. M. could be told differently; it often is.
>
> (1992: 55)

Yet as if in anticipation of critiques like Leary's, Schafer adds: 'I am not proposing that any account is as acceptable as any other.' What he does propose, in a hermeneutically postmodern argument, is that 'when we speak of true and false accounts of actions, we are positioning ourselves in a matrix of narratives that are always open to examination as to their precritical assumptions and values and as to their usefulness in one or another project' (1992: 56).

Where Schafer is interested in how the analyst's theory reshapes the patient's account of her or his history (which account is itself already one of many possible narratives), Hoffman talks about how the analyst chooses to shape the evolving relationship with the patient by doing or not doing, saying or not saying certain things at specific junctures. The analyst can no longer be certain that unwavering adherence to a specific technical stance (whether empathy or resistance analysis) simply serves to bring forth a clear picture of what has been inside the patient's psyche or guarantees the most effective route to what has been called structural change. Further, such unwavering adherence does not mean that the analyst is not deciding over and over to shape the analytic relationship in a specific way.

As an example of a specific decision he made in his own work, Hoffman (1994) reports that when he called an angry patient's internist during a session in response to the patient's demand that he do something immediately to help her get Valium, the

> enactment helped me and the patient to begin to see how much she wanted me to be frantic about her in a way similar to how she thought her mother

was frantic about [a sister], the difference being that my 'getting hysterical' was also an object of curiosity and critical reflection. Thus there was reason to believe that the quality of my attention, taken as a whole, was better than what either the patient or [the sister] got from their mother.

(1994: 212–13)

What Hoffman emphasizes here is his awareness that his choices are rooted in his subjectivity, which includes countertransference even when it is theoretically informed. The choice therefore invites critical reflection as to its meaning in the relationship. The countertransference is not condemned since the entire transference–countertransference enactment is an object of critical reflection.

Neither Schafer nor Hoffman has been implying that analysands have no enduring unconscious psychology, nor that people are an endless flow of abruptly appearing selves unrelated to each other in time and space. What each, in quite different ways, has argued at times is that his clinical observations have led him to think that one enduring feature of human unconscious psychology is a greater sense of discontinuity and contingency than was recognized by previous theories.

By the time Leary was ready to move from Hoffman and Schafer to the realms of body and gender, she was in high positivist and objectivist gears. Postmodernists, she says, forget that people have bodies and that these bodies come in male and female versions – an especially intriguing criticism, given that the contemporary focus on the body and its pleasures by the social sciences and the humanities is generally understood to have derived great impetus from postmodernism as a theoretical and political current (see Butler, 1993). Having forgotten this, they probably talk to their female patients as if these patients are free to forget those realities as well. Further, she suggests, postmodernists probably tell patients that death is just another version of life, just as they must believe that Terry Anderson could have made anything he wanted out of his captivity once he got past putting too much stock in treating as real such facts as his captors' controlling when he could use the toilet (Leary, 1994: 458).

Leary argues that Hoffman, after briefly considering it, gives up on the idea of an external reality. He does not. He simply argues that the variations of what we claim is out there are not constructed privately by each mind but by minds in interaction. Similarly, Hoffman's emphasis does not argue that every account of the analysand must be treated by the analyst as credible and tenable. He suggests a shift in technique in which the analyst is much more likely, than was once (in the history of psychoanalysis) the case, to treat as plausible that the patient did in fact evoke and then find some element of the analyst's experience (including unconscious experience) or behaviour on which to hang the enduring representation of a ragefully attacking other. Further, Hoffman nowhere says that he automatically agrees with his patients that everything they say about him is true. He portrays himself as doing exactly what Leary suggests analysts should do: he appreciates the patient's view of the analyst by more often treating it as plausible than theories of transference-as-distortion had encouraged us to do. He argues, however, that such appreciation has been crude when embedded by analysts in clear statements that while they appreciate the patient's infantile view of them, there is simply not a shred of current truth in it.

If an analyst was persuaded by Hoffman's writings and if that analyst gradually internalized a constructivist attitude, we might expect a shift to more often and more automatically considering the possibility that a patient's statement about the analyst's experience (including the analyst's unconscious experience) has captured something true not only about the analyst but also about the patient's ability to evoke experience in others and the patient's selective attention to certain aspects of the experience of others. Similarly, such an analyst might also feel more free to judge (out loud) the patient's assessments of the analyst's experience with the proviso that the analyst understands such judgements as arising out of subjective experience and as having the potential to contribute in part to the enactment of transference–countertransference patterns. What makes the difference in Hoffman's view is that the analyst appreciates that his or her judgement is born out of his or her full subjective participation in the process.

What is unfortunate about articles such as those by sceptics of 'postmodern psychoanalysis' like Glass and Leary is that they raise important issues about the psychical and social implications of postmodernism in such a divisive and dismissive way. Their respective critiques of the 'inescapable fragmentation' which postmodernity promotes does specify quite well a dilemma which psychoanalysts face today: the contemporary world is marked by constant turmoil and dislocation, yet to embrace the insights of postmodernism risks a further escalation of fragmentation itself – of knowledge, expertise and meaning.

Such an understanding of postmodernism, it is argued, is misplaced (even if the anxiety registered is expressive of a fear of 'not-knowing'). In fact, the critiques made by Glass and Leary are critiques that many postmodernists would make against the extreme forms of postmodernism that Glass and Leary set up for criticism. Leary, especially, having set things up this way, then simply claims that any non-positivist, non-objectivist theorist of the analytic process must, prima facie, be one of those extreme postmodernists; since she can see only those two places for a theorist to stand. Because, as noted, those points of view labelled as postmodern are heterogeneous, postmodernity permits other conceptual options than those imagined by Glass and Leary.

In the next two sections of this chapter, it is necessary to go beyond the specific arguments of Glass or Leary and take up two general categories of critique written against attempts to use postmodern discourse to reshape psychoanalytic theory: that it forces on us an untenable notion of the self as inescapably fragmented, and that it leaves us with no hope or even ambition of finding the truth about anything. In each case the aim is to show that these criticisms should not frighten away or deter interested analysts from pursuing the possibility that a study of postmodern ideas will enhance their clinical effectiveness. In considering each of these criticisms, distinctions between what is and what is not being said about selfhood and subjectivity in the postmodern discourse are offered. In brief, postmodern thought does not force upon us the notion that the self is incoherently fragmented (rather, it is decentred); and postmodern thought does not leave us lost in the belief that any interpretation is as good as any other (rather, all views are interpretive and perspectival).

The critique of 'inescapable fragmentation'

Postmodern conceptions of plural selves and worlds are informed, in broad terms, by the poststructuralist notion of the decentring of the subject. This is a decentring initiated by Freud himself, who suggested in the strongest theoretical terms that the ego is not master in its own house, and this is an insight that has been fruitfully extended by Lacan to include a focus on the creative and coercive effects of language.

The central point to note at this stage is that this decentring should not be equated with a disintegration of the human subject. The criticism that the postmodernist decentring of selves amounts to a wiping out of subjectivity is perhaps better seen as a defensive reaction to the dislocation of modernist fantasies of self-control and mastery. The postmodernist stress on ambiguity, ambivalence, difference, plurality and fragmentation, on the contrary, under-lines the psychical capacities and resources that are needed to register such forms of subjectivity, or, psychoanalytically speaking, to attach meaning to experience in open-ended ways.

Seen in this light, postmodern conceptions of multiple selves actually situate the subject in a context of heightened self-reflexivity, a reflectiveness that is used for exploring personal experience and fantasy. This intertwining of experience, fantasy and reflexivity is conceptualized in terms of the capacity to think about – that is, to symbolize and to process – unconscious communications in the interpersonal world, of projective and introjective identifications, splitting, denial, and the like. Broadly speaking, what is being stressed here is the prising open of a space between fantasy and words (the chain of significations) in which meaning is constituted, such that the subject can reflect upon this self-constitution and creatively alter it.

In some circumstances, of course, self-reflexivity is debilitating rather than emancipatory. An openness to multiple worlds of fantasy can produce extreme pain and anxiety, as well as a dislocation of the capacity of the mind to register thinking itself (Bion, 1962; Ogden, 1989b). In general terms though, and in a diversity of contexts, it produces the contrary: an 'opening out' to the multiplicity of fantasy and imagination at the intersection of self and world. This is conceptualized, as we will examine later in this chapter, in differing ways by postmodern analysts. Cornelius Castoriadis speaks of a self-understanding of 'radical imagination', Julia Kristeva of 'semiotic subversion', and Christopher Bollas of our 'personal idiom'. This focus highlights a reflexive awareness of imagination, and of the key role of ambivalence, difference and otherness in human relations.

Criticisms of the postmodern collapse of signification

What about 'reality' and 'truth'? Some critics of postmodernism have reached the erroneous conclusion that so-called hermeneutic, relational, deconstructionist, intersubjective, or constructivist perspectives imply that the conditions of interpretation are such that no true or correct interpretations are possible – a position that some philosophers (Bohman, 1991) label 'interpretive skepticism' (136) or 'strong holism' (130). These terms refer to the arguments by certain postmodern thinkers that all cognitive activity is interpretive and so warrants deep scepticism and that it is holistic in the sense of always taking place against the background of all our beliefs and practices. 'Together these two theses imply that no interpretation can be singled out as uniquely correct, since the assertion that it is so would itself be an interpretation within a particular context' (Bohman, 1991: 130) – the so-called hermeneutic circle.

A number of philosophers and literary critics have strongly identified with this epistemological claim while others have partially or moderately embraced it at times in their writings. We do not, however, believe that postmodern analysts have to embrace this strongly sceptical and strongly holistic position on interpretation. To varying degrees Schafer and Hoffman (who are as much modern as postmodern), along with other analysts who work within the modern/postmodern dialectic, seem to agree that interpretation is indeterminate and perspectival, while also maintaining that interpretations can produce revisable, shared knowledge based on identifiable evidence. Thus, in the clinical situation a postmodern attitude does nothing so radical as to force the abandonment of the quest for truth about the patient's unconscious psychology. It does, however, question and make problematic any rigidly modernist pursuit of this truth. Consider, for example, this clinical event:

> A 25-year-old woman fell silent after I made an interpretation. After a few minutes, she said she felt my voice was too 'insistent,' and she became silent again.
>
> (Busch, 1995: 47)

One could easily imagine any analyst influenced by postmodern trends asking the patient to tell him or her about his or her insistence. Busch almost does that, but the contrast is vital. He reports: 'I immediately recognized what she was responding to' (1995: 47). Postmodernism would urge a little less certainty about what the patient was responding to until the patient had a chance to elaborate (or associate to) her representation of the analyst as too insistent.

What happens next is, at first, a bit confusing. We might expect that Busch would tell us, the readers, what it was that he immediately recognized; but he only tells us that the 'interpretation was one that I had speculated about for some time, and the analysand's associations confirmed it in a way that she seemed ready to understand' (1995: 47). We read this in two ways. First Busch wants us to know that he has waited until the patient was already saying whatever it was he told her in the interpretation she claimed he made too insistently. Second, he wants us to know that he was not speculating about the unconscious wishes that make her anxious. This matters because in most of his writings Busch identifies himself as working along the lines suggested by Paul Gray, and Gray has made it clear throughout his writings that he does not think analysts should do that sort of speculating about what *absent content* catalyses defences – just interpret resistance, especially in the form of superego projections onto the analyst, and the patient will get to the anxiety that triggers the resistance and the sexual excitement or rage that triggers the anxiety. Busch has to make this apologetic because sooner or later he will say something about that *absent content*, and he does not want to emphasize the subjective nature of the judgement call involved in deciding when one is simply pointing to it in the patient's associations and when one is getting it from one's own thought. Like Leary, he wants there to be a ground in the data of the patient's associations upon which we stand free of constructions or narratives.

Having made these points, Busch then tells us that what he immediately recognized was that he, too, thought there had been a shift from his more questioning voice to another kind of voice. It is crucial here, however, that he does not label that new voice. It is hard to imagine that he does not have a label for it in his mind, just as the patient has the label 'too insistent' attached to it in hers. He does, after all, have a label for the voice he shifted from: it was 'questioning'. What a postmodern analyst might say at this point is that Busch has his shift in voice constructed one way in his mind and the patient has it constructed in another. How can Busch be so positive (as in positivistic) that her construction ('too insistent') is wrong? This does not mean that Hoffman or Schafer thinks every construction is as plausible here as any other, simply that if Busch shifted from questioning to telling or from questioning to asserting, there is a range of constructions that might make sense of what he had done.

What Busch does next is return to his questioning voice. A bit later in his article he complains that object relational analysts, whom he believes he is critiquing in his essay, might simply 'turn down the volume' of their voice to make the patient feel safe, so we assume he wants us to understand that, while he too did that, he also did more. No object relational analyst whose work we have read has suggested that if the patient complains about something we are doing, we simply stop doing it and do not try to work with the patient to understand the complaint.

What matters here is that Busch, too, changed his voice but attributes little or no significance to this as influencing what happens next. Further complicating things, his lack of attention to how he is participating in constructing this complex relational event with his patient allows him to say simply in passing that the first thing he did after returning to his *questioning* voice was to *tell* her something: that he could see how she heard his voice as 'different'. Finally, he has been forced to do what we have been suggesting, from a postmodern perspective, cannot be avoided: he tells us how he has constructed his changing of his voice. He has applied the word 'different' to it. He will implicitly claim that anything more descriptive than that is entirely the patient's resistance. We believe that this is precisely the sort of clinical work, in counterpoint to which theories such as Hoffman's stand. Leary's use of the extreme example of a patient's claiming the analyst is always ragefully attacking her, when he has never overtly done so, masked this problem of the clinical position her stance implies.

What critics of postmodernism such as Glass and Leary fail to do

Some of the most important changes taking place in postmodern culture concern the restructuring of emotional relationships, sexuality, intimacy, gender and love (Beck and Beck-Gernsheim, 1995; Giddens, 1992). In the light of the postmodernist critique of the grand narratives of Western rationality, how can psychoanalysts rethink the relationship between subjectivity, unconscious desire, and interpersonal processes? (For an extended treatment of these issues, see Elliott, 1999.)

Critiques such as those of Glass and Leary, in our opinion, occlude the epistemological interest of postmodernism in psychoanalysis. That is, they fail to deal with what is most important and significant in the postmodernity debate as regards psychoanalysis.

Glass focuses on the work of Michel Foucault and his thesis that 'subject positions' are determined by networks of power/knowledge relations. He then makes the criticism – quite rightly against Foucault – that the unconscious and libidinal desires are rendered mere products of wider social forces, of power and knowledge. But the critical point here is that this is not a criticism of postmodernism: Foucault was not a postmodernist, and in fact rejected the notion of a transition from modernity to postmodernity (see Macey, 1993).

Leary makes use of the term 'postmodern' to marginalize the potential usefulness to analysts of the theorizing of Hoffman and Schafer (rather than, say, showing how their clinical work links them to specific modern or postmodern thinkers). She then implies that because they are postmodern, they would be inclined to do various absurd things during analytic hours. Her suggestion – that if we consider Schafer and Hoffman as gadflies for positivistically inclined analysts (rather than purveyors of clinical theories of their own), then maybe they are useful after all – hardly mitigates her previous severe criticizing of them, which is based on having first linked them, via labelling them 'postmodern', with total fragmentation of the self and total relativism in the assignment of meaning to experience.

Postmodernity and psychoanalytic heterogeneity

Whereas Glass and Leary proceed by bundling very divergent postmodern social theories together and then developing a negative assessment of this shift in thinking as regards psychoanalysis as a discipline, we propose a different tack.

In our opinion, it is too simple, and indeed erroneous, to imagine that divergent postmodern theories can either be imported into, or excluded from, psychoanalysis at the level of theory as well as the level of clinical practice. Such an approach treats the very nature of psychoanalytic thought as something that develops outside of our general culture. That thing known as 'postmodernism' appears as something that does not really affect the structure of mind; and if its conceptual and practical implications seem a little too threatening, then it is something that psychoanalysis would also do well to avoid. Postmodernity and psychoanalysis, in this reading, have absolutely nothing to do with each other, unless it is decided otherwise by the psychoanalytic community at some point when the profession might more actively consider a radical change in its system of beliefs.

In our view, the development of psychoanalysis is not so self-contained. On the contrary, recent trends in psychoanalysis indicate a transformation in theorizing as regards subjectivity, the status of the unconscious, the nature of intersubjectivity, and of thinking in terms of what analyst and patient know about themselves and each other (Elliott and Frosh, 1995; Mitchell, 1993; Spezzano, 1993). Such changes in theorizing take many forms throughout contemporary psychoanalytic literature, and it is a central aspect of our argument that this direction in psychoanalytic theorizing is part of our postmodern world-view.

Consider, for example, the question of epistemology. In traditional psychoanalysis, practitioners tended to pride themselves on their knowledge of the unconscious as a distinct psychical system. The unconscious, having been fully explored and colonized by Freud, was seen as a realm of mind that can be known and subsequently placed under rational control, once patient and analyst are brave enough to face sexual repression and its difficulty. In post-Freudian psychoanalysis, however, there is a range of approaches to thinking of the unconscious and the anxiety-provoking nature of desire, which generally displace this emphasis on certitude toward more open-ended forms of knowledge and of experience. Indeed, the capacity to tolerate periods of 'not-knowing', at both subjective and theoretical levels is positively valued in some contemporary versions of psychoanalysis (see Hoffman, 1987; Ogden, 1989b).

Here the focus is on a suspension of preconceived thoughts and beliefs, coupled with the intersubjective exploration of fantasy and desire. Human knowledge is no longer understood as being subject to singular, rationalistic control (once the secrets of the unconscious are unlocked); on the contrary, knowledge is regarded as perspectival and decentred. Knowledge, of the self and of others, is discovered, according to Winnicott, in that 'transitional space' of intermediate experience; the connections between subjectivity and truth unfold at the margins of thinking and in intersubjective reverie, according to Bion; and fantasy is embedded in human relationships through a dialectical interplay of paranoid-schizoid and depressive positions of generating experience, according to Klein. We mention Winnicott, Bion, and Klein in this context to highlight the beginnings of that psychoanalytic shift away from understanding knowledge as rationality and control. The point is not that any of these psycho-analysts may, at the current historical juncture, be reread as 'postmodern'. Rather, the point is that the development of psychoanalytic theory, to which their contributions are seminal, at once contributes to and reflects our postmodern world-view and culture.

Many psychoanalysts have been contributing to a shift away from realist aspirations or impersonal objectivity. They have rejected the traditional view that the clearest form of understanding occurs when secondary-process thinking is separated out from the unconscious fantasy. Instead, they pay explicit atten-tion to the creative power of human imagination as regards issues of subjectivity, intersubjectivity, truth, desire, fantasy and personal meaning, and authenticity. As Stephen Mitchell (1993: 21) summarizes this rescaffolding of the discipline:

> What is inspiring about psychoanalysis today is not the renunciation of illusion in the hope of joining a common, progressively realistic knowledge and control, but rather the hope of fashioning a personal reality that feels authentic and enriching. . . . The hope inspired by psychoanalysis in our time is grounded in personal meaning, not rational consensus. The bridge supporting connections with others is not built out of a rationality superseding fantasy and the imagination, but out of feelings experienced as real, authentic, generated from the inside, rather than imposed externally, in close relationship with fantasy and the imagination.

It is this explicit attention given to fantasy and the imagination that, in our opinion, helps to define the stakes of contemporary psychoanalysis. The stakes are necessarily high if only because no one knows with any degree of certainty how, and with what success, contemporary selves and societies will frame meaning and truth based on an appreciation of the ambivalence, ambiguity and plurality of human experience.

All of this raises the thorny question: has psychoanalysis, whether it likes it or not, become postmodern? Is there such a thing as 'postmodern psycho-analysis'? To this, we would respond with a qualified 'yes'; save that the issue cannot really be understood adequately if put in such terms. To grasp the trajectories of psychoanalysis today, we suggest, it is necessary to understand that the self-reflexivity which psychoanalysis uncovers and promotes (and which, according to Jürgen Habermas [1968], is Freud's central discovery) is radicalized and transformed in postmodern culture. With the eclipse of custom and tradition as embedded in modernity, the relationship between self and society becomes self-referential in postmodern times. Without the binding cultural, symbolic norms of modernity in arenas such as sexuality, love, relation-ships, gender and work, people become increasingly aware of the contingency of the self, of relationships, and of society itself. They also become profoundly aware of the contingency of meaning and of the sign; they see that meaning is not fixed once and for all, but rather that signification is creatively made and remade by desire-and-anxiety-driven human relationships. In this sense, postmodern culture can be said to directly incorporate certain core insights of psychoanalysis into its framing assumptions, especially as concerns the role of fantasy as being at the root of our traffic with social meaning. (For a detailed discussion of the intricate connections between postmodernity and psycho-analysis see Elliott, 1996.)

There are strong indications that this cultural self-awareness of contingency, ambivalence, and plurality – key features of the postmodern world-view – are theorized in contemporary psychoanalytic dialogues. In contemporary psychoanalysis, in the work of its most radical clinicians and theoreticians, the subjectivity of the self is approached as comprising multivalent psychical forms, embedded in a field of interpersonal relationships, and in close connection with unconscious fantasy. In recent years, such writers as Castoriadis, Kristeva, Anzieu, Ogden and Bollas have radically reconceptualized the nature of psychic processing, and in particular of the constitution of psychic meanings. It is beyond the scope of this chapter to discuss in any detail the specific contri-butions of these authors, or of the significant conceptual differences between their approaches to psychoanalysis. However, some of the common threads in their visions of psychoanalysis, and of their understandings of psychic constitution and meaning, will be briefly touched on here, in order to draw out the wider cultural links to postmodernism.

Cornelius Castoriadis (1987, 1995) theorizes subjectivity in terms of a 'radical imaginary', by which he means an unconscious architecture of representations, drives, and affects in and through which psychic space is constituted and perpetuated. The precondition for the self-reflection upon subjectivity, says Castoriadis, is fantasy: the capacity of the psyche to posit figuration *ex nihilo*. 'The original narcissistic cathexis or investment,' he writes, 'is necessarily representation . . . (otherwise it would not be psychical) and it can then be nothing other than a "representation" (unimaginable and unrepresentable for us) of the Self' (1987: 287).

In Castoriadis's reading of Freud, the unconscious is not so much the psychic depository of that which cannot be held in consciousness, but rather the essential psychical flux which underpins all representations of the self, of others, and of the social and cultural world. Such psychical flux, necessarily plural, multiple and discontinuous, is that which renders identity non-identical with itself, as Adorno would have it, or, in more psychoanalytic terms, it is that which means that every self-representation is intrinsically incomplete and lacking since the subject arises from a primary loss which remains traumatic at the level of the unconscious. Here Castoriadis's emphasis on the radically imaginary dimensions of self and society parallels the postmodernist stress on the demise of external foundations as an anchoring mechanism for thought, and his stress on psychical flux mirrors certain postmodernist themes which highlight the ambiguity, ambivalence, and radical otherness of contemporary social life.

So too Kristeva (1984, 1989) underscores the profoundly imaginary dimen-sions of unconscious experience in terms of her notion of the 'semiotic', a realm of prelinguistic experience (including drives, affects and primal rhythms) which is necessarily prior to symbolic representation and entry into cultural processes. Seeking to account for an internally disruptive presence as regards the space of the Other in Lacanian psychoanalysis, Kristeva argues that contemporary psychoanalysis is increasingly concerned with the complexities of semiotic displacement, or unconscious rupture, as that point of otherness which derails symbolism and intersubjectivity. One way of understanding Kristeva's reconceptualization of the unconscious in post-Lacanian theory is as an explicit attempt to account for the multiplication of fantasy (and of multiple selves) in its trading with received social meanings, or external reality.

Extending Kristeva, I (1995) argue that this multiplication of fantasy is underlined by a 'representational wrapping of self and other', a preliminary ordering of pre-self experience, otherness and difference. Such wrapping lies at the core of intersubjective space – indeed it is the unconscious investment in the shapes, textures, surfaces and pre-objects that comprise psychic space itself – and it functions as a kind of perpetual self-constitution, or what is termed 'rolling identification' (1995: 45–7). In a Kleinian vein, Thomas Ogden (1989b) also speaks of such a preliminary ordering of pre-object relations as the 'autistic-contiguous mode of generating experience' (1989b: 30), the sensory floor of psychic space which underlies paranoid-schizoid and depressive processes.

Along similar lines, Anzieu (1985) links fantasy and interpersonal experience with the notion of a 'skin ego', an imaginary registration of maternal holding. Influenced by Klein and Winnicott, Anzieu argues that the skin ego is constituted in relation to maternal bodily experiences, a contact from which the beginning separation of inner and outer worlds takes place through introjective and projective identification. The skin ego is thus a kind of 'containing envelope' for the holding of emotional states in fantasy, from which human experience can become known, symbolized and developed. So too Bollas (1992) argues that selfhood is generated in and through our 'personal idiom', a psychical grid (or unconscious space) between experience and fantasy.

In the preceding accounts, psychical life is portrayed as a non-linear movement of fantasies, containers, introjects, representational wrappings, semiotic sensations, envelopes and memories. Such a focus has much in common with postmodernist theory insofar as the radical imagination of the psyche is treated as central to the constitution and reproduction of subjectivity; a self-reflexive subjectivity. This is not to say, however, that the subject of contemporary psychoanalysis is without grounding, set adrift within the logics of disintegration. On the contrary, the multivalent psychical forms of contemporary selves are said to be patterned in and through an interpersonal field of interactions with significant others, theorized variously as the Lacanian Symbolic Order, the Kleinian depressive position, or social imaginary significations.

Beyond hermeneutics and constructivism

The hermeneutic and constructivist perspectives of Hoffman and Schafer are not the whole story of a 'postmodern turn' in psychoanalysis. We emphasized their work because authors such as Leary (1994) and Glass (1993) had risked leaving an impression that might easily limit interest not only in the important work of these two analysts but also in anything else associated with post-modernism. As we argued above, psychoanalysts cannot remain impervious to the postmodern ideas swirling around them – any more than any domain of twentieth century Western thought was able to decide not to be bothered by psychoanalysis.

Psychoanalysts believed, for most of this century, that we could choose not to study outside our discipline. We needed only to master our techniques and theories. Then came a period of time during which some analysts looked to philosophy, neuropsychology, infant research, or literary criticism to adjudicate our theoretical and clinical debates. Leary's essay, although we disputed it, might be treated as a harbinger of a third phase in the relationship between psychoanalysis and other disciplines. In this emerging third phase, we would neither ignore nor annex ideas from, say, contemporary philosophy. Instead, we would recognize that as broad cultural shifts occur in our way of viewing the human condition (and in our way of understanding our ways of viewing the human condition), then psychoanalysis will both contribute to and be moved by these shifts. As a result we would understand that we are thrown into relationships with activities in other disciplines – from rereadings of Hegel to studies of affect and intersubjectivity by neuropsychologists and infant researchers – through which psychoanalysis (clinical and applied) both reacts to and shapes the human world.

6 Social theory, psychoanalysis and the politics of postmodernity

Anthony Elliott talks with Sean Homer

SH: Let me begin with a rather broad question. Your work is situated in the interstices of psychoanalysis, politics and sociology; what is the importance of psychoanalysis to these other two disciplines?

AE: As a first approximation, psychoanalysis is of core importance to sociology and politics, or social and political theory, in terms of providing an enriched account of subjectivity, agency and the human agent. Now the model against which classical social theory took its cue was primarily from economic conceptualizations of action. Utilitarian norms of maximizing or minimizing behavioural/economic risks dominated, and still do in such approaches as rational choice theory. Parsons' critique of economistic modes of sociological thought is important because he stresses so clearly the role of values and norms in the constitution of the acting self. Parsons is also interesting since he was one of the first major sociologists in the US to deploy psychoanalysis for rethinking agency and the agent. The sociological tradition represented by, say, Anthony Giddens (structuration theory) and Jürgen Habermas (communications theory) has similarly drawn from Freud and psychoanalysis to rethink agency, but usually in partial and limited ways: Giddens for a residual account of the unconscious as the other side of discursive and practical consciousness, and Habermas mostly in methodological terms.

There are of course other important sociological thinkers that should be mentioned here, including Marcuse and Adorno, but the point is that sociology and politics as disciplines have for the most part used only very partial and restrictive accounts of the unconscious in social relations. This is a matter of some social-theoretical and cultural-political importance, since as Freud so strongly emphasized the unconscious continually disrupts reason-dictated rules and regulations. That's to say, you can't really have a residual use of the unconscious – in the manner, say, that Giddens invokes at the level of ontology, and that Habermas invokes at the level of epistemology. Once you admit a space for unconscious processes it becomes evident, I think, that these processes affect not only social relationships and contemporary culture but also all attempts at conceptualization. The unconscious, in effect, plays tricks with cognitive, conceptual, and all theoretical/poetic forms of thinking. This isn't a new insight of course. If you look at Freud's writings throughout his career, it is evident why he needed to revise his conceptual schemes and topographies or mappings of the mind, the reason being that every time he thought he had circumscribed the operations of the unconscious he subsequently discovered the unconscious at work, invading other spheres of psychic life that he had held to be free of such influence.

A reading of the importance of Freud for sociology and politics – as I tried to do in my *Social Theory and Psychoanalysis in Transition* (1992, second edition 1999) and *Psychoanalytic Theory: An Introduction* (1994, second edition 2002) – is of basic importance to reworking the concepts of agent, agency and action in the social sciences and social theory. My argument, bluntly put, is that we can find in Freud a radical account of the creativity of the psyche, an account that can be used to theorize the role of human creation and innovation in society, history and politics. When I speak of creation I refer to its constitution, reproduction and transformation in the strongest sense. That is, the creation of fantasy, representation, symbol, affect. Human creation, as I have argued at length, operates on the level of the singular individual subject and at the level of society and institutions. Trying to think through what this creativity of the psyche and of radical imagination means in the aftermath of our era's obsession with the 'death of man', 'end of history', and 'decentring of the subject', is a principle objective of my social/theoretical work. From this angle, while I have engaged with Lacanian-orientated social theory, and the currents of post-structuralism and postmodernism more generally, I argue that the decentring of the subject need not be made equivalent to the person's disappearance in social analysis. This differentiates my position in important, substantive ways, I think, from many working in psychoanalytically-orientated social theory.

Now, at a deeper level, psychoanalysis is also of crucial significance to sociology and politics, not simply for rethinking subjectivity and agency, but for reassessing both the object of study, namely society, the social, or politics and the political, as well as for self-reflection upon these disciplinary positions. Psychoanalysis in the reading I am undertaking highlights the fantasmatic dimension of cultural practices, social institutions, political norms, and the like. This takes us directly into immense conceptual problematics of the relationship of the psyche and social (not the individual and society, as Habermas and others have wrongly asserted). The opposition between the individual and society is, in a strictly psychoanalytical sense, meaningless. For the individual is on the side of the social – the self is a social/historical construction through and through: as Foucault rightly asserts. The psyche, obviously, plays a fundamental role in this process of construction (something Foucault simply fails to grant): the psyche invests, images, represents, and transfigures the raw social materials that it finds at its disposal.

SH: You say that psychoanalysis is important for your work in two key respects
   – it provides us with a theory of subjectivity or agency and it raises the question, or more accurately poses the problem of the relationship of the psyche
   and the social. Let me leave to one side the question of the psyche for
   the time being and address the first of these issues. You have argued, quite
   rightly I think, that the deployment of psychoanalysis by previous
   generations of social theorists has been rather one-sided and partial; in
   your early books in particular you have countered this approach through
   a reading of Freud and, just as importantly I think, Cornelius Castoriadis.
   Could you say something about the significance of Castoriadis on your
   reading of Freud and in particular to the creative potential of subjectivity
   and human agency?

   You also say that what differentiates you from Lacanian approaches
   to social theory is that the subject does not completely disappear in your
   work and in the books you mention, *Social Theory and Psychoanalysis in
   Transition* and *Psychoanalytic Theory: An Introduction* you take a very critical
   position in relation to Lacanian theory. In a more recent book, however –
   Subject to Ourselves – I thought I detected a much more sympathetic view of
   Lacanianism, especially in relation to its account of the fragmentation
   of the subject within postmodernity. Is this a fair reading of your work?

AE: First, my interest in Castoriadis developed from his critique of Lacan's
   mirror stage, and also his broader critique of Lacanian practice. Castoriadis's
   split from the Lacanian *Ecole freudienne* led to the establishment of the
   'Fourth Group' in Paris, which developed the philosophical position that
   psychoanalysis is a practical-poetic activity which involves second-order
   reflections on human imagination in the search and struggle for autonomy.
   Now Castoriadis's critique of Lacan is crucial to my work because it permits
   a shift away from the Lacanian obsession with the scopic – Lacan always
   tends to equate the imaginary with the image, the visual, the optical. By
   contrast, Castoriadis argues that the imaginary is the capacity to create
   something that is not the 'real', such as common perception. The psyche
   in this viewpoint is the endless creation of a world for itself, which at one
   stroke puts Castoriadis at odds with the manner in which imagination
   has been deployed in its inherited sense, and especially from Husserl's
   and Heidegger's sense of imagination. Of key importance is Castoriadis's
   opposition to Lacan's fixation on the scopic; he instead says that the radical
   imaginary is principally kinetic, auditory and rhythmic. This of course
   comes close to what neo-Lacanians such as Kristeva have been arguing
   for some time. But I think the importance of Castoriadis's reading of Freud
   is that it returns us, with full force, to the problem of representation and
   affect – a problem which Kristeva and others coming to psychoanalysis
   from linguistics have not been able to satisfactorily elucidate.

   The relevance of Castoriadis's account of radical imagination is of the
   utmost importance to rethinking the state of the subject in the aftermath
   of the post-structuralist decentring of subjectivity. I have used Castoriadis's

philosophy in my own work to elaborate a conception of self-identity in which agency and being are understood as a surging forth of the creative – which, incidentally, has nothing to do with the Californian cult of creativity which Foucault so much despised. The creativity of the psyche is unhinged from ethics and morality; the interweaving of unconscious representation, drive and affect can give rise to inventive social forms and institutions (the United Nations, Amnesty International, the International Society of Psychoanalysts for Nuclear Disarmament, etc.) or to destructive, schizo-pathological ones (Auschwitz, Stalinism, Pol Pot, etc.). The issue of the social and political structuring of unconscious mental activity however must be situated on another plane altogether. This is one of the most vexing and difficult issues of contemporary theory and politics.

As to your second question, you rightly detect a different response to Lacanian theory in my *Subject to Ourselves*. The reasons being that I was concerned there to analyse different relational configurations with reference to modernity and postmodernity. Now it so happens that much of the more interesting work that's been done on postmodernism in psychoanalysis has taken a Lacanian direction. For that reason, I wanted to take up on that work and view it through a slightly different optic. My doing so in no way led me to change my views on the philosophical and political limitations of Lacan's teaching, the so-called 'return to Freud'.

I guess what I wanted to do was to try to show that late capitalism requires, and indeed instantiates, both modernist and postmodernist relational configurations of subjectivity. That is, Lacanian postmodernists are wrong to say that fragmentation, lack and dislocation define the subject *in toto* in the postmodern. It is true that the culture of simulation and globalization promotes fragmentation up to a point, and well beyond the confines of modernity. But the point is that the current social order requires a subject that continually shifts between centring and decentring, integration and fragmentation. The state of the subject is thus complex, contradictory and conflictual.

SH: I agree with what you say about the status of the subject within a postmodern world and my argument with enthusiasts of Deleuze and Guattari, for example, is that schizoid fragmentation and nomadic subjectivity is precisely what late capitalism requires today. Globalization and what Castells has called the network society, or the informational age, requires just those kinds of decentred and mobile subjects the postmodernists celebrate. I can see nothing, therefore, as inherently radical in the celebration of fragmentation as this merely legitimates the present state of affairs.

My difficulty with Castoriadis' work here is that I also do not see the kind of 'autonomy' that he speaks about as a viable possibility today. Now I think you address this when you say that postmodernism instantiates both modernist and postmodernist forms of subjectivity but my question is what confers upon the subject a degree of consistency to resist the fragmentation of a globalized, informational economy? I am perhaps less certain here than you are of the possibilities of integration and what you have called hyper-reflexivity in the postmodern era.

AE: Yes, I agree with much of what you say. Although the division between the centred, unified human subject of market capitalism and the dispersed, fragmented self of monopoly capitalism surely isn't clear cut. Nomadic subjectivity and psychic fragmentation, in its various forms, clearly says something about the late capitalist economy itself – although what this 'something' is has been handled poorly in many strands of contemporary theory, especially Lacanian and deconstructionist theory. I say poorly since, while psychic dispersal, fragmentation, schizoid and paranoid modes of generating experience are ideologically essential to processes of post-modernization, the more centred and reflective – and hence depressive – modes of generating experience are equally demanded for the reproduction of the socio-symbolic orders of the political system itself. This is why I argue that postmodernists such as Baudrillard, Virilio and Lyotard are best approached as providing an angle on one key mode of psychic experience in conditions of late modernity. Try going to work, going out with friends to the pub, or writing a cheque to assist refugees in Albania in the 'modes' of fragmentation and dispersal that many postmodernists celebrate, and you'll quickly discover it can't be done. Our immersion in everyday life – what people do in their day-to-day practical lives – is constituted to its roots in dialectical relations of consciousness and unconscious, practical agency and non-conscious properties of psychic processing.

So what I'm suggesting is that the simplistic antithesis raised about subjectivity in the debate over modernity and postmodernity is bound to overlook the internal complexity of the psyche. I think this happens, in part, because it has become very fashionable to dismiss discussion about autonomy in various debates occurring in the social sciences and the humanities. In our postmodern age of anxiety, intellectuals seem to have a knee-jerk reaction against analysing the reflective and reflexive forms of agency that subjects produce and reproduce in their everyday actions. There are of course exceptions to this. One only has to think of the work of Pierre Bourdieu and Anthony Giddens in sociology, Julia Kristeva, Jessica Benjamin and Thomas Ogden in psychoanalysis, and – as you say – the late writings of Castoriadis. Castoriadis is especially interesting on the issue of autonomy, I think, since he so radically questioned and subverted the notion of the centred, autonomous human subject of liberal political theory, while wanting to keep open a space for the notion of autonomy in his theorization of the conscious/unconscious duality at the level of the psyche and the individual subject. As he points out continually throughout his mature writings, to speak of autonomy at the level of the psyche is not to speak of the well adjusted self, or of 'the Californian cult of the self' (Foucault). Rather autonomy, in the view of Castoriadis, concerns the interplay between consciousness and unconsciousness – the communication between these two psychic strata – in the reflective deliberations of the individual subject. Such a formulation raises complex issues about repression at the psychic level, and also issues about the ideal of personal identity and selfhood promoted by cultural processes and upheld at the level of the socialization of the psyche. They are complex because they go to the heart of the question of autonomy, and also necessarily of the project for collective autonomy of which Castoriadis said so much. I think it is important, however, to bracket issues of social institutions and cultural forms for thinking through the reflective constitution of the subject, at least on an analytical level. So I'm not sure the issue of modernity/postmodernity is one that I would bring in at this stage. I also think it is not a matter of talk about 'consistency'. The psychoanalytical account of the subject that I develop in my work is one that does away with notions of consistency and of unity; it is an account which instead stresses the decentring of the self from subjectivity, the radical nature of imagination and fantasy, and the reflective capabilities of the subject in the weaving together of consciousness and unconsciousness in everyday life. I am speaking, of course, of the minimum requirements that Freud and psychoanalysts posit for therapy: the capacity of the subject to put something into question, to bracket and hold or tolerate their representational and affective activity, and thus the transformation of the relation between consciousness and unconsciousness. One needs also to consider issues of severe schizoid processing, autism and the like, but these are other matters.

SH: Now this is where I think you see the centrality of Castoriadis' notion of radical imagination, but as you point out unconscious representation, or fantasy, can give rise to either the UN or Auschwitz. So in what sense do you see the usefulness of fantasy, to use Žižek's phrase, as a political category?

AE: I am not very sympathetic to Žižek's 'theory' of fantasy as a political category, if only because fantasy is not a 'category' and I don't think it can be talked about in terms of usefulness. In *Social Theory and Psychoanalysis in Transition*, I argued that Žižek's 'return to Lacan' was no more and no less than sheer academic noise. The notion of fantasy as concealment of a constitutive 'lack' or 'void' or 'gap' is only one way of conceptualizing the constitution of fantasy, and even then the Lacanian account is misguided since it can provide no proper grasp of the relation of the 'subject of the unconscious' from the imaginary realm (misrecognition) of the speaking subject. (The imaginary is not created through the reflecting surface of the mirror; the mirror itself is the work of fantasization.) I have written about this extensively, and I have found nothing in the views of some of my critics that might lead me to alter my critique of Lacanian theory.

I give much more weight to Castoriadis's rereading of Freud because he makes explicit much of what traditional psychoanalysis was trying to get at: the radically imaginary dimensions of human subjectivity and of culture. It is when Freud speaks of the small infant as having 'created an object out of the mother' that we come close to grasping the radical imagination of the psyche. Imagination, and its dissimulation in fantasy, involves a configuration of representational and affective elements – elements that at a single stroke create and define identity, otherness and their relational mode to culture and institutions. Through thinking and in thought individuals create representations, elaborate figures, modes of affectivity and the like. Imagination is thus tied to ontological creation. In more detail, imaginary creation takes place within the context of given horizons, yet the 'given' is itself created (i.e. creation has a relationship to what has already been created, which can now be seen in the debate, for example, over post-traditional forms of life in current sociology), figured and refigured as part of that process known as the constitution and reproduction of society. As you say, creation, as part of our history, can be Beethoven, the Beatles, the democratization of daily life and intimacy, and it can equally infuse political corruption, the Gulag and global warming. However, it makes no sense in this context to talk of fantasy as a 'political category'. For the moment that one tries to inject a formula like 'the personal is political', the radical dimensions of imagination and imaginary creation are lost from view. The social-historical world, in its creation of misery and destruction, is not something that can be 'deconstructed', 'dispersed by the Real', or other such notions that pervade much of contemporary theory. The social-historical is engaged with, is entered into, is figured and refigured, is given elucidation; it is a complex structuration of agency and structure, a patterning of the already figured and other figures – all filtered through imaginary fabrications and articulations, which of course includes the limitations and distortions of reason which contemporary culture increasingly reflects upon in our postmodern engagement with modernization and modernity.

SH: Castoriadis's work, especially in relation to the creative potential of the psyche, is clearly central to your understanding and account not only of the fragmentation and splitting of the subject in postmodernity but also for the possibility of integration and reflexivity. You mentioned above the work of Thomas Ogden who has become much more prominent in your writing recently. I could also mention Christopher Bollas in this respect. The work of these analysts is probably not so well known in psychoanalytic social or cultural theory as that deriving from the Lacanian tradition. What is it in particular that you think Ogden and the object relations theorists can bring to our current concerns and work in psychoanalytic social and cultural theory?

AE: Notwithstanding the use that I make of Castoriadis's reading of Freud, there are a number of difficulties that pervade his conceptual approach to self and society – most especially those that arise from his monadic approach to the psyche (and which I examine in some detail in my *Critical Visions: New Directions in Social Theory*, 2003). I think that Castoriadis's starting position – that is, that the psyche is initially closed in upon itself

– ultimately puts him in a position connected to the Lacanians when it comes to thinking about the Symbolic order or Oedipal relationships. Perhaps this is why Castoriadis approves of Lacan's linguistic reading of the Oedipus complex – it's the one area where he has something positive to say about Lacan. What Castoriadis calls 'the break-up of the monad' occurs in a typically masculinist, rationalist sense: the father intrudes into the mother–child dyad to disrupt imaginary wholeness, and to refer the child to symbols, language, difference, diversity, otherness, culture. Now from one angle, I wouldn't want to contest this. I think that, unless one wants to hold that human beings are just magically preordained to take up social and cultural positions as speaking subjects, some such socio-symbolic process (the Oedipus complex, castration, decentration) must occur. On the other hand, I don't think that the symbolic has to be theorized as such a violent intrusion from the outside. That is to say, I think that the work of psychoanalysts such as Winnicott and Bion highlight the links between the psyche and culture in a very interesting manner – interesting because their clinical work shows that small infants negotiate transitional space, process reveries, and interact with preliminary draftings of the symbolic. Kristeva has, perhaps more than anyone (with the exception of Laplanche), excavated this terrain in her notion of the 'imaginary father' – understood as the mother's desire for the phallus, and as such a desire referring the infant to symbolic cues prior to the onset of the Oedipus complex. I should also say that, while I think Kristeva is on the right track here, I have made detailed criticisms of her account of 'the Father of personal prehistory' in several places, including sections of this book. In developing this critique, I have substituted the emphasis of Kristeva and Laplanche on the imaginary father or primal seduction for the notion of 'rolling representations' and 'representational wrappings of self and other'. In developing these concepts, I am seeking to elucidate the pre-Oedipal, imaginary figurations of the psyche through which a 'world' is constituted, primarily the forms, figures, fantasies and fabrications which permit the valorization of pre-self and pre-object investment and counter-investment. This is what Castoriadis refers to as the 'break-up of the psychical monad', but I am using the notions of rolling identifications and representational wrappings to suggest that this 'break-up' happens well before the onset of the Oedipal phase, and also – pace Kristeva and Laplanche – that this occurs prior to primary narcissism (as this is a later development, one in which the subject invests in an image of itself).

Now to Ogden. His work is, in the American context, important – if only because he has done so much to address misunderstandings and misreadings of Klein. More than that, however, he has shown – through detailed clinical profiles – that the paranoid-schizoid and depressive positions interact in complex and crosscutting ways. Depressive anxiety, involving a mix of integration and containment on the one side and stagnation and closure on the other, is broken up, according to Ogden, by paranoid anxiety, through the splitting of linkages. This in turn leads to the depressive position once more, in order to limit the chaos of thought and the discontinuity of experience. Importantly, Ogden theorizes a space underpinning these psychic processes: the autistic-contiguous position. This pre-self experience – that is pre-Oedipal and imaginary formations – is built out of the affective impressions of bounded surfaces, the very building blocks of warmth, coldness, texture, hardness. These self-as-object and pre-object valorizations underpin imaginary and symbolic processing, and contribute to what I term representational wrappings of identity and difference. I think this work is important to current social and cultural theory because (1) it provides a way out of the determinism and pessimism of the Lacanian account, and (2) it provides a crucial handle on the management of psychotic/non-psychotic aspects of social formations and cultural reproduction. These primitive, autistic, radically imaginary figurations of pre-self and pre-object experience are in fact highly relevant to the subject's construction of self-constitution, self/other relations, and forms of cultural association more generally. I believe that it is when these primitive psychic forms are reactivated in frightening and alarming ways that social anxieties and cultural terrors can be unleashed with pathological political consequences.

SH: I want to shift topics now, and ask about your research on celebrity, particularly your book *The Mourning of John Lennon*. This book is unlike your previous work in the sense that it represents a study of the cultural significance of a single figure. But also in its tone and style it is unlike your previous books, Lennon seems to have a strong personal significance for you, is that right?

AE: *The Mourning of John Lennon* was written against the backdrop of my theoretical and cultural interests in celebrity, fame and mass culture. This is an area of research with which I want to continue, as it strikes me as increasingly central to some of the most far-reaching intimate and political transformations occurring today against the backdrop of modern communications, globalization and new information technologies.

The present surge of interest in celebrity and fame in cultural studies and critical theory signifies something important in social life. For with the collapse of the big stories or grand narratives of culture and history, people look for other ways of making sense of their personal and cultural experience. The old story of cultural progress and social emancipation has taken such a battering in recent times that, for many people on the political left at least, it seems increasingly difficult to move beyond the narcissistic preoccupations of daily life and to make meaningful contact with broader public issues. Celebrity is very interesting in this context, and I do not think it can be adequately analysed as a mindless form of cultural domination or subjection. This is not to say that there are not very disturbing social pathologies associated with the cult of celebrity. For clearly there are, and one needs only to get hold of the latest copy of *Who Weekly* to get a sense of just how superficial, narcissistic and episodic the public's engagement with the culture of celebrity often is. However, I'm trying to take a radically different tack in my approach to cultural studies and cultural theory, and my book on John Lennon is an attempt to develop a sustained and serious reflection upon the social consequences of what happens when a cultural icon rejects the adoration of the public. Lennon is an exemplary figure in this respect, given that his celebrity was of epic proportions, such that his withdrawal from, and rejection of, fame could not but generate a crisis in received social meanings surrounding the cult of celebrity.

You are right about the personal significance: Lennon loomed large for me, and I have always pondered why he meant so much, how someone I had never met could exercise such a strong influence, and why the death of a celebrity could provoke grief on a global scale. My aim was also to bring theory and biography, cultural studies and celebrity into a more reflective dialogue; the book is very anti-cultural studies as many post-structuralists and postmodernists practise it. I draw throughout on Freud, Kristeva, Bauman and others: I am out to recover the authentic in Lennon's cultural productions and conception of the aesthetic; I draw from Freud and contemporary psychoanalysis to link this personal grief and loss with mourning and melancholia in the public sphere; and I problematize postmodernism by looking at the Beatles hi-tech 'reunion' in 1994–5. The reader can dip in and out of the various chapters as she or he pleases; each chapter is self-contained. But there is a strong connecting thread: the deconstruction that Lennon made of his celebrity in the late 1970s, and of how threatening and disturbing this was for him and, crucially, for his fans and the public.

SH: Turning now to *Concepts of the Self*. This work struck me as at once a kind of history of the discourse of subjectivity in critical theory and modern European philosophy and a sustained critique of social-constructivism, especially Foucaultian interpretations of identity. Can you comment?

AE: Yes, the book sought to trace various discourses of the self in sociology, political science, philosophy, cultural studies, feminism, and psycho-analysis. From one angle, that was conventional enough, and there have of course been some very interesting interventions on the topic of the self in recent years, especially from Foucaultians and deconstructionists. It is, I think at any rate, impossible to write about the history of the self without taking on board what Foucault says in particular. However the point of the book – at once psychoanalytical and political – was to underline that various discourses of the self function as discourses to the extent that they are passionately invested, imagined and reimagined. I tried to deconstruct contextualizations of the self to uncover the psychic stakes of the complex, contradictory ways in which the self is produced, performed and trans-figured. The book is, in a sense, very anti-Foucault in its conclusions.

SH: There is an increasing sense in your most recent work that Kristeva, Castoriadis, and maybe Laplanche, are central thinkers for you. I wonder here about what has produced the extended dialogue with these three psychoanalysts. Does it arise from the series of reflections each has offered on the transformed conditions of subjectivity and the psyche? Or is the prompt more broadly cultural, more systematically theoretical?

AE: There's a passage in *Revolt, She Said* where Kristeva remarks that people today (psychoanalysts, patients, theorists and other interested parties) aren't necessarily prisoners of Lacan's judgements. I for one certainly welcomed Kristeva's courage in exposing some of the core psychological and philosophical deficiencies of Lacanian psychoanalysis, not only in her early writings on 'abjection' and the 'semiotic' but also in her more recent work (especially where she turns to analyse the proto-fantasy or what's termed the status of the 'representative prior to representation'). Kristeva has suggested, in various places, that motivating her critique of the French psychoanalytic orthodoxy are the new symptoms patients today display. Now the problems are not so much those of sexual repression, denial and subjugation of life energies and but rather those stemming from extreme narcissism, borderline personalities and the retreat towards privatism. She traces these discontents, partly, to the symbolic decline of the father in modern families, somewhat akin to the Frankfurt School analysis; while I think this aspect of her analysis is perhaps the least innovative part of her recent writings, I nonetheless can see the logic of her argument, and of what motivates her ongoing interest in pre-symbolic, imaginary modes of generating affective experience.

But the transformed cultural conditions in which the modern patient finds herself today is only part of the story here, or so I would argue. There are other central reasons – at once theoretical and political – why the turn to the imaginary constitution of psychic space (which Kristeva has certainly helped initiate) has become an especially pressing dilemma in our time. One concerns the insufficiency of doctrines of imagination, which for the most part consists in the reduction of radically creative elements of the psyche to predetermined forces, sometimes specular and negative implantations, sometimes purely instrumental operations. This relegation of the imaginary to a lethal negativism, in which the products of mind are cast as copies, illusions, snares and deceptions, has rendered mainstream accounts unfit for engaging with both the conditions and consequences of our shared imaginative life. Another reason concerns the cultural landscape of postmodernity. The postmodern prejudice against the radical character of the imagination is, in many ways, politically catastrophic. As long as we think of the radical imaginary and social imagination as little more than effects of discourse, a ludic mirage of signs, we remain under the sway of flagrantly superficial ideas. Yet there is a truth-value to the postmodern experiment (which Fredric Jameson has done a great deal to unearth), and here I refer to the fact that current social conditions indicate the extent of flattening of genuine psychic creation, of an imaginary colonized, controlled, hyped and parodied. The so-called postmodern 'play' of infinite multiplication may indeed fit hand-in-glove with the global narrative of capitalism, but perhaps above all it also underlines that our present political order is based upon the suppression or non-being of radical imagination, of autonomous individuals.

The matter is obviously enormously complex, and I've only really touched upon the problem here in a very one-sided way. But yes, again, you're correct: Kristeva is central to many aspects of my work (especially the books *Subject to Ourselves* and *Critical Visions*), and I draw extensively from her devastating critique of Lacan (set out in her tract *The Sense and Non-Sense of Revolt*) in developing several central arguments in this book. As I indicated before, Castoriadis is, to my mind, a different case. He helped me greatly to understand why an excavation or archaeology of the productive imagination should have come about as a new topic in our own time. Compared to Kristeva, his corpus elucidates crossroads in social imaginaries and radical imaginaries. What I have taken from Castoriadis is not only an appreciation of how individual-radical imaginaries and social-collective imaginaries are mutually constitutive, but also of the utter centrality of human creation in the making of how things are as well as in the making of how things might be different.

Laplanche? I was seeking a way of approaching intersubjective issues otherwise from the Habermasian reading of Freud and also of object-relational approaches. What I learned from Laplanche is a way of theorizing intersubjectivity that doesn't lose sight of the work of the psychical economy of the subject in attempting to decipher, translate and bind messages from the Other. Ogden too is central here, perhaps even more so than Laplanche. As I mentioned previously, Ogden's excavation of the autistic valorization of sensory experience, though not developed by him in any social-theoretical detail, is exceptionally interesting I think. I draw from his account of the autistic-contiguous mode of generating experience to rethink the imaginary constitution of the subject, as well as the mutual imbrication of radical and social imaginaries.

Notes

Introduction: imagination in the service of the new

1 It might be helpful to provide a few brief biographical details. Castoriadis studied in Athens before moving to France in 1945. He worked for many years as a professional economist at the Organization of Economic Co-operation and Development. He left his post at the OECD in 1970 and began training as a psychoanalyst. He undertook his training with the French-language psychoanalytic organization known as the 'fourth group', a break-away association from the Lacanian *ecole freudienne*. For further details see Thompson, 1984; Elliott, 2002, 2003.

2 Kristeva, now Professor of Linguistics at the University of Paris VII, did her psychoanalytic training with Lacan. Already in her earliest theoretical work, however, she indicated a determination to move beyond the conceptual terrain of Lacanianism narrowly defined. For example, her doctoral dissertation, which was subsequently published as her first book *Revolution in Poetic Language*, blends linguistics and psychoanalytical theory to advance a novel account of how pre-verbal experience – infantile, maternal, poetic – enters into, shapes, distorts and disrupts language through processes of art, literature and psychoanalysis. In her more recent work, which I trace throughout this book, Kristeva has turned away from Lacan and back to classical Freudianism, and especially toward Kleinian psychoanalysis. (See Elliott, 2003.)

3 Having trained with Lacan, Laplanche's early writings indicate a strong conceptual debt to his former analyst. Indeed, the book for which Laplanche is perhaps best known in the Anglo-American world is *The Language of Psychoanalysis* (1980), co-authored with J. B. Pontalis – an encyclopedic coverage of core psychoanalytic concepts through the lens of French Freudianism. Further works of psychoanalytic exposition and critique followed, including the influential tract *Life and Death in Psychoanalysis* (1976), in which Laplanche struggled to remain faithful to the Lacanian modifications to psychoanalysis, principally through expressing his general suspicion of structural theory. It seems likely, however, that Laplanche's lasting contribution to psychoanalysis will be his reflections on otherness in the formation of human subjectivity, as developed in his 'general theory of seduction', set out in the five-volume *Problématiques* (1980–7). A summary of Laplanche's post-Lacanian theory of seduction has appeared in English, in the volumes *New Foundations for Psychoanalysis* (1987) and *Essays on Otherness* (1999). (See Fletcher, 1992.)

3 The psychic constitution of the subject: imagination, identification, primary repression

1 This intersubjective recasting of the relation of desire to the nascent subject differentiates the work of psychoanalytic feminists such as Jessica Benjamin from Habermas's highly cognitive and linguistic version of intersubjectivity. This perspective is also radically different from the work of neo-Lacanians, such as Laplanche, who have developed intersubjective accounts of Freudian theory by stressing that sexuality and repressed desire are inscribed into the child's psychic world from without by the socio-symbolic network. The view that the child imbibes what parents unknowingly express of their own fantasies and fears concerning sexuality makes the nascent subject a passive recipient of the Other – or so I have argued. In this connection, Benjamin's stress on mutuality and recognition in the child/mother dyad offers an alternative theorization to neo-Lacanians. What relational analysts generally failed to theorize, however, are the sources of psychic creativity and representation that allow the nascent subject to gather meaning and make something of the intersubjective field for itself. This is where Castoriadis's formulations on radical imagination are most pertinent to recent debates about intersubjectivity.

References

Adorno, T. (1974) *Minima Moralia*. London: Verso.

Adorno, T. and Horkheimer, M. (1973) *Dialectic of Enlightenment*. London: Allen Lane.

Althusser, L. [1971[(1984) *Essays on Ideology*. London: Verso.

Altman, D. (1996) 'On global queering'. *Australian Humanities Review*.

Anzieu, D. (1989) *The Skin Ego*. New Haven, CT: Yale University Press.

Appignanesi, L. and Forrester, J. (1992) *Freud's Women*. London: Virago.

Arendt, H. (1978) *The Life of the Mind*. New York and London: Harcourt Brace Jovanovich.

Barratt, B. B. (1993) *Psychoanalysis and the Postmodern Impulse: Knowing and Being since Freud's Psychology*, Baltimore, MD/London: Johns Hopkins University Press.

Barrett, M. (1991) *The Politics of Truth*. Cambridge: Polity Press.

Barthes, R. (1974) *Writing Degree Zero*. London: Jonathan Cape.

Bauman, Z. (1991) *Modernity and Ambivalence*. Cambridge: Polity Press.

Bauman, Z. (1991) *Intimations of Postmodernity*. London: Routledge.

Bauman, Z. (1992) *Mortality, Immortality, and Other Life Strategies*. Cambridge: Polity Press.

Bauman, Z. (1993) *Postmodern Ethics*. Oxford: Blackwell.

Bauman, Z. (1995) *Life in Fragments*. Oxford: Blackwell.

Bauman, Z. (2000) *Liquid Modernity*. Cambridge: Polity Press.

Bauman, Z. (2001) *The Individualized Society*. Cambridge: Polity Press.

Beck, U. (1992) *Risk Society: Towards a New Modernity*. London: Sage.

Beck, U. and Beck-Gernsheim, E. (1995) *The Normal Chaos of Love*. Cambridge: Polity Press.

Benhabib, S. and Cornell, D. (eds) (1987) *Feminism as Critique*. Cambridge: Polity Press.

Benjamin, J. (1977) 'The end of internalization: Adorno's social psychology'. *Telos*, 32.

Benjamin, J. (1990) *The Bonds of Love*. London: Virago.

Benjamin, J. (1995) *Like Subjects, Love Objects*. New Haven: Yale University Press.

Benjamin, J. (1998) *Shadow of the Other*. New York: Routledge.

Bion, W. R. (1961) *Learning from Experience*. New York: Basic Books.

Blackburn, S. (1993) *Essays in Quasi-Realism*. Oxford: Oxford University Press.

Bohman, J. (1991) 'Holism without skepticism', in D. Hiley, J. Dorman and R. Shusterman (eds) *The Interpretive Turn*. Ithaca, NY: Cornell University Press, pp. 129–34.

Bollas, C. (1992) *Being a Character*. New York: Hill and Wang.

Bollas, C. (1995) *Cracking Up*. New York: Hill and Wang.

Borch-Jacobsen, M. (1988) *The Freudian Subject*. Stanford, CA: Stanford University Press.

Bourdieu, P. (1977) *Outline of a Theory of Practice*. Cambridge: Cambridge University Press.

Bourguignon, A. *et al.* (1989) *Traduire Freud*. Paris: Presses Universitaire de France.

Busch, F. (1995) 'Resistance analysis and object relations theory'. *Psychoanalytic Psychology*, 12: 43–54.

Bradotti, R. (1992) *Patterns of Dissonance*. Cambridge: Polity.

Brenkman, J. (1987) *Culture and Domination*. Ithaca, NY: Cornell University Press.

Burr, V. and Butt, T. (2000) 'Psychological distress and postmodern thought', in D. See (ed.) *Pathology in the Postmodern*. London and Thousand Oaks: Sage.

Butler, J. (1993) *Bodies That Matter*. New York: Routledge.

Calvet, L.-J. (1994) *Roland Barthes: A Biography*. Cambridge: Polity Press.

Castoriadis, C. (1984) *Crossroads in the Labyrinth*. Cambridge, MA: MIT Press.

Castoriadis, C. (1987) *The Imaginary Institution of Society*. Cambridge: Polity Press.

Castoriadis, C. (1989) 'The state of the subject today'. *Thesis Eleven*, 24: 5–43.

Castoriadis, C. (1991) *Philosophy, Politic, Autonomy*. Oxford: Oxford University Press.

Castoriadis, C. (1995) 'Logic, imagination, reflection', in A. Elliott and S. Frosh (eds) *Psychoanalysis in Contexts: Paths between Theory and Modern Culture*. London: Routledge, pp. 15–35.

Castoriadis, C. (1997) *World in Fragments: Writing on Politics, Society, Psychoanalysis and the Imagination*. Stanford, CA: Stanford University Press.

Chamberlain, D. (1987) 'The cognitive newborn: a scientific update'. *British Journal of Psychotherapy*, 4: 30–71.

Chodorow, N. (1978) *The Reproduction of Mothering*. Berkeley: University of California Press.

Chodorow, N. (1989) *Feminism and Psychoanalytic Theory*. Cambridge: Polity Press.

Cixous, H. [1976] (1981) 'The laugh of the Medusa', in E. Marks and I. de Courtivon (eds) *New French Feminisms*. Sussex: Harvester Press.

Copjec, J. (1994) *Read my Desire: Lacan Against the Historicists*. Cambridge, MA: MIT Press.

Cornell, D. (1991) *Beyond Accommodation*. New York: Routledge.

Cornell, D. (1993) *Transformations*. New York: Routledge.

Crews, F. (1986) *Skeptical Engagements*. New York: Oxford University Press.

Crews, F. (1993) 'The unknown Freud'. *New York Review of Books*, 18 November: 55–66.

Deleuze, G. and Guattari, E. (1977) *Anti-Oedipus: Capitalism and Schizophrenia*. New York: Viking.

Delrieu, A. (1977) *Sigmund Freud: Index Thématique*. Paris: Editions Anthropos.

Derrida, J. (1978) *Writing and Difference*, translated by A. Bass. Chicago: University of Chicago Press, 1980.

Derrida, J. (1981) *Positions*, translated by A. Bass. Chicago: University of Chicago Press.

Dews, P. (1987) *Logics of Disintegration*. London: Verso.

Dews, P. (1995) 'The crisis of Oedipal identity', in A. Elliott and S. Frosh (eds) *Psychoanalysis in Contexts*. London and New York: Routledge.

Eagleton, T. (1990) *The Ideology of the Aesthetic*. Oxford: Blackwell.

Edmundson, M. (1990) *Towards Reading Freud*. Princeton, NJ: Princeton University Press.

Elliott, A. (1992) *Social Theory and Psychoanalysis in Transition: Self and Society from Freud to Kristeva*. Oxford: Blackwell.

Elliott, A. (1993) 'The self-destructive subject'. *Free Associations*, 3(4): 504–44.

Elliott, A. (1994) *Psychoanalytic Theory: An Introduction*. Oxford: Blackwell.

Elliott, A. (1995) 'The affirmation of primary repression rethought: reflections on the state of the self in its unconscious relational world'. *American Imago*, 52: 55–79.

Elliott, A. (1996) *Subject To Ourselves: Social Theory, Psychoanalysis and Postmodernity*. Cambridge: Polity Press.

Elliott, A. (1999) *Social Theory and Psychoanalysis in Transition: Self and Society from Freud to Kristeva*. London: Free Association Books.

Elliott, A. (2001) *Concepts of the Self*. Cambridge: Polity Press.

Elliott, A. (2002) *Psychoanalytic Theory: An introduction*, 2nd edn. Durham, NC: Duke University Press.

Elliott, A. (2003) *Critical Visions: New Directions in Social Theory*. New York: Rowan and Littlefield.

Elliott, A. (2004) *Subject to Ourselves: Social Theory, Psychoanalysis and Postmodernity*. Boulder: Paradigm Press.

Elliott, A. and Frosh, S. (eds) (1995) *Psychoanalysis in Contexts: Paths Between Theory and Modern Culture*. London: Routledge.

Ferguson, H. (1996) *The Love of Dreams: Sigmund Freud on the Construction of Modernity*. London and New York: Routledge.

Fish, S. (1989) 'Rhetoric', in F. Lentricchia and T. McLaughlin (eds) *Critical Terms for Literary Study*. Chicago: University of Chicago Press, pp. 203–22.

Flax, J. (1990) *Thinking Fragments: Psychoanalysis, Feminism, and Postmodernism in the Contemporary West*. Berkeley: University of California Press.

Fletcher, J. (1992) 'The letter in the unconscious: the enigmatic signifier in the work of Jean Laplanche', in J. Fletcher and M. Stanton (eds) *Seduction, Translation and the Drives*. London: ICA, pp. 93–120.

Fletcher, J. and Stanton, M. (eds) (1992) *Jean Laplanche: Seduction, Translation and The Drives*. London: ICA.

Forrester, J. (1997) *Dispatches from the Freud Wars: Psychoanalysis and its Passions*. Cambridge, MA: Harvard University Press.

Frank, M. [1984] (1989) *What is Neostructuralism?*. Minneapolis: University of Minnesota Press.

Freud, S. (1900) *The Interpretation of Dreams*. S.E. 4 and 5.

Freud, S. (1911) 'Formulations on the two principles of mental functioning'. S.E. 12.

Freud, S. (1913) 'Totem and taboo'. S.E. 13, pp. 1–161.

Freud, S. (1914) 'The unconscious', in Freud (1935–74), 14, pp. 159–215.

Freud, S. (1915a) 'The unconscious'. S.E. 14.

Freud, S. (1915b) 'Repression'. S.E. 14.

Freud, S. (1921) 'Group psychology and the analysis of the ego'. S.E. 18, pp. 69–143.

Freud, S. (1923) *The Ego and the Id*. S.E. 19, pp. 1–66.

Freud, S. (1924) 'Neurosis and psychosis'. S.E. 19, pp. 148–53.

Freud, S. (1926) *Inhibitions, Symptoms and Anxiety*. S.E. 20.

Freud, S. (1926) 'Psycho-analysis'. S.E. 20.

Freud, S. (1931) 'Female sexuality'. S.E. 21, pp. 223–43.

Freud, S. (1932) 'Why war?'. S.E. 22, pp. 197–215.

Freud, S. (1935–74) *The Standard Edition of the Complete Psychological Works of Sigmund Freud*. (S.E.) London: Hogarth Press.

Freud, S. (1940) *An Outline of Psycho-Analysis*. S.E. 23, pp. 141–207.

Friel, B. (1981) *Translations*. London: Faber.

Fromm, E. [1932] (1982) 'The method and function of an analytic social psychology', in A. Arato and E. Gebhardt (eds) *The Essential Frankfurt School Reader*. New York: Continuum.

Fromm, E. [1956] (1991) *The Sane Society*. London: Routledge.

Frosh, S. (1987) *The Politics of Psychoanalysis*. London: Macmillan.

Frosh, S. (1991) *Identity Crisis: Modernity, Psychoanalysis and the Self*. London: Macmillan.

Frosh, S. (1994) *Sexual Difference*. London: Routledge.

Frosh, S. (1997) *For and Against Psychoanalysis*. London and New York: Routledge.

Frosh, S. (1999) *The Politics of Psychoanalysis*, 2nd edn. London: Palgrave.

Frosh, S. (2002) *After Words*. London: Palgrave.

Gay, P. (1988) *Freud: A Life For Our Time*. London: Dent.

Giddens, A. (1979) *Central Problems in Social Theory*. London: Macmillan.

Giddens, A. (1991) *Modernity and Self-Identity: Self and Society in the Late Modern Age*. Stanford, CA: Stanford University Press.

Giddens, A. (1992) *The Transformation of Intimacy: Sexuality, Love, and Eroticism in Modern Societies*. Stanford, CA: Stanford University Press.

Glass, J. M. (1993) *Shattered Selves: Multiple Personality in a Postmodern World*. Ithaca, NY and London: Cornell University Press.

Green, A. [1985] (1995) 'Réflexions libres sur la représentation de l'affect', in *Propédeutique. La métapsychologie revistée*. Seyssel: Éditions Champ Vallon.

Greenberg, J. (1991) *Oedipus and Beyond*. Cambridge, MA: Harvard University Press.

Greenberg, J. and Mitchell, S. A. (1983) *Object Relations in Psychoanalytic Theory*. Cambridge, MA: Harvard University Press.

Grosz, E. (1995) *Space, Time and Perversion*. London: Routledge.

Habermas, J. (1968) *Knowledge and Human Interests*, translated by J. J. Shapiro. Boston: Beacon, 1971.

Habermas, J. [1970] (1988) *On the Logic of the Social Sciences*, translated by S. W. Nicholson and J. A Stark, Cambridge, MA: MIT Press.

Habermas, J. (1972) *Knowledge and Human Interests*. London: Heinemann.

Harvey, D. (1990) *The Condition of Postmodernity*. Cambridge, MA: Blackwell.

Held, D. (1980) *Introduction to Critical Theory*. London: Hutchinson.

Hoffman, I. Z. (1987) 'The value of uncertainty in psychoanalytic practice'. *Contemporary Psychoanalysis*, 23: 205–15.

Hoffman, I. Z. (1994) 'Dialectical thinking and therapeutic action in the psychoanalytic process'. *Psychoanalytic Quarterly*, 63: 187–218.

Irigaray, L. [1977] (1981): 'Ce sexe qui n'est pas un', in E. Marks and I. de Courtivon (eds) *New French Feminisms*. Sussex: Harvester Press.

Irigaray, L. (1993) *An Ethics of Sexual Difference*. London: Athlone Press.

Irigaray, L. (1999) *To Be Two*. London: Athlone Press.

Jacoby, R. (1975) *Social Amnesia*. Sussex: Harvester Press.

Jameson, F. (1988) *The Ideologies of Theory*. London: Routledge.

Jameson, F. (1991) *Postmodernism: Or, The Cultural Logics of Late Capitalism*. London: Verso.

Jay, M. (1973) *The Dialectical Imagination*. Boston: Little, Brown.

Kirsner, D. (2000) *Unfree Associations*. London: Process Press.

Kristeva, J. (1984) *Revolution in Poetic Language*. New York: Columbia University Press.

Kristeva, J. (1986) *The Kristeva Reader*, ed. T. Moi. Oxford: Blackwell.

Kristeva, J. (1987) *Tales of Love*. New York: Columbia University Press.

Kristeva, J. (1988) *In the Beginning was Love*. New York: Columbia University Press.

Kristeva, J. (1989) *Black Sun: Depression and Melancholia*. New York: Columbia University Press.

Kristeva, J. (1991) *Strangers to Ourselves*. London: Harvester.

Kristeva, J. (1993) *New Maladies of the Soul*. New York: Columbia University Press.

Kristeva, J. (1994) 'Psychosis in Times of Distress', in S. Shamdazani and M. Munchow (eds) *Speculations after Freud: Psychoanalysis, Philosophy and Culture*. London: Routledge.

Kristeva, J. (1995) 'Psychoanalysis in times of distress', in S. Shandasani and M. Munchow (eds) *Speculations after Freud*. London: Routledge.

Kristeva, J. (2000a) *The Sense and Non-Sense of Revolt: The Powers and Limits of Psychoanalysis*. New York: Columbia University Press.

Kristeva, J. (2000b) *Crisis of the European Subject*. New York: Other Press.

Kristeva, J. (2001a) *Melanie Klein*. New York: Columbia University Press.

Kristeva, J. (2001b) *Hannah Arendt: Life is a Narrative*. Toronto: University of Toronto Press.

Kristeva, J. (2001c) *Hannah Arendt*. New York: Columbia University Press.

Kristeva, J. (2002) *Revolt, She Said*. New York: Semiotext(e).

Lacan, J. (1949) 'The Mirror Stage as Formative of the Function of the I' in *Ecrits: A Selection*. London: Tavistock, 1977.

Lacan, J. (1966) *Ecrits*. Paris: Seuil.

Lacan, J. [1975] (1988) *The Seminar of Jacques Lacan, Book I (1953–4)*. Cambridge: Cambridge University Press.

Lacan, J. (1975) *Le Seminaire, Livre I, Les Ecrits techniques de Freud*. Paris: Seuil.

Lacan, J. (1977) *Ecrits: A Selection*. London: Tavistock.

Lacan, J. (1991) *Le Seminaire: Livre XVII. L'envers de la psychanalyse (1969–70)*, ed. J.-A. Miller. Paris: Seuil.

Laplanche, J. (1976) *Life and Death in Psychoanalysis*. Baltimore, MD: Johns Hopkins University Press.

Laplanche, J. (1980–7) *Problematiques*. Paris: Presses Universitaire de France.

Laplanche, J. (1987) *New Foundations for Psychoanalysis*. Oxford: Blackwell.

Laplanche, J. (1997) 'The theory of seducation and the problem of the other', *International Journal of Psycho-Analysis*, **78**, 4.

Laplanche, J. (1999) *Essays on Otherness*. London: Routledge.

Laplanche, J. and Pontalis, J. B. (1980) *The Language of Psychoanalysis*. London: Hogarth Press.

Laplanche, J. and Pontalis, J. B. (1986) 'Phantasy and the origins of sexuality', *International Journal of Psycho-Analysis*, **49**, 1:1–18.

Lear, J. (1991) *Love and Its Place in Nature*. New York: Farrar, Straus & Giroux.

Leary, K. (1994) 'Psychoanalytic "problems" and postmodern "solutions"'. *Psychoanalytic Quarterly*, **63**: 433–65.

Lemert, C. (1997) *Postmodernism is Not What You Think*. Oxford: Blackwell.

Leupin, A. (ed.) (1991) *Lacan and the Human Sciences*. Lincoln: University of Nebraska Press.

Lyotard, J.-F. (1974) *Economie libidinale*. Paris: Seuil.

Lyotard, J.-F. (1984) *The Postmodern Condition: A Report on Knowledge*, translated by G. Bennington and B. Massumi. Minneapolis: University of Minnesota Press.

Lyotard, J.-F. (1993) *Libidinal Economy*. London: Athlone Press.

Lyotard, J. F. (1989) *The Lyotard Reader*, edited by A. Benjamin. Oxford: Blackwell.

Macey, D. (1988) *Lacan in Contexts*. London: Verso.

Macey, D. (1993) *The Lives of Michel Foucault*. London: Hutchinson.

Malcolm, J. (1984) *In the Freud Archives*. New York: Knopf.

Marcuse, H. [1956] (1987) *Eros and Civilization*. London: Ark.

Marcuse, H. (1970) *Five Lectures: Psychoanalysis, Politics, and Utopia*. London: Allen Lane.

Masson, J. (1984) *The Assault on Truth: Freud's Suppression of the Seduction Theory*. New York: Farrar, Straus & Giroux.

Masson, J. (1988) *Against Therapy*. London: Fontana.

McGowan, J. (1991) *Postmodernism and Its Critics*. Ithaca, NY: Cornell University Press.

McNay, L. (1992) *Foucault and Feminism*. Cambridge: Polity Press.

Mitchell, J. (1974) *Psychoanalysis and Feminism*. Harmondsworth: Penguin.

Mitchell, S. (1988) *Relational Concepts in Psychoanalysis*. Cambridge, MA: Harvard University Press.

Mitchell, S. (1993) *Hope and Dread in Psychoanalysis*. New York: Basic Books.

Mitchell, J. and Rose, J. (1982) *Feminine Sexuality: Jacques Lacan and the Ecole Freudienne*. London: Routledge.

Moi, T. (1985) *Sexual/Textual Politics*. London: Routledge.

Murdoch, I. [1993] (1994) *Metaphysics as a Guide to Morals: Philosophical Reflections*. New York: Viking Penguin.

Nietzsche, F. (1983) *Untimely Meditations*. New York: Cambridge University Press.

Norris, C. (1987) *Derrida*. Cambridge, MA: Harvard University Press.

Norris, C. (1993) *The Truth about Postmodernism*. Oxford: Blackwell.

Ogden, T. 1989a 'On the concept of an autistic-contiguous position'. *International Journal of Psycho-Analysis*, 70, 1: 127–40.

Ogden, T. 1989b *The Primitive Edge of Experience*. Northvale, NJ: Jason Aronson.

Phillips, A. (1994) *On Flirtation*. London: Faber.

Prager, J. (1998) *Presenting the Past: Psychoanalysis and the Sociology of Misremembering*. Cambridge, MA: Harvard University Press.

Ragland-Sullivan, E. (1986) *Jacques Lacan and the Philosophy of Psychoanalysis*. Chicago: University of Illinois Press.

Ragland-Sullivan, E. and Bracher, M. (eds) (1991) *Lacan and the Subject of Language*. New York: Routledge.

Ricoeur, P. (1970) *Freud and Philosophy: An Essay on Interpretation*. New Haven, CT: Yale University Press.

Rieff, P. [1959] (1979) *Freud: The Mind of the Moralist*. Chicago: University of Chicago Press.

Rorty, R. (1982) *The Consequences of Pragmatism: Essays 1972–1980*. Minneapolis: University of Minnesota Press.

Rose, J. (1975) *The Psychoanalysis of War*. London: Indiana University Press.

Rose, J. (1985) *Sexuality in the Field of Vision*. London: Verso.

Rose, J. (1993a) *Why War?* Oxford: Blackwell.

Rose, J. (1993b) 'Where does the misery come from?' in J. Rose, *Why War?* Oxford: Blackwell.

Rose, J. (1996) *States of Fantasy*. Oxford: Oxford University Press.

Rose, N. (1990) *Governing the Soul: The Shaping of the Private Self*. London: Routledge.

Rustin, M. (1991) *The Good Society and the Inner World: Psychoanalysis, Politics and Culture*. London: Verso.

Sandler, J. (1989) 'Toward a reconsideration of the psychoanalytic theory of motivation', in A. Cooper, O. Kernberg and E. Person (eds) *Psychoanalysis*. New Haven, CT: Yale University Press, pp. 91–110.

Schafer, R. (1983) *The Analytic Attitude*. New York: Basic Books.

Schafer, R. (1992) *Retelling a Life: Narration and Dialogue in Psychoanalysis*. New York: Basic Books.

Schimek, J. (1987) 'Fact and fantasy in the seduction theory: a historical review'. *Journal of the American Psychoanalytic Association*, 35, 937–65.

Scruton, R. (1994) *Modern Philosophy*. London: Sinclair-Stevenson.

Segal, L. (1987) *Is the Future Female? Troubled Thoughts on Contemporary Feminism*. London: Virago.

Segal, L. (1999) *Why Feminism?* Cambridge: Polity Press.

Smelser, N. (1998) *The Social Edges of Psychoanalysis*. Berkeley: University of California Press.

Spezzano, C. (1992) *Affect in Psychoanalysis: A Clinical Synthesis*. Hillsdale, NJ: The Analytic Press.

Sprengnether, M. (1990) *The Spectral Mother: Freud, Feminism and Psychoanalysis*. Ithaca, NY: Cornell University Press.

Stern, D. (1985) *The Interpersonal World of the Infant*. New York: Basic Books.

Thompson, J. B. (1984) *Studies in the Theory of Ideology*. Cambridge: Polity Press.

Thompson, J. B. (1990) *Ideology and Modern Culture: Critical Social Theory in the Era of Mass Communication*. Stanford, CA: Stanford University Press.

Toews, J. (1991) 'Historicizing Psycho-Analysis: Freud in his time and for our time', *Journal of Modern History*, G3: 504–45.

Trachtenberg, A. (1979) 'Intellectual background', in D. Hoffman (ed.) *Harvard Guide to Contemporary American Writing*. Cambridge, MA: Harvard University Press.

Tustin, E. (1980) 'Autistic objects'. *International Review of Psycho-Analysis*, 7: 2740.

Tustin, E. (1984) 'Autistic shapes'. *International Review of Psycho-Analysis*, 11: 279–90.

Vattimo, G. (1980) *The Adventure of Difference: Philosophy after Nietzche and Heidegger*, translated by C. Blamires and T. Harrison. Baltimore, MD: Johns Hopkins University Press.

Wellmer, A. (1991) *The Persistence of Modernity*. Cambridge: Polity Press.

Whitebook, J. (1989) 'Intersubjectivity and the monadic core of the psyche: Habermas and Castoriadis on the unconscious'. *Revue européenne des sciences sociales*, 27: 226–45.

Whitebook, J. (1995) *Perversion and Utopia*. Cambridge, MA: MIT Press.

Winnicott, D. (1956) 'Primary maternal preoccupation', in *Through Paediatrics to Psycho-Analysis*. New York: Basic Books.

Winnicott, D. (1971) *Playing and Reality*. New York: Basic Books.

Wolf, N. (1994) *Fire With Fire*. London: Vintage.

Žižek, S. (1989) *The Sublime Object of Ideology*. London: Verso.

Žižek, S. (1991) *Looking Awry: An Introduction to Jacques Lacan through Popular Culture*. Cambridge, MA: MIT Press.

Žižek, S. (1994) *The Metastases of Enjoyment*. London: Verso.

Index